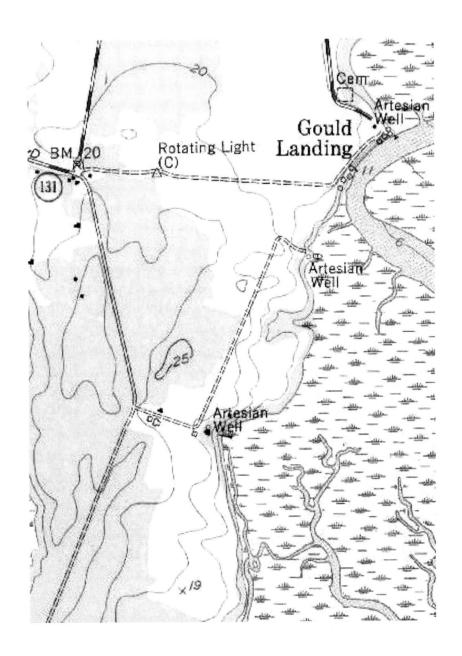

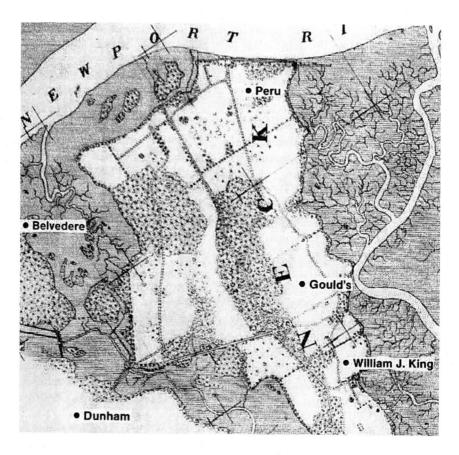

Upper Harris Neck in the antebellum plantation period.

Harris Neck & Its Environs

Land Use & Landscape in North McIntosh County, Georgia

BUDDY SULLIVAN

*Environmental Influences on Life & Labor in
McIntosh County, Georgia, one of a series*

2020

3

Table of Contents

Preface

This monograph comprising a survey of the history of Harris Neck, interwoven with that of the northeastern and central sections of McIntosh County, Georgia, is largely extrapolated from my research from 2016 to 2019 contained in two books—a revised and expanded edition of the county history, *Early Days on the Georgia Tidewater*, and a new volume, *Environmental Influences on Life & Labor in McIntosh County, Georgia.*

The thematic intent of this study rests upon land use patterns and land ownership during the eighteenth and nineteenth centuries in the section under discussion. While Harris Neck is the area most extensively covered, there is ample material relating to tracts, settlements and land use along the South Newport and Sapelo rivers, and the central sections of McIntosh County, including the settlements of Eulonia, Fairhope and Pine Harbor.

Due to the paucity of county land records prior to 1873 because of two courthouse fires in a 10-year period, and conflicting data in nineteenth century federal census records, there is a degree of confusion—and uncertainty—regarding the chains of title for some tracts and the persons occupying them during parts of the antebellum period before the Civil War. I would like to acknowledge with gratitude my thanks to Jim McMahon for his diligent detective work in bringing to light many of the genealogical obscurities pertaining to the antebellum Harris and allied families.

Buddy Sullivan

Cedar Point, March 2020

Abbreviations Used in Notes

GDAH   Georgia Department of Archives and History

GDNR   Georgia Department of Natural Resources

GHS   Georgia Historical Society, Savannah

NARA   National Archives and Records Administration

RMCG   Records of McIntosh County, Georgia

1

The Ecological Perspective

From Charleston to the Georgia-Florida border, the south Atlantic tidewater is fringed by low-lying sea islands in a section ecologically unique to the American landscape. The islands are typified by sub-tropical vegetation dominated by maritime forests comprised of live oak, pine and red cedar, anchored by thick understories of palmetto and myrtle. Between the islands and mainland are belts of salt marshes, chiefly the cordgrass *Spartina alterniflora*, penetrated by tidal creeks and rivers. These streams flow into estuaries created by the several fresh water streams entering the sounds and embayments between the islands.

Few places on the U.S. eastern seaboard better exemplify the economic and societal utilization of a local ecosystem by human populations than the tidewater sections of South Carolina and Georgia. For four centuries Euro-and-Afro-centric cultures in that region have assiduously adapted to their particular environmental circumstances—salt marsh ecosystem, fresh water and tidal systems and their hydrology, soil fertility, and meteorological considerations, among other prevailing conditions—to effectuate the enhancement of

9

their lifestyles and life-ways. An antebellum agrarian economy, interwoven with a distinct maritime culture—all linked to the land and water resources of the region—has spanned more than two centuries, and is set against the fascinating backdrop of coastal history. The *ecology as history* in this book resonates with a recurrent theme, one that relates the story of community—particularly that which involves the use of its land, its economy and the dynamics of its labor—from the perspective of the local environment. It blends the natural dynamics of the local ecosystem with human pursuits from rice cultivation, to waterborne commerce, to oyster harvesting, to scientific investigation, all impelled amidst a diverse array of peoples.

This is a story of *land use* in association with the intangibles of *place* and *permanence*—and by extension, *perseverance*—as they relate to the north section of McIntosh County. It is a story that is applicable to all of coastal Georgia and lower South Carolina. It will be argued here that the human occupants of the county simultaneously *adapted* to the ecological circumstances of their locale while *utilizing* local environmental conditions as an increasingly effective, and resourceful, means of furthering their economic and cultural well-being. The relevance of a communal and cultural sense of place is an important blended theme, as is the significance of the applied scientific research relating to the ecosystem that has evolved since the 1950s in determining the effects of ecology on human life-ways.

Ecology, for the purposes of the following discussion, entails the salt marshes and their tidal cycles, and the biological and chemical processes within those elements, along with other ecological considerations: soil types, river hydrology, upland forests, etc. that pertain to the section of McIntosh County under discussion in this

10

narrative. It is important to understand the environmental circumstances of the county here, particularly with respect to the large amount of agriculture and commercial fishing that dominated the economy and lifestyles of the peoples of Harris Neck and north McIntosh County for two centuries. The salt marshes, the tidal waterways, the soil types and the weather all had measurable impacts on the sustainability of people's lives and livelihoods.

Tides have a pronounced effect on the shorelines of McIntosh County, including Sapelo Island and the inshore marshes. There is a tidal amplitude around Sapelo ranging about seven feet up to about eleven feet on spring tides. Not surprisingly, the hydraulics of the tides affects the ecology of the marshes to a great extent.

Tidal rise and fall is a key factor in the active processes that occur in the marshes, and constitute the diversity of habitats for a number of organisms in the intertidal area. Most tidal creeks lie within steep mud banks and natural levees that create a pattern for the movement of water preceding its eventual dissipation in headwaters on the marsh surface. Tidal waters flow across the low marsh levees only on the highest spring tides. There are two tidal cycles daily with about 600 square miles of marsh and creeks in coastal Georgia being inundated, drained and refilled.[1]

---

[1] Much of this chapter is based upon Albert Sydney Johnson, Hilburn O. Hillestad, Sheryl Fanning Shanholtzer and G. Frederick Shanholtzer, eds., *An Ecological Survey of the Coastal Region of Georgia* (National Park Service Scientific Monograph Series 3, 1974) which is an excellent overview of the ecological characteristics of the Georgia coast. The twenty-eight volumes of *Collected Reprints*, 1962-2004, University of Georgia Marine Institute (School of Marine Sciences, Athens), containing the published papers of UGAMI scientists, is the primary source for findings and conclusions based on forty years of scientific field investigations in the salt marsh ecosystem of Sapelo Island and environs.

An important component of the tidal interactions within the coastal ecosystem is the phenomena between the barrier islands and the mainland called "dividings." These are areas in which several streams meet and their tidal flows converge—tides meet from different directions and "divide." Most of the barrier islands of Georgia and South Carolina have these convergence areas, dividings, as tidal streams flow though the marshes between the islands and the mainland. Often, changing shoal areas are created at dividings at which the tides flow in different directions. Sandbars shift and the areas of shoaling can create hazards for the unwary mariner. There is one notable area of tidewater McIntosh County where this phenomenon occurs: the Dividings east of Valona is that confluence of several streams where the ebbing and flooding tides meet. If these streams were the points of a compass then Mud River would be to the east, Old Teakettle Creek to the south, Shellbluff Creek from Valona to the west, and the South Sapelo River (Crescent River) to the northwest, all meeting in the middle. Add to these a fifth waterway that has tidal influence, the lower end of Creighton Narrows just north of the Dividings where it meets the lower end of South Sapelo River.

Mud River, west of Sapelo Island and separating it from the mainland, is aptly named. It is one of coastal Georgia's most distinctive—and unusual—tidal streams. This broad, shallow river was for over a hundred years the principal connection between its confluence with Sapelo Sound on the north and New Teakettle Creek for coasting traffic between Savannah and Darien. It has always been notorious for its difficulty of navigation on anything but high tide, or very nearly high tide. Northeasterly and southwesterly winds (both are prevalent at varying times of the year) tend to practically empty Mud River on an ebbing tide. Much of the mud bottom of the river is exposed at low tide, although locals in anything smaller than a shrimp boat know how to navigate the passage through a narrow channel hugging the marsh. Tides below half-tide are the most unforgiving to those not familiar with local conditions, for the mud bottom can't be seen, yet is only a foot or less below the surface. There are numerous examples of the problems encountered with this waterway.

Perhaps the best example of a tidal waterway and its interaction with, and influence by, tidal cycles is the Duplin River which flows within Sapelo Island. The Duplin, largest of the streams lying entirely within the marshes of Sapelo, transits the western side of the island, emptying on its southern end into Doboy Sound. Except for rainfall and groundwater discharge from the nearby uplands, the Duplin receives no freshwater, and thus can be more accurately defined as a large tidal creek or embayment. Along its six-and-a-half mile length, the Duplin has three distinct sections, or tidal "prisms." The lower component ends near Pumpkin Hammock, the second extends northward to Moses Hammock, and the third comprises the several tidal creek branches of the upper Duplin.

The strong tidal currents and the lack of freshwater input generally keep the hydrological dynamics of the upper Duplin excluded from those of the lower section of the river nearer Doboy Sound. Occasionally, during especially high spring tides, water in the upper Duplin may merge with that of Mud River a short distance to the north. Conversely, the lower Duplin can sometimes have lower salinity levels than that of the upper sections during times of heavy

13

discharge from the Altamaha River into Doboy Sound. The Duplin estuary covers 3,300 acres, about fifteen per cent of which remains submerged at mean low water with a tidal excursion of about three miles.[2]

A survey of the Duplin by University of Georgia Marine Institute scientists in the 1950s determined that the river's water surface was relatively narrow at low tide. When the water rises to six feet above mean low tide, however, it begins to leave the banks and flow in a sheet across the marsh. Small increases in tidal height impel increased volumes of water into the estuary, and as a consequence the tidal flow is turbulent. This promotes greater turbidity, though marsh flushing is incomplete with very little fresh water entering the system. Most water in the estuary merely oscillates back and forth, rather than draining away to be replaced. The sediments in the bed of the Duplin are low in mud content and contain accumulations of shell material, much of which is deposited from the oyster banks along the river. At Little Sapelo Island and Pumpkin Hammock the river is eroding sandy Pleistocene deposits.[3]

The intertidal habitat of the Duplin, and its largest tributary, Barn Creek, is teeming with marine organisms that receive nutrients from the marshes, and in turn, provide food sources for saltwater fish species. The Marine Institute has conducted much of its research in these marshes, and over the last half century has made important

---

[2] Johnson, Hillestad, et.al., *Ecological Survey of the Coastal Region of Georgia*, 91.

[3] R.G. Wiegert and B.J. Freeman, *Tidal Salt Marshes of the Southeast Atlantic Coast: A Community Profile* (Washington, DC: U.S. Department of the Interior, Fish and Wildlife Service, 1990); R.A. Ragotzkie and R.A. Bryson, "Hydrography of the Duplin River, Sapelo Island, Georgia," *Bulletin of Marine Science of the Gulf and Caribbean* 5 (1955): 297-314.

discoveries relative to the feeding habits of subtidal species. Microalgae are productive in the river, and these and other organisms provide a food source for juvenile menhaden, a plankton feeder. Menhaden, in turn, are preyed upon by larger fish and birds. Flounder, bluefish and yellowtail are other finfish predators in the estuary; mullet are deposit feeders, and mummichog live in the shallower creeks and headwaters where they are rarely threatened by larger fish. Shrimp utilize the creeks off the Duplin throughout the year, and are especially prevalent during the summer. Larger predators, such as dolphins that feed around Marsh Landing dock on the lower Duplin, and mink and otter forage in the smaller creeks and marsh edges; birds feed in the tidal waters as well—pelicans, gulls and terns nearer the sound, and blue herons, ospreys and egrets further up the Duplin.

Eugene P. Odum, ecologist of the University of Georgia, and regarded as the "father of modern ecology," once described tidal creeks as a great circulatory system driven by the pumping "heart" of the tides. Tidal creeks and smaller rivers provide new water input to the marshes on each high tide, while flushing out and removing many of the by-products of marsh growth and marsh decay—detritus— on the ebbing tide. Some of the creeks are almost bare at low tide leaving exposed mud banks that serve as habitat to a variety of consumers such as fiddler crabs, herons, egrets, and marsh hens. On a flooding tide, snails become active while periwinkles and insects graze on the stems of the marsh cordgrass. Plankton and juveniles of various species enter the creeks with incoming tides, as do shrimp and fish when the water becomes deep enough.

McIntosh County's salt marshes are composed of many plant species, but the most prevalent by far is smooth cordgrass–*Spartina alterniflora*–which comprises about ninety per cent of the marsh system, and receives the greatest amount of tidal inundation. Despite its low diversity the marsh is considered to be one of the most productive natural areas on earth.[4] The basis for the marsh food chain is detritus originating from the dominant vascular plant, the cordgrass. There are differences in the *Spartina* along the creek banks, and that of the high marsh nearer the transitional zone that is comprised of a mix of short *Spartina*, and *Salicornia* marsh. Low marsh *Spartina* is taller and more luxuriant than other marshes, and prevails along the creek and river fringes. All life requires fresh water to carry on metabolic processes, and the marshes have unique mechanisms that allow them to extract fresh water from the saline waters of the estuary.[5]

Marsh soils are anaerobic except near the surface and around the roots. Soil bacteria that breaks down accumulated organic matter require an anaerobic environment with the rate of breakdown, and that in which plant nutrients become available for new marsh growth, being related to water-flow characteristics and the dispersal

---

[4] E.P. Odum and C.L. Schelske, "Mechanisms Maintaining High Productivity in Georgia Estuaries," *Proceedings* of the Gulf and Caribbean Fish Institute 14 (1961): 75-80.

[5] The most lucid study of the *Spartina* marsh ecosystem, minus the technical jargon, is Charles Seabrook, *The World of the Salt Marsh: Appreciating and Protecting the Tidal Marshes of the Southeastern Atlantic Coast* (Athens: University of Georgia Press, 2012). See also Mildred Teal and John Teal, *Portrait of an Island* (New York: Atheneum, 1964) and Teal and Teal, *Life and Death of a Salt Marsh* (New York: Atlantic, 1969).

Profile of a Salt Marsh

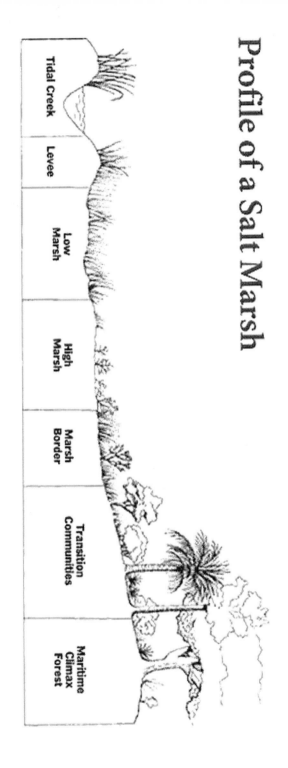

Tidal Creek | Levee | Low Marsh | High Marsh | Marsh Border | Transition Communities | Maritime Climax Forest

of waste products.[6] Plant zonation is always subject to elevation and hydrology but there is a water table that maintains the marsh sediments in a near waterlogged state in all but the highest intertidal elevations.[7] Consequently, there is a high diversity of plant, soil, and microbial attributes between the low and high *Spartina* zones.

Salt marsh requires nitrogen and phosphorus as nutrients, the latter of which is abundantly available in both the soil and the tidal waters. Nitrogen availability is more complicated. The use of this common air element by *Spartina* requires its conversion to ammonia, nitrate or nitrite by the marsh through blue-green algae on the marsh surface, and bacteria within the soil.[8] Thus, the adaptability of the marsh to natural processes in a salt water environment makes it one of the more unique plant species of any ecosystem.

Twice-daily tidal cycles convey nutrients into the marshes, export detritus and nutrients back into the estuary, and provide a large surface area for phytoplankton production. Tidal flushing maintains a desirable vertical distribution of nutrients and detritus; the base of the detritus food chain is decayed *Spartina,* which is attacked by microorganisms.

Marine Institute research has determined that bacteria found in Sapelo's marsh mud are an important link in the food chain. In the

---

[6] J.R. Wadsworth, "Geomorphic Characteristics of Tidal Drainage Networks in the Duplin River System, Sapelo Island, Georgia," PhD diss., University of Georgia, 1980; R.W. Frey and P. Basan, "Coastal Salt Marshes," in R.A. Davis, Jr., ed. *Coastal Sedimentary Environments,* 2nd edit. (New York: Springer-Verlag, 1985), 225-301.

[7] Wiegert and Freeman, *Tidal Salt Marshes of the Southeast Atlantic Coast.* See also the many technical papers relating to marsh studies in *Collected Reprints,* UGAMI.

[8] L.R. Pomeroy and R.G. Wiegert, *The Ecology of a Salt Marsh* (New York: Springer-Verlag, 1981).

late 1950s, John Teal found the important detritus-algae feeders to be fiddler crabs, periwinkle snails and nematodes among Sapelo's deposit feeders. The utilization of marsh organic matter accounts for about fifty-five per cent of production, leaving about forty-five per cent available for support of finfish, crabs, shrimp, oysters, and other estuarine species.[9] Further investigations found that marsh algae form a thin stratum between a dark, nutrient-rich, anaerobic sediment, and either an illuminated, aerobic, comparatively nutrient-poor water column. Thus, the algae habitat is subjected to rapid changes in light, temperature, pH, salinity, and nutrients that can have correspondingly rapid effects on the photosynthetic rate. Benthic productivity was found to represent about twelve per cent of the net primary production of the macrophytes in the marsh. About seventy-five per cent of this production occurs during ebbing tides, with the exposed creek banks being the most productive areas.[10]

In the higher intertidal zone between the *Spartina* and the upland, areas subjected to less frequent tidal inundation, other marsh-type plants are prevalent. Glasswort and saltgrass appear mixed with the shorter cordgrass. Black needlerush (*Juncus roemerianus*) develops as patches amid the cordgrass with its thin grey-brown stalks and sharp points. Other salt-tolerant plants mixed with the short *Spartina* in this zone are marsh bulrush and sea oxeye. Also featured in the higher zones are salt pans—barren sections of flat, packed soil that is free of vegetation because of its excessively high salinity.

---

[9] John M. Teal, "Energy Flow in the Salt Marsh Ecosystem of Georgia," *Ecology* 43 (1962): 614-24.
[10] L.R. Pomeroy, W.M. Darley, E.L. Dunn, J.L. Gallagher, E.B. Haines and D.M. Whitney, "Primary Production," in Pomeroy and Wiegert, *Ecology of a Salt Marsh*, 39-67.

Areas of vegetation lying amid *Spartina* marsh along the fringe abutting a tidal creek, or even a short distance apart from the uplands, are clumps of vegetation of varying size known as hammocks. These formations of high ground feature a mix of similar vegetation, including red cedar, sabal palm, wax myrtle, and yaupon holly. Hammock characteristics are similar, and they range in size from less than an acre to several acres. Many coastal hammocks have Pleistocene bases surrounded by their Holocene marshes. Other hammocks are more recent, being comprised of dredge spoil deposited on the marsh banks with the development of vegetation increasing with the passage of time, primarily red cedar, scrub oak, sabal palm and wax myrtle.

A variety of marine organisms utilize the marshes for nutrients as decomposing *Spartina* detritus gradually dissolves and is flushed by the tides to provide food. Numerous consumer species inhabit the marsh ecosystem with the major groups being comprised of zooplankton, benthic invertebrates, insects, fishes, reptiles, birds and mammals. Benthic macro-invertebrates are the most conspicuous of the consumers, particularly fiddler crabs (*Uca* species), marsh mussel (*Geukensia demissa*), and marsh periwinkle (*Littorino irrorata*). Noticeable along some creek banks are oyster reefs. Oysters (*Crassostrea virginica*) settle on solid surfaces along the banks and subtidal water; as filter feeders they use marsh nutrients as an important food source. Oyster beds can alter tidal flow in the creeks by creating pools and small breakwaters.

In the early decades of the twentieth century, Georgia salt marshes supported a sizeable oyster industry but over-exploitation, and the failure to replace shell, led to its near-collapse by the 1950s.

Another beneficiary of marsh nutrients directly related to commercial use is the Atlantic blue crab (*Callinectus sapidus*), the majority of which are taken in the sounds and the smaller rivers and creeks. Crabs use the marshes and creeks as habitat during their juvenile and sub-adult stages.

Of even greater economic significance, the marsh is critical in supporting the coastal shrimp fishery, long a multi-million-dollar industry on the Georgia coast, with peak production in the middle decades of the twentieth century. While coastal shrimp (*Penaeus*) spawn in the open ocean, they migrate to the inshore waters as juveniles, and depend on marsh-produced nutrients during their growth stages before returning to the sea.

At low tide, the ubiquitous fiddler crab, particularly the sand fiddler (*Uca pugilator*), is frequently observed scuttling along the mudflats foraging for food near its burrow. Fiddlers extract food from the substrate based on differing feeding stimulants in response to levels in the food resource.[11] Gradients in biotic and abiotic factors resulting from tidal flooding affect the distribution of marsh organisms with the structural characteristics of *Spartina* providing refuge for some species from predators and submergence. The periwinkle prevalent in the marshes is a favorite of predators, particularly the blue crab.

Much of the current understanding of the salt marsh ecosystem and its attendant rivers, creeks and dividings, and the biological and chemical processes that occur within these systems, began to be

---

[11] J.R. Robertson, K. Bancroft, G. Vermeer, and K. Plaiser, "Experimental Studies on the Foraging Behavior of the Sand Fiddler Crab," *Journal of Experimental Marine Biology and Ecology* 52 (1980): 47-64.

formulated after 1953 with the establishment of the University of Georgia Marine Institute on Sapelo Island. A young biology professor at the University of Georgia, Eugene P. Odum (1913-2002), who was laying the foundation for the first serious investigations of saltmarsh ecosystems on the southeastern coast, and several of his colleagues, worked with Sapelo owner Richard J. Reynolds, Jr. to make it possible for the marine biological laboratory to come to Sapelo.[12]

Ecological research in the first forty years often entailed field studies stemming from two basic considerations: determining the water flow characteristics of *Spartina alterniflora* (smooth cordgrass marsh), and the chemical and biological processes associated with *Spartina*, in concert with the marine organisms that proliferate the marsh ecosystem, or are directly affected by the marsh. Eventually, an important connection was made between the dynamics of the natural processes occurring in the salt marshes, and the sustainability of marine life in the nearshore and estuarine waters, as Emory Thomas points out:

"This transmittal through tidal action of organic matter is primarily in the form of detritus which is mostly decomposed *Spartina*. The process by which detritus enters the ocean is called 'outwelling' and the initial hypothesis among Odum and the other scientists at the University of Georgia Marine Institute was that this outwelling from salt marshes and estuaries lay at the base of the food chain which supported the abundant marine life found off the east

---

[12] Betty Jean Craige, *Eugene Odum: Ecosystem Ecologist & Environmentalist* (Athens: University of Georgia Press, 2001). 54-58. An overview of the first forty years of research at the UGA Marine Institute is found in Buddy Sullivan, *Sapelo, People and Place on a Georgia Sea Island* (Athens: University of Georgia Press, 2017).

coast. Thus there seemed to be an empirical connection between *Spartina* and shrimp cocktail at least. In very recent years, however, scientists have challenged the assumption that 'outwelling' from salt marshes is vital to the food chain in coastal waters."[13]

Odum's research in those early years at Sapelo had important ramifications for the work of the Marine Institute in its first two decades. It also influenced his own evolving attitudes about ecology and environmentalism. Odum expresses an almost spiritual connection to the marsh and tides:

"We moved up tidal creeks in small outboard motor boats on ebbing tides; we found ourselves in deep canyons of golden mud banks, topped by six-foot high stands of marsh grass looking for all the world like a well-fertilized stand of sugar cane. The notion came to us in those early days that we were in the arteries of a remarkable energy-absorbing natural system whose heart was the pumping action of the tides. The entire tideland complex of barrier islands, marshes, creeks, and river mouths was a single operational unit linked together by the tide. If we were right, each part of the system would have to be dependent for its life-sustaining energy not only on the direct rays of the sun, but also on the energy of the tides...Does nature routinely exploit tidal power as men have dreamed of doing for centuries? In the past, biologists who studied estuarine and seashore organisms had been preoccupied with how such life adapts to the obvious stresses; that some of the stresses might be converted to subsidies was, and still is, something of a new theory. This germ of an idea, subsequently developed by twenty years of team research on Sapelo, will, we hope, provide the basis for man to design with, rather than against, nature on this remarkable sea coast."[14]

---

[13] Emory M. Thomas, "The South and the Sea: Some Thoughts on the Southern Maritime Tradition," *Georgia Historical Quarterly* 67 (Summer 1983).

[14] Eugene P. Odum, "Living Marsh," in Robert Hanie, *Guale: The Golden Coast of Georgia* (San Francisco: Friends of the Earth, 1974), Introduction.

The upland wooded areas contiguous to the marshes on the McIntosh County mainland, as well as areas of Sapelo Island and Blackbeard islands, are characterized by a mixed maritime forest dominated by stands of mature live oak (*Quercus virginiana*), and several varieties of pine (*Pinus*). Other sections of the upland forest comprise a mixed oak-hardwood community, but with less presence of pine. Here there are live oak, laurel oak, water oak, hickory, bay, holly, magnolia, and some slash pine. The oaks with their low, spreading limbs support various vines and epiphytes (air plants), the latter dominated by Spanish moss and resurrection fern. The latter epiphyte appears dead and dried out in its dormant phase but springs to life, lush and green, during periods of rainfall. Wending their way around the gnarled thick lower trunks and limbs of the oaks are grapevines and Virginia creeper. Spanish moss is a bromeliad and features tiny green flowers, hardly visible. Moss is a distinctive feature of the oaks but can also be observed on other tree species. Often seen on or near the marsh fringes are stands of native cabbage palm (*Sabal palmetto*) with an understory dominated by wax myrtle, broomsedge and panic grass in uncleared areas.

Along the tidal areas of Harris Neck and the South Newport River section, there are several distinct ecologies and forest zones: upland hardwood maritime forests, lowland hardwood forests, old and new pine plantations, and grassy savannahs. The lowland forests are typically found in wetter areas, and are comprised of live oak, water oak, loblolly pine, hickory, blackgum, sweetgum, and sweetbay, set amidst thick understorys of palmetto and wax myrtle.

Proper timber management provides open food habitat for deer and other species, and facilitates the healthy growth of the maritime forest and commercial pine plantations. Mixed stands of oak and pine are scattered in many areas of McIntosh County's uplands, with closed oak canopies beneath many of the pines. The selective cutting of pine usually results in cleared habitat for deer herds, and has hastened the regeneration of natural oak and other hardwood species in parts of the timbered areas. Large sections of the maritime forest on the McIntosh mainland and the larger islands are dominated by pine-palmetto vegetation with the pine canopy rarely closed. Though pine is cut selectively, natural seeding remains effective in some areas. Saw palmetto form dense thickets four to five feet tall amid the pine forests and is often interspersed with other vegetation.

In a number of areas along highway 99 in McIntosh County between Meridian and Eulonia, and on either side of the road between South Newport and Harris Neck, will be observed cleared, grassy meadows, some being open grasslands, or savannahs, usually the result of manmade modifications for agriculture and cattle pasturage in the nineteenth and early twentieth centuries. Some of these areas have thick stands of bahia grass (*Poaceae notatum*) planted earlier as forage for cattle herds. Many areas of the islands, particularly Sapelo and Creighton, and the eastern mainland tidewater are clear and open, evidence of earlier crop cultivation.

One of the best means of exemplifying the connectedness of ecology and land use in McIntosh County is through a review of its soil types, particularly in areas of the county that will come under scrutiny in future chapters of this study. The soils of Sapelo and Creighton islands and other tidewater sections of the county, such as Harris Neck and west along the South Newport River, Sutherland's Bluff and other Sapelo River tracts, and areas along either side of

highway 99 from Crescent to just north of Darien, are derived
primarily from quartz sands. These generally have high permeability,
a condition that results in low water-holding capacity and rapid
leaching. These soils range from deep, well-drained sands to poorly
drained thick black loam surfaces and subsurface horizons of gray
sands. Most of the soils, however, range from moderately well-
drained to poorly-drained. These coastal soils are generally highly
acidic, whether they are well-drained or poorly-drained. According to
the most recent soil survey of McIntosh County (1959), the pH of
the soil in the county's tidewater areas range from 4.1 to 7.4 among
the twelve identified soil types inventoried. Additionally, nineteenth
and early-to-mid- twentieth century agriculture and cattle operations
resulted in the clearing, ditching, and draining of many upland areas,
thus altering both the natural hydrology as well as the soil dynamics
in some areas. This is particularly true of parts of Sapelo Island, the
Altamaha delta bottomlands and large areas of the western sections
of McIntosh County, which is dominated by low-lying swamps and
forested timber land.[15]

Hydrological factors especially come into play in McIntosh
County's eastern tidewater areas, including the islands. On the
beaches of Sapelo, Blackbeard and Wolf islands, high salt
concentrations in dune sands inhibit the vertical percolation of
rainwater through the dunes. This limited water supply reduces the
amount of vegetation on the seaward side of the county's islands. On
the inshore islands, the western sides of the larger barrier islands,

---

[15] Hubert J. Byrd, D.G. Aydelott, et. al., *Soil Survey of McIntosh County,
Georgia*, Series 1959 (Washington, DC: U.S. Department of Agriculture,
1961). The discussion here is based on the 1959 survey.

and along the eastern mainland tidewater the salts exert an influence on vegetation in the intertidal zone between the marshes and the upland, and tend to limit species diversity. The abundant nutrients, however, enable the relatively few species in these areas to be highly productive. Conversely, as noted earlier, there are hard salt pans in the high marsh in some areas that are so concentrated in salts, usually two or more times that of sea water, that few vascular plants can grow there. Good examples are seen along the Valona road on the mainland and near Dean Creek on the South End of Sapelo.

The most cultivable soils in McIntosh County are the "fine sands" of the Galestown, St. Johns, Palm Beach and Ona-Scranton series, all of which are moderately well-drained with a sandy surface. McIntosh County's greatest agricultural productivity in the nineteenth century, outside of rice production in the Altamaha delta, was in the areas of these four fine sands. On Sapelo Island, Galestown, Ona-Scranton and pockets of Leon fine sand especially supported the cultivation of sea island cotton, sugar cane and provision crops at Kenan Field, High Point, Bourbon Field and Long Tabby. Palm Beach fine sand is dark and well drained, and found on level areas of sand ridges near tidal marsh. With proper fertilization, this soil was also of utility for cotton cultivation, for example on Sapelo at parts of Kenan Field, Dumoussay Field, Long Row Field (Chocolate) and Little Sapelo Island. Although it supported provision and subsistence crop cultivation in many areas, St. Johns fine sand is relatively poorly drained and is often found in damp areas, with vegetation of sabal palm, palmetto, huckleberry, gallberry, and scattered pines. On the McIntosh tidal mainland and on Sapelo Island many of the Ona-Scranton and Palm Beach soils are now forested with pine, chiefly

27

loblolly pine, with mixed stands of live oak, areas often indicative of earlier agricultural activities.

Palm Beach sand dominates the northeast side of Harris Neck, from the South Newport River southward to below Gould's Landing, an area known to have had a high production of sea island cotton. Palm Beach sand is also identified in a relatively confined area south of Gould's Landing on the east side of Harris Neck where the Harris and King families cultivated sea island cotton; the same soil prevails on the southern tip of the Neck at Julianton. There are pockets of Palm Beach sand at Sutherland's Bluff, Shellman Bluff and Contentment Bluff, all being areas where cotton was grown as a cash crop. Galestown fine sand, however, is the dominant soil at Sutherland's Bluff as well as at Belleville, both being areas of high crop productivity. Another moderately well-drained soil type, the Ona-Scranton fine sand soil series, is typically found in areas (but not all) where agriculture was productive. On both the north and south ends of Creighton Island are Ona-Scranton and Palm Beach fine soils in areas where cotton was cultivated. Ona-Scranton is also found at Kenan Field and Long Row Field on Sapelo Island, and in sections of the McIntosh County eastern tidewater from Crescent to Darien, including Black Island, all being areas of crop production. Oddly, however, very little Ona-Scranton sand is to be found anywhere on Harris Neck. The prevailing soils on the upper end of Harris Neck are Palm Beach and Rutledge, while along the South Newport River, on tracts west of the Neck, Ona-Scranton, Leon fine sand, and Galestown are prevalent. Rutledge fine sand is fairly extensive on the eastern tidewater and the islands. However, it is generally poorly drained, and is covered by water part of the year with vegetation of blackgum, cypress, and pine. Examples are a long strip of Rutledge soil along the eastern side of Creighton Island, and pockets of the soil on the upper end of Harris Neck in the wetter areas. With adequate drainage Rutledge is well-suited for pine plantations, but is usually too wet for most crops.

Eastern McIntosh County's soils, including those on the islands, include many areas of high-phase tidal marsh soil in zones close to the marsh that are non-cultivable but are sufficiently above the frequent influence of tidal inundation to allow vegetation of red cedar, small oaks and coarse grasses. These areas include the marsh zones of the smaller islands, such as Creighton and Little Sapelo, where tidal inundation occasionally occurs, and on the eastern shore of the mainland along the coast from the South Newport River, Harris Neck, lower Bruro Neck, White Chimney, and from Belleville southward to the Darien River, including areas around Baisden's Bluff, Cedar Point, Valona, Hudson, the Thicket, the Ridge and the marsh islands of Hird, Black and Mayhall. Soils identified as High tidal marsh, and subject to more frequent periods of tidal inundation, such as on spring tides, fringe the upland marsh transition zones and have vegetation of wax myrtle, marsh elder, saltwort and sea oxeye. Low tidal marsh is comprised almost exclusively of smooth cordgrass (*Spartina*) with pockets of black needlerush (*Juncus*) in the higher areas. The prevailing soil on the seaward sides of the barrier islands is Coastal beach sand, a wide strip that runs along the entire easternmost edge of McIntosh County, including Blackbeard and Cabretta islands, Nannygoat Beach on Sapelo Island's South End, and Wolf Island. Strips of porous Blanton and Lakeland sands are featured on the upland sand ridges

29

on both the north and south ends of Blackbeard Island. However, on a sand ridge in Blackbeard's northwest corner there is a strip of Palm Beach fine sand, validating the use of that small section of the island for cotton cultivation in the early 1800s.

There are two other areas of McIntosh County that should be mentioned for their soil types. In the Altamaha delta the only soil is that identified as Wet Alluvial land, found nowhere else in the county. In an earlier 1929 soil survey this rich bottomland was labeled as Altamaha clay. It includes the western part of Broughton Island, all of Champneys, Butler's, Cambers, Generals and Carr's islands, the western half of Rhett's Island, and along both sides of Cathead Creek to about three miles west of Darien. These were all areas of rice cultivation in the nineteenth century. The other area is the western section of the county which is largely comprised of soils labeled as Swamp, in addition to the Bladen series of sands and clays, which are not conducive to large-scale agriculture such as that practiced in the Altamaha bottomlands, the coastal islands and the county's eastern tidewater. Much of the western part of the county is comprised of large swampy areas, along with drier sandy areas commonly called the pine flatwoods. One interesting soil type stands out from the others mentioned here, that being Lakeland coarse sand. It is prevalent in only two areas of McIntosh County, one being an extensive strip in the southwest section of the county immediately north of Buffalo Swamp, running west to the Long County line. It is an area known as the "sand hills," part of which touch on the Altamaha River at Fort Barrington and Barrington and Harper's lakes, and at Possum Point at the headwaters of Lewis Creek. The only other area Lakeland sand is found in the county is on the sand ridges of Blackbeard Island.

Relevant to the forgoing discussion it must be kept in mind that sizeable sections of McIntosh County have been subjected to modification of varying degrees by human activity over the last two-and-a-half centuries, primarily for agriculture, cattle-herding, and timbering. Successive private owners in areas of the county and on the islands constructed irrigation canals and ditches to drain off low-lying sections, particularly in the Altamaha delta and on Sapelo Island, and built levees and embankments to facilitate agriculture and timbering. Irrigation ditches were dug by slave labor in the nineteenth century to facilitate crop production and the watering of livestock. Some of the nineteenth century ditches on Sapelo Island were improved and enlarged in the 1920s through dynamiting operations during H.E. Coffin's ownership. Evidence of the ditches made or enlarged with dynamite is conspicuous in places on the south and central portions of Sapelo. Pursuant to modifications for truck farming, there was also ditching on Butler's and Champneys islands in the 1930s and 1940s to improve drainage provided by earlier irrigation ditches associated with nineteenth century rice planting.

About one third of McIntosh County is salt marsh, islands, marsh hammocks and a complex network of sounds, tidal rivers and creeks, some of which penetrate well inland, such as the South Newport and Sapelo rivers. From the beginning of the county's English settlement, human populations have tended to inhabit upland tracts on or near the rivers and creeks—areas such as South Newport, Priester, Harris Neck, Shellman Bluff, Sutherland's Bluff, Belleville, Pine Harbor,

31

Baisden's Bluff, Cedar Point, Valona, Hudson, the Thicket, Ridgeville and Darien. These areas of the coast are largely drained by Sapelo and Doboy sounds, the South Newport and Sapelo rivers, the tidal tributaries attached thereto, and the freshwater-influenced Altamaha River and its estuary.

West of the tidewater is an altogether different ecosystem, particularly with respect to that section west of U.S. highway 17. Compared to the tidewater, the western half of the county is very sparsely populated. Here there are fresh-water swamps, pine flatwoods, palmetto thickets, pockets of sand hill ridges, and open meadows that once served as cattle pasturage. The larger swamps are occasionally flooded by seasonal spring freshets from the Altamaha, and consequently are regarded as some of the most inaccessible areas of McIntosh County. The largest are Buffalo Swamp on the south, drained by the Altamaha River, Lewis Creek and Cathead Creek, Young's Swamp in the central part of the county, Big Mortar and Oscar swamps in the western section and Bull Town Swamp between McIntosh and Liberty counties, drained by the South Newport River.

The ecological dynamic of the Altamaha delta is vastly different from that of the tidewater and pine flatwoods. The delta is an area that, prior to English settlement, was dominated by dense cypress hardwood swamps and other wetlands. After the Revolution the cypress swamps in the lower Altamaha gave way to large-scale rice production with planters utilizing the soils of the rich river bottomlands washed down to the coast from middle Georgia. Here the nineteenth century planters produced rice as a money staple, with cotton and sugar cane as rotation crops. These areas are unpopulated now, being under state administration as protected waterfowl management areas.

Animal species common to the McIntosh islands and tidewater areas are white-tailed deer, raccoons, opossum, squirrels, otters, minks, armadillos, and feral hogs and cattle. Eastern diamondback rattlesnakes populate the uplands and beach dunes, cottonmouth water moccasins are in the wetter areas, and numerous species of non-venomous snakes are commonly encountered in the less-cleared areas. It is likely that much, perhaps most, of the flora and fauna encountered today is not the same as that of the Archaic period (10,000-3,000 B.P.). During the Archaic most of the area was covered by a climax forest, which would have reduced the available food supply in the spring and summer. There would have been browsing areas available in the shrub-herb layers of the ecosystem but it would not have supported the large deer herds, and other wildlife that prevail today with open pastures and second-and-third generation forest growth. As oak species matured in the Archaic, the fall and winter months would have produced sufficient acorn fall to support deer in greater numbers as time went along; Spanish moss and plants growing in the high marsh would have provided additional food sources. The remaining vestiges of the maritime climax forest from that period disappeared when large areas of the islands and coastal mainland were cleared for agriculture and oak timbering in the eighteenth and nineteenth centuries. If the early climax forest was not seriously depleted during the proto-historic and aboriginal agricultural eras, then it almost certainly was during the colonial period and after.

Weather is an important component of local environmental considerations. McIntosh County's climate is classified as sub-tropical, consisting of brief, relatively mild winters, and warm, humid summers. Cold temperatures in some winters prevent tropical or sub-tropical vegetation to persist but are sufficiently mild to allow some species characteristic of warmer areas to grow and reproduce naturally. The average date of the earliest frost is December 3, with the latest being March 2, allowing an average growing season of 276 days. Intense summer showers account for much of the county's annual precipitation, which averages about 52 inches. The wettest months are June, July, and August with the driest being October and November. One of the driest years on record was 1954 when only 32.9 inches of rainfall was recorded on Sapelo Island. The wettest was seventy-five inches in 1964, a hurricane year. Several hurricanes from 1989-2005 passed near the Georgia coast but none caused serious damage. Most east coast hurricanes tend to follow the warmer waters of the offshore Gulf Stream. Brunswick, Georgia, just south of McIntosh County, is the westernmost point from the Gulf Stream of any section of the south Atlantic coast. Several historic hurricanes, however, have created extreme conditions that precipitated temporary economic chaos. The storms directly impacting McIntosh County with either landfall or severe effects, occurred in 1804, 1824, 1854, 1893, 1896, 1898, 1944, 1964 (Dora), 1979 (David), 2016 (Matthew) and 2017 (Irma). The worst of these were the 1824 and 1898 cyclones that left much of Sapelo and the nearby islands under several feet of water due to high tidal surge.

No review of McIntosh County ecology in relation to its history can omit at least some mention of the eighteenth-century naturalist

34

William Bartram (1739-1823). Bartram made the first serious assessment, based on scientific rigor, of the ecology of coastal Georgia, including the area that later became McIntosh County. He was the son of well-known Quaker botanist John Bartram. After completing his formal education in Philadelphia, William accompanied his father as assistant on a botanical exploration and plant-gathering tour through the Carolinas, Georgia and East Florida in 1765-66. William Bartram later travelled the southern wilderness with much of his time being spent in Georgia from 1773-77.

McIntosh County's role in his findings is significant, for it was here that Bartram discovered the rare and beautiful flowering shrub, *Franklinia Alatamaha,* named for Benjamin Franklin and the nearby Altamaha River. The *Franklinia* was originally discovered by William and his father on October 1, 1765 growing near the Altamaha between present-day Cox and Fort Barrington in the county's south-west section. This unique flowering shrub was the so-called "Lost Gordonia" of botanical fame.

On his second expedition in 1773, William Bartram again visited Fort Barrington at which time he classified and named the shrub. In the autumn 1765 visit with his father the flower was not in bloom, thus they had been unable to classify it. Bartram collected specimens and sent them to Philadelphia where they became the source of the present-day plants of *Franklinia* in botanical gardens. Bartram published his observations in a classic work, *Travels through North and South Carolina, Georgia, East and West Florida,* completed in 1791. In *Travels,* Bartram provides notes on his exploration of the area that would become McIntosh County. The following passage relates to his visit in the spring of 1773:

"The next morning I set off for the settlements on the Alatamaha [sic], still pursuing the high road for Fort Barrington, till towards noon, when I turned off to the left, following the road to Darien, a settlement on the river, twenty miles lower down, and near the coast. The fore part of this day's journey was pleasant, the plantations frequent, and the roads in tolerable good repair. But the country being now less cultivated, the roads became bad, pursuing my journey almost continually, through swamps and creeks, till night, when I lost my way; but coming up to a fence, I saw a glimmering light, which conducted me to a house; there I stayed all night. Early next morning, I set off again towards Darien. I rode several miles through a high forest of pines, thinly growing on a level plain, which admitted an ample view, and a free circulation of air, to another swamp; and crossing a considerable branch of river [South Newport River], I then came to a small plantation by the side of another swamp: the people were remarkably civil and hospitable. The man's name was M'Intosh,[16] in a family of the first colony established in Georgia, under the conduct of General Oglethorpe. I was treated there with some excellent venison, and here found friendly and secure shelter from a tremendous thunderstorm. The tempest being over, I took leave of my friends and departed. The air was now cool and salubrious, and riding seven or eight miles, through a pine forest, I came to Sapello bridge, to which the salt tide flows. I [proceeded] to Mr. L. M'Intosh's at Darien..."[17]

In *Travels of William Bartram* (Naturalist's Edition), editor Francis Harper provides insightful commentary on this stage of Bartram's journey, based on his 1930s analysis of Bartram:

"Bartram's route from the Midway district to Darien is rather puzzling, but it may be tentatively defined somewhat as follows: south

---

[16] Donald McIntosh of Bain whose farm was a land grant at the later site of the South Newport settlement. Donald McIntosh was the patriarch of this branch of the family that were among the original Scots Highlander families that settled Darien in early 1736.
[17] Lachlan McIntosh (1727-1806) was the most famous of the McIntosh family of coastal Georgia.

along the Barrington Road to Bull Town Swamp at the southern border of Liberty County; then for several additional miles on the same road along the boundary between Long and McIntosh counties; then 3 miles southeastward to the vicinity of Jones, where he may have lost his way toward night in a westerly branch of Big Mortar Swamp; then, the next day, 5 miles eastward, across 'a considerable branch of Sapello river' to South Newport, where a 'small plantation' belonging to a McIntosh was located; then 'seven or eight miles' southward along the present U.S. Highway 17 to 'Sapello bridge,' which was doubtless at or near present Eulonia; then, continuing southward along the same highway, a dozen miles more to Lachlan McIntosh's home in Darien on the banks of the Altamaha. Bartram's route from Darien to Fort Barrington was probably by way of Chisholm Swamp, McClendon School, and Cox. The 'two new beautiful shrubs' (Franklinia) had been discovered on October 1, 1765, by John and William Bartram in the same spot where William now notes them again. This spot is believed to be a sand-hill bog on the north side of the road at a point about 1.7 miles northwest of Cox. There is considerable doubt as to whether these shrubs were actually in bloom at the time of Bartram's present visit, which was probably about April 24 or 25, 1773."[18]

---

[18] William Bartram, *Travels of William Bartram*, Naturalist's Edition, Francis Harper, ed. (Athens: University of Georgia Press, 1958).

2

Harris Neck: Pre-History to Emancipation

Some 4,000 years ago Native American peoples thrived in the areas that now comprise northern McIntosh County and Harris Neck, as well as on the barrier islands along Georgia's coast. Burial mounds of the Guale chiefdom once proliferated this section of the coast, until most of them were eradicated through agricultural and forestry operations in the eighteenth and nineteenth centuries.

Archaeological investigations have been conducted at Harris Neck and Bruro Neck since the 1890s, the findings conveying a wealth of burials and artifacts from the Native American and Spanish periods of habitation of the region.

The first archaeologist to employ scholarly rigor to investigative field research on Sapelo was Clarence Bloomfield Moore, a Philadelphia academic who conducted studies on the south Atlantic and Gulf coasts in the 1890s and early 1900s. His detailed field notes and drawings, when published in 1897 as *Certain Aboriginal Mounds of the Georgia Coast*, documented for the first time Native American societal life in the region. This compendium included an assessment of his work at Sapelo and Creighton islands, and the Harris Neck area in 1896.[19] Moore's observations, in tandem with the validity of his detailed field notes and reports on mound complexes and shell rings, provided later generations of researchers with critically important insights into aspects of pre-Columbian life on the coast of Georgia.

Moore's interest in Southeastern coastal aboriginal societies was inspired by a series of articles published in the *American Naturalist* from 1892 to 1894 on the "Shell Heaps of the St. Johns River." Moore's meticulous attention to detail in the methodology of his field collection, and subsequent documentation of aboriginal sites visited between 1894 and 1918, has enabled his findings to be used continuously through the years. He and his staff traveled the Gulf of Mexico, and the southeastern Atlantic coasts, in addition to making trips along several interior rivers. The annual field work was usually conducted from October through April after which Moore returned to Philadelphia for the summer to collate and rewrite his field notes, and make public his latest research.

During his investigations of Sapelo and Creighton islands, and other sites along McIntosh County's tidewater, Moore visited the Walker Mound, about a mile and a half west of present-day Shellman Bluff. Based on his notes, Moore and his assistants apparently went up the Sapelo River to Belleville Point at the end of each day's field work, then returned the next morning to Shellman Bluff. There the *Gopher* was moored in the Bruro River during Moore's day trips to Creighton Island and the Walker Mound on the mainland near Shellman.

---

[19] Clarence B. Moore, *Certain Aboriginal Mounds of the Georgia Coast* (Philadelphia: Journal of the Academy of Natural Sciences, 1897).

Moore described the Walker Mound as being almost six feet high with a base diameter of forty-six feet:

"The mound had previously been dug into to an inconsiderable extent. On its northern margin grew a live-oak 5 feet in diameter, 3 feet from the ground. This tree was not removed, though otherwise the mound was totally demolished...The mound was composed of rich, loamy brown sand with many local layers of oyster shells. The usual charcoal and fireplaces were present... A black layer from 3 inches to 1 foot thickness, made up of sand mingled with charcoal in minute particles, ran through the mound at about the level of the surrounding territory...the layer [being] 5 feet 9 inches below the surface."[20]

Moore discovered the remains of seventy-five individuals in thirty-six burials. Some of the burials were cremations in urns based on Moore's discovery of charred bones, in addition to the remains of bones placed in the pits that were then filled with oyster shell. Shell beads were catalogued within the mound, as were other grave goods including whelk bowls, shell ear pins and cups. Irene-incised bowls and other pottery vessels and jars were recovered, one of which yielded Irene Complicated Stamped decoration.

Georgia state archaeologist Lewis H. Larson visited the Walker Mound site in 1953 and noted that the live oak tree described by Moore a half century earlier was still standing, among other oaks. The trees were likely on the site to provide shade for cattle herds or workers cultivating the fields, a common practice on coastal farm tracts in the nineteenth and early twentieth centuries.[21] Larson noted

---

[20] Moore, quoted in Larson, ibid., 23.

[21] For a review of nineteenth century agriculture in northern McIntosh County, including the Shellman Bluff area, see Buddy Sullivan, *Early Days on the Georgia Tidewater*, op. cit., all editions.

that the site had disappeared and has not been relocated, largely due to the extensive planting of a pine plantation on and around the site. Large expanses of slash pine have made the Walker Mound all but impossible to find in the present-day. During this time Moore also investigated a mound near Contentment Bluff about a mile and a half mile north of Shellman Bluff on the Bruro River.

During this same field season, the upper end of Harris Neck drew Moore's attention, particularly an area on the Barbour Island River at Gould's Landing on the site of the former antebellum Bahama plantation of Thomas K. Gould.[22] Moore describes Bahama as a place-name in his report, it then being the post office for the Harris Neck African American settlement nearby.[23] The African American community of freedmen on the upper end of Harris Neck was begun in the early 1870s and was self-sufficient and stable with the population engaged in agriculture, oyster harvesting, and timber-related pursuits in the late nineteenth and early twentieth centuries. The settlement was later condemned and the people relocated when the federal government made plans to develop an army airfield on the site just as World War II was beginning.[24]

The results of Moore's investigation at Bahama apparently were not particularly fruitful. He made note of "numerous low shell heaps" that yielded little in the way of artifacts, and he excavated two small mounds in which were found several burials.

In 1952 and 1953, Larson excavated a site several hundred feet

[22] An area of Harris Neck later occupied by the World War II airfield, and still later by the Wildlife Refuge docks.
[23] The Bahama post office was established in 1891, and was re-designated as Lacey in 1896 at the same location.
[24] Sullivan, *Early Days on the Georgia Tidewater*, all editions.

southeast of the Livingston house at Thomas Landing on the South Newport River, almost two miles north of Moore's Bahama site. He reported finding Spanish majolica and olive jar ware sherds dating from the sixteenth and seventeenth centuries.

In 1986, the U.S. Fish and Wildlife Service, which administered the Harris Neck National Wildlife Refuge, contracted Southeastern Archaeological Services, Inc. to conduct field surveys at Gould's Landing, as mitigation of the adverse efforts of the construction of a service road to the Refuge's docks and storage facilities on the Barbour Island River.[25] These investigations yielded artifacts from all periods of pre-Columbian and historic periods of occupancy, including Native American, Spanish and plantation eras. A large amount of materials were recovered at the site relating to the antebellum Gould cotton plantation located there overlooking the Barbour Island River.[26] The field work of Larson in 1952-53 and that of Southeastern in the mid-1980s has provided substantive credence to relatively recent theories that the upper end Harris Neck was an important settlement of the Espogache/Tupiqui kingdom, and the possibility of its association with the Tolomato Mission prior to the 1597 Guale uprising.[27]

---

[25] Chad O. Braley, Lisa D. O'Steen, and Irvy R. Quitmyer, "Archaeological Investigations at 9Mc14 1, Harris Neck National Wildlife Refuge, McIntosh County, Georgia," Southeastern Archaeological Services, Inc., Athens, Georgia, 1986.

[26] Material later in this chapter discusses the Gould plantation at Bahama and further elaborates on the 1986 archaeological report.

[27] Tolomato and the 1597 revolt are discussed in J. Michael Francis and Kathleen M. Kole, *Murder and Martyrdom in in Spanish Florida: Don Juan and the Guale Uprising of 1597* (New York: American Museum of Natural History Anthropological Papers 95, 2011).

18th Century Settlement at Harris Neck

Stephen Dickenson, Daniel Demetre, David Delegal, William Thomas Harris, William Jones, and later, Francis Levett, are some of the early names associated with the settlement and development of Harris Neck and lands near the South Newport River in the latter half of the eighteenth century. Many of the cultivated tracts were at what came to be known as Harris Neck, in the northeastern section of McIntosh County, Georgia. Harris Neck and the plantations along the South Newport River prospered in the antebellum period, and represent some of the most fascinating history associated with McIntosh County. This section, comprising the 22nd General Militia District of the county, was almost thirty miles distant from the county seat at Darien where the business, social, religious and commercial affairs of the county were centered. Thus, the South Newport River and Harris Neck sections probably had more connection to Savannah and Liberty County than with Darien.

While members of the McIntosh family were the recipients of many of the land grants in the District of Darien and St. Andrew Parish in the 1740s and 1750s, others who served the British in the recently-ended war with Spain also acquired acreage in the region, particularly in what later became Harris Neck and north McIntosh County.

Oldnor and Barbour islands, off Sapelo Sound and east of Harris Neck, were granted as early as 1744, and were under cultivation soon after. At Dickenson's Neck, later Harris Neck, land grants were awarded to William Thomas Harris, Roderick McIntosh, David Delegal, Daniel Demetre, John Todd, John Jones, and others. Demetre, coxswain on the English scout boats during the Spanish war, received additional acreage in the 1750s, including Smith

Island, later Creighton. The McIntoshes of Bain, and other McDonalds, settled along the South Newport River; Norman McDonald had a plantation at Turkey Camp Swamp. Further north, near the Broad Road, was Robert McDonald. The Baillies, Alexander and Robert, had tracts at the headwaters of the Sapelo River, portions of which they cleared for farming near the later site of Sapelo Bridge.

John McIntosh Mohr, and his four sons, William, Lachlan, John and George, and daughter Anne, were known as the Borlum McIntoshes, and their land grants as the Borlum lands. The McDonalds and the McIntoshes of Bain settled near the South Newport River in the northern part of later McIntosh County. Donald McIntosh Bain lived in the area of the present-day South Newport community, his grant including the swamp that he called "Strathlachlan," later corrupted to Strawlathlan. Between the South Newport and Sapelo rivers was the plantation of Angus McIntosh while John Polson and Roderick McLeod were granted land on Bruro Neck in the present-day Shellman Buff area. Sir Patrick Houstoun was granted 1,000 acres of upland and tidal rice lands on Cathead Creek west of Darien, and land near the South Newport River that he named Marengo. James Wright, third royal governor of Georgia, also had holdings in the Altamaha delta, including the tract that came to be known as Wright's Island.

Land Grants in the Upper District of Darien to 1755

Daniel Demetre: 500 acres on the South Newport River, May 1750; John McIntosh (Benjamin): 500 acres on the south side of the Sapelo River, 1750; Roderick McIntosh: 500 acres on a north branch of the Sapelo River, 1754; George McDonald: 150 acres at the head of a

creek on the north side of Sapelo River; Donald Kennedy: 150 acres
on the north side of Sapelo River; James Steward (Stuart): 50 acres
on the north branch of Sapelo River, 1749; Peter Grant: 50 acres on
the south side of Sapelo River; Gilbert Grant: unspecified amount of
acreage on the Sapelo River; Patrick Sutherland: 500 acres on the
north side of Sapelo River; Ann Demetre (as guardian to William
Thomas Harris, her son): 350 acres on a creek north of Sapelo River;
Hugh Morrison: 150 acres at the head of Sapelo River; Hugh Clark:
500 acres on the head of Sapelo River; Lachlan McIntosh: 500 acres
on the Newport River, 1750; Angus Clarke: 500 acres on the north
side of Sapelo River; George McIntosh: 500 acres at the head of
Sapelo River, 1753; William Clarke: 500 acres on the south side of
Sapelo River known by the name of Cedar Bluff, 1750; Henry
Calwell: 500 acres on the northeast side of Sapelo River, 1753;
Alexander Mackdonald: 150 acres on the north side of Sapelo River,
1744; John McIntosh (Benjamin): 500 acres situated on the
northeast side of Sapelo River; William Low: 500 acres on the south
side of the south branch of Newport River, 1754; John Gray: by
James Mackay: 500 acres on the north side of Sapelo River.[28]

Crown Grants in Upper St. Andrew Parish, 1755-1775

Robert Baillie: 1,000 acres bounded on the northwest by Burgon
Bird, John Mackay and the Sapelo River, 1767; Robert Baillie: 150
acres bounded on the southeast by Anne McIntosh, 1768; Robert
Baillie: 150 acres bounded on the west by John McDonald and John
Ponshare and on the northwest by Anne McIntosh, 1772; Donald
McDonald: 300 acres bounded on the southwest by Sapelo River,
1774; George McIntosh: 500 acres bounded on the north by
Roderick McLeod, east by John McIntosh, south by the Sapelo River,
1767; John McIntosh: 500 acres bounded on the south and east by
Sapelo River and the marshes thereof, 1760; Roderick McIntosh:
100 acres bounded on the northeast by land of the said guarantee.
The plat of survey shows this to be bounded on the northeast by
John McIntosh, 1771; George McIntosh: 1,000 acres bounded on all
sides by lands run out for the said guarantee, 1774; David Delegal:
300 acres bounded on the west by South Newport River, south by
Roderick McIntosh, east by salt marsh, north by Barber and lands
said to belong to Roderick McIntosh, 1771; Daniel Demetre: 500

---

[28] Extracted from Pat Bryant, comp., *Entry of Claims for Georgia Landholders,
1733-1755* (Atlanta: Georgia Surveyor General Department, 1975).

acres bounded on the north by said Daniel Demetre and on all other sides by creeks and marshes of Sapelo River, 1756 [lower section of Creighton Island]; Daniel Demetre: 400 acres on an island in the Sapelo River, bounded on the northeast by Sapelo River, south by lands formerly belonging to John Smith and on all other sides by marsh, 1756 [upper half of Creighton Island]; Daniel Demetre: 200 acres bounded on the east by William Harris, southwest by marshes of South Newport River, 1758: William [Thomas] Harris: 350 acres bounded on the north by John Rutledge, and east by creeks and marshes of the Sapelo River; John Jones: 200 acres bounded on the north by William Harris, east by marshes of Sapelo River, west by marshes of South Newport River; William LeConte: 500 acres bounded on all sides by vacant land, 1770; Roderick Mackay: 500 acres bounded on the southwest by land formerly surveyed for John McIntosh, northwest by land granted Hugh Clark, and northwest by the Sapelo River, 1767; Moses Way: 150 acres bounded on all sides by vacant land, 1761; Robert Stewart: 300 acres bounded on the north by the South Newport River, 1757; Captain Patrick Sutherland: 500 acres on Sapelo River bounded on the west by Lieut. John Gray, north by vacant lands, 1756.[29]

Crown Grants for Islands in Upper St. Andrew Parish

Barbers [Barbour] Island: Grant to John Barber on May 5, 1767 of 111 acres being small islands in the Sapelo River and bounded on every side by the marshes and creeks of the said river. Plat shows that this tract includes Richard Oldnors Island, John Barbers Island and Wahoo Island. Original warrant states that this includes "sundry hammocks between South Newport and Sapelo rivers at the head of Sapelo Sound."

Wahoo Island: Grant to John Barber on May 5, 1767 of 111 acres [see Barbers Island above].

Unnamed islands:

Daniel Demetre: 500 acres on May 15, 1756 on an island in the Sapelo River bounded on the north by the said Daniel Demetre and on all other sides by the creeks and marshes of the Sapelo River [southern half of Creighton Island].

---

[29] Extracted from Pat Bryant, comp., *English Crown Grants in St. Andrew Parish in Georgia, 1755-1775* (Atlanta: Georgia Surveyor General Department, 1972).

46

Wahoo Island is a McIntosh County placename that dates to the colonial period. The earliest use of Wahoo occurred in 1760 on petition by John Barber to the Provincial Council for a grant to a group of "hammocks" on the lower side of South Newport River. Barber was applying for ownership of lands he claimed to have settled since ca. 1740 with the permission of Oglethorpe. South of Wahoo are Barbour and Oldnor islands, a pair of marsh hammocks overlooking Sapelo Sound to the south.

The first Harris Neck land claimants petitioned for their tracts in the late 1740s. One of the earliest grantees at Harris Neck was Stephen Dickinson who claimed 200 acres on the lower end of the Neck in 1757. However, evidence points to Dickinson possessing a generally recognized claim, if not title, to land in this area before 1750, as grants to the first two major landholders in that year identify those tracts as being located on "Dickerson's Neck" near "Sappola Sound." In the granting process, years could pass between the time a person entered his initial petition and the time he actually received title to the land. Harris Neck was known as Dickinson's Neck until shortly after 1770.

One of the early grantees at the upper end of Dickinson's Neck was Daniel Demetre (d.1758), who in the early 1750s, acquired sections of land there totaling more than 1,200 acres. The *Colonial Records of the State of Georgia* identify Demetre as a public servant who had been in the colony since its inception. Demetre was a mariner, being coxswain of the scout boat in the service of Frederica. Demetre also filed claims for acreage on Creighton Island. In 1750, Demetre was granted 500 acres on Dickenson's Neck, the Bethany tract, which was inherited by his stepson, William Thomas Harris in 1758. Demetre was subsequently awarded an additional 250 acres that were added to Bethany making it a 750-acre tract by 1758. In 1750, John Rutledge was granted fifty acres near Bethany, a tract applied for and received by Ann Harris in the name of her son, William Thomas Harris, the same year.[30]

William Harris (ca. 1718-1737) came to Savannah from England in 1734 or 1735. A young clerk, Harris married Ann Cassell (ca. 1719-1758) in Savannah in 1736 or 1737. Harris died of unknown causes in Savannah in 1737. The young couple had a son, William Thomas Harris (1738-1786), born after his father's death. While still living in Savannah with her mother, Anna Cassells Coles Salter and her third husband, Thomas Salter, Harris' widow Ann was awarded a town lot in Frederica by James Oglethorpe in December 1742. She moved there with her son, William Thomas Harris, and her widowed mother, Anna Salter. In April 1752, Ann Harris married Daniel Demetre, also of Frederica. Ann Harris Demetre was apparently quite resourceful, easily the most enterprising woman at Frederica, as she ran a store in the town, and with her husband Daniel Demetre, operated a freight boat between Savannah and St. Simons, and engaged in the timber business for construction at Frederica. In 1753, after the death of Ann's mother, the Demetres removed to Savannah. Daniel and Ann Harris Demetre both died in 1758.

On December 8, 1752, Ann Demetre petitioned for a grant of 500 acres at the upper end of Dickenson's Neck "adjoining land of Daniel Demetre" in the name of her son, William Thomas Harris, still a minor at the time, since women were not allowed to petition for land in their name. A grant of 350 acres was awarded the same month, a tract that went to William Thomas Harris upon the deaths of his mother and step-father in 1758. He acquired an

---

[30] "Meeting of the President and Assistants in Council for the Colony of Georgia," November 29, 1749," in Allen D. Candler, ed., *Colonial Records of the State of Georgia* (Atlanta: 1906), 6:298-99; Pat Bryant, comp., *English Crown Grants in St. Andrew Parish, 1755-1775* (Atlanta: Surveyor General Department, GDAH, 1972), 23; Bessie Mary Lewis Papers, Collection 2138, GHS.

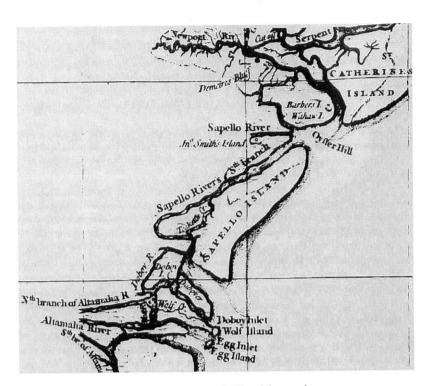

Ca. 1757 map of the coast. "Demetres Bluff" is delineated top center.

additional 200 acres in his own right in 1758. At the time of his death in 1758, Daniel Demetre had acquired about 1,200 acres on Dickinson's Neck, including the Bethany tract. His stepson, William T. Harris, inherited the 750-acre Bethany tract from Demetre in 1758. Ann Demetre's will, dated February 20, 1755, noted that Bethany had become a joint property of she and Daniel Demetre, and "was to go to the longest lived of us" then to William Thomas Harris. Demetre's will, dated July 12, 1758, identified William Thomas Harris's residence as Bethany, although it is unclear whether the latter's mother and stepfather ever lived at Bethany themselves. When William T. Harris took residence at Bethany as a young man in ca. 1757 or 1758 (possibly earlier) he may have been the first permanent white resident of Harris Neck. In 1758, several slaves lived and worked at Bethany, which may then have been used primarily as livestock range. The inter-relationship of the

49

Harris and Demetre families is clarified in the following extract from *Colonial Records* documenting an estate settlement of January 5, 1759, an agreement between James Habersham and Francis Harris (brother of the deceased first William Harris), both of Savannah, and William Thomas Harris, "planter of Bethany Plantation, Parish of Saint Andrew." The agreement stated:

"James Habersham and Francis Harris, executors of the will of Daniel Demetre, Marriner, deceased, who intermarried with Ann Harris, Widow, since deceased, who was the widow of William Harris and daughter of [William] Cassell and Anna Cassell, afterwards Anna Salter, also deceased,' agree to convey specified property to William Thomas Harris in satisfaction of the latter's demands against Demetre's estate. In his will, dated July 12, 1758, Demetre bequeathed to William Thomas Harris a 750-acre plantation called Bethany, 'on Dickinson's Neck in the district of Sapala and Newport' with all appurtenances, livestock, and plantation tools and the following slaves: Nicholas, Hagar, Tony, Prince, Belinda, Dinah, James and Silvia, and their issue. By virtue of the will, dated December 19, 1753, of his now-deceased grandmother, Anna Salter, William Thomas Harris lays claim to the aforementioned slaves and their issue and the profit that has accrued by their labor, sundry household goods, and two young valuable Negro men slaves whom Demetre was obliged to buy for Harris in accordance with Anna Salter's will. To prevent suits against Demetre's estate, Habersham and Francis Harris pay William Thomas Harris 20 pounds lawful money of Great Britain and sell to Harris for 10 shillings lawful money of Great Britain ten Negro slaves and the household goods, furniture, and plate at Bethany Plantation."[31]

William Thomas Harris (1737-1786) married Mary Landree (1738-1817), had several children, and cultivated crops at Bethany until shortly after the Revolution, in which he had served the continental cause as an officer; after the war, Harris was the first speaker of the Georgia general assembly. He died at Bethany in 1786 at the age of forty-eight. William and Mary Harris had

---

[31] "Marriage Settlement of Ann Harris & Daniel Demetrie," Conveyance Book I (1751-1761), 40-41, GDAH; "Will of Ann Harris Demetrie: Declaration of Uses," Bonds, Bills of Sale. Deeds of Gifts, Powers of Attorney, Book I, 1755-1762, 199-203, GDAH; Bryant, comp., *English Crown Grants in St. Andrew Parish.*

three sons, William Thomas Harris, Jr. (1759-1818), James Harris (1760-
1804), and John Harris, Sr. (ca. 1770-1839), all who later lived on family lands
at Harris Neck.[32]

Following is a summary of the most relevant colonial grants in the South
Newport River-Harris Neck region:

Button Gwinnett, 10,000 acres on the east side of the White Chimney River,
1767; Donald Mackintosh, 200 acres on the present site of South Newport
near the headwaters of the South Newport River; Sir Patrick Houstoun's
Marengo plantation, near the South Newport River west of Harris Neck;
Edward Baker's Lebanon plantation, 100 acres west of Harris Neck on the
South Newport River, 1773; John Williams, 500 acres on the Bruro River east
of Sutherland's Bluff and south of present-day Shellman Bluff, 1771; Henry
Calwell, 500 acres on the lower end of Dickenson's Neck, 1753; William
Thomas Harris, 350 acres on upper end of Dickenson's Neck, 1752 (with his
mother, Ann Harris, as guardian); David Delegal, 300 acres on Dickinson's
Neck, fronting on the Julianton River, 1771; John Todd, Sr. and John Todd,
Jr., lands west of the upper end of Dickenson's Neck on the South Newport
River (Todd's Bluff), 1754; John McDonald, Belvedere Island west of the
upper end of Harris Neck on the South Newport River, 1758 (tract
subsequently acquired by James Gignilliat); James Gignilliat, Contentment
Bluff near present-day Shellman Bluff.[33]

The earliest determined reference to "Harris Neck" supplanting the name of
Dickinson's Neck, appears in the Savannah *Georgia Gazette* of October 11,
1775. The pre-Revolutionary plantation activities that began along the South
Newport River were largely the cultivation of indigo and small quantities of
rice. Livestock activities were actively pursued by most of the early settlers. The
system of open ranges eliminated the need for extensive fencing, but there is
evidence that some enclosure did occur. In 1775, two Harris Neck
landowners, David and Philip Delegal, advertised in the *Georgia Gazette*

---

[32] See Isabel Thorpe Mealing, comp., *Charles Thorpe of Georgia and His
Descendants, The Harris Family* (Darien, Ga., privately printed, 1993), 107-153,
for deeds, wills and other genealogical material on the colonial Harris family.
[33] Extracted from Bryant, comp., *English Crown Grants in St. Andrew Parish.*

referenced above that since "evil disposed persons" were engaged in poaching cattle and hogs, and in illegal timber cutting on the Neck, they had found it necessary to post their "inclosures" against trespassers.[34] Several plantations, including Bethany and the Delegals' Delta plantation, were active on Harris Neck in the years before and after the Revolution before the introduction of sea island cotton led to wider plantation development in the 1790s. There is evidence of dwellings for owners, overseers, and slaves, along with the usual assortment of mill houses, barns, poultry sheds, kitchens and wash houses, all needed for the operation of even the smaller plantations.

By 1792 activities in the Harris Neck region merited the construction of a road from Julianton plantation on the south end of the Neck, through Eagle Neck, and along the South Newport River westward to a junction with the Stage Road at South Newport Bridge. Francis Levett joined William Thomas Harris, Jr., David Delegal, John Bradford, and William Myddleton (Middleton) as commissioners of the new road, a conveyor still in use. Charles Thorpe of Sunbury oversaw the road's construction.[35] From 1800 to 1820, cattle raising was an important activity in the area, so much so, that the state legislature approved an "Act for Better Regulating the Fences on Harris Neck."[36] Timbering took place at Harris Neck and its environs in the post-Revolutionary period; live oak was cut for sale to shipbuilders, a frequent practice on the southeast coast, particularly on the sea islands such as Ossabaw, Sapelo, St. Simons and Cumberland. Although it is unclear to what degree this activity was pursued at Harris Neck, it is known that in 1811 William Thomas Harris, Jr. advertised prime oak and cedar for sale with "a convenient landing for loading same."[37] Vessels transporting cotton on the

---

[34] *Georgia Gazette*, October 11, 1775.

[35] Ibid., August 30, 1792; Mealing, *Charles Thorpe of Georgia*, 8.

[36] *Columbian Museum and Savannah Advertiser*, December 21, 1809.

[37] Ibid., October 17, 1811.

inland waterway from Darien to Savannah often called at intermediate points to take on additional cargoes of agricultural staples as well as to deliver manufactured goods to the local plantations. Vessels transited the South Newport River from its juncture with Sapelo Sound upriver to the South Newport settlement about twelve miles distant, making stops along the way to load cotton from Harris Neck and nearby plantations.[38] Access to Harris Neck via the South Newport was as practicable as the new road that had been constructed in the 1790s.

By 1820 a sufficient number of white children resided in the South Newport River-Harris Neck region to require a school. Records of the McIntosh County Academy indicate a branch of that institution being established that year at Harris Neck. Classes possibly met in a church or a private home rather than an actual school building.[39] Presbyterian and Baptist congregations were active at Harris Neck from 1820 to 1861. One document notes:

"It being represented by letter & other information to be depended on to this Session that a Religious excitement & revival had commenced on Harris Neck within the jurisdiction of this church & a request made by our members in that quarter that our Pastor should visit them & administer the Sacrament of Our Lord's Supper among them, it was determined to set apart the next Sabbath for that purpose, and that this Session meet on the Saturday previous at Harris Neck at 10 o'clock A.M. in order to receive & examine such applicants as might be anxious of coming forward."[40]

Harris Neck residents who "came forward" to join the branch Presbyterian congregation in that section included Jonathan Thomas, Augustus

---

[38] Ibid., February 9, 1820.
[39] Virginia Steele Wood, ed., *McIntosh County Academy, Minutes of the Commissioners, 1820-1875 and Account Book of Students* (privately printed, 1973), 3.
[40] Minutes of Session, Darien Presbyterian Church, May 12, 1824, v. 1 (1821-1869).

Myddleton, Robert Houstoun, Mrs. Frances L. Baker, Miss Emily Myddleton, Mrs. Mary Ann Houstoun, Miss Eliza Harper, John Forbes, Daniel Young, William Todd, William Dunham and John Calder. Harris Neck planter Edward B. Baker was elected as an elder of the Darien Presbyterian Church in 1830. The Baptist congregation at Harris Neck was admitted to the Sunbury Baptist Association in November 1824. The church was organized by the Rev. Charles O. Screven. In 1831, the Baptist church was moved seven miles west to South Newport where it became South Newport Baptist Church. Trustees of the church that year were Charles J. W. Thorpe, Thomas K. Gould, William J. Cannon, George Rentz, Gideon B. Dean and Henry J. White.

Francis Levett & Julianton Plantation

The land encompassing the lower half of Harris Neck was originally awarded as Crown grants to Roderick McIntosh and Henry Calwell. About 1754, Calwell was granted 500 acres on the southernmost end of the Neck, a claim not registered until 1763 after Calwell had died. Calwell's tract was bounded on the north by a 500-acre grant issued to Roderick McIntosh.

Based on post-Revolutionary Loyalist documents Francis Levett, Sr. apparently owned property in Georgia, presumably at Harris Neck, prior to his establishment in British East Florida in 1769. It is known that Levett, Sr. was in London in 1767. On May 8, 1767, Levett, Sr. was granted 10,000 acres on the east side of the St. Johns River, land which became his Julianton plantation in East Florida. This tract, near the present-day town of Mandarin, Florida, was bounded on one side by a 1,250-acre grant claimed by Alexander

Creighton.[41] In 1778 Creighton acquired Demetre's Island, later Creighton Island, in St. Andrew Parish.

Removing to East Florida in 1769, Francis Levett, Sr. served on the British Council from 1771-73, also being appointed an assistant judge, possibly because of familial ties with his brother-in-law, the governor of East Florida, Patrick Tonyn. Levett died in late 1774 or early 1775 following his resignation from the British Council amid allegations of fraudulent practices relating to landlord rents and the sale of slaves; he is not listed in subsequent East Florida records.

London-born Francis Levett, Jr. (1753-1802) assumed the management of his father's plantation at the age of twenty-one and was appointed one of nineteen members of the East Florida House of Assembly in March 1781 and served a period as a provost marshal.[42] While in East Florida, Levett married Charlotte Box, daughter of a Loyalist Savannah attorney. She had inherited her father's considerable Florida property, making her independently wealthy. Most British citizens, including some 13,000 Loyalist refugees who migrated from South Carolina and Georgia during the Revolution, left East Florida for the Bahamas, Jamaica, or England from 1783-85 during the transition of the province back to Spanish authority as stipulated in the Treaty of Paris.

In 1785, Levett abandoned the St. John's River plantation and left St. Augustine for the Bahamas with 100 slaves, house frames, household silver and other belongings, briefly attempting to produce

---

[41] Mary B. Graff, *Mandarin on the St. Johns* (Gainesville: University of Florida Press, 1963), 10.

[42] Wilbur Henry Siebert, *Loyalists in East Florida, 1774 to 1785* (Deland, FL: Florida State Historical Society, 1929), v. 2, 228.

cotton there while making Loyalist claims on his late father's estate.[43] It would appear that sometime in 1786 Levett and his family established themselves at Julianton on the lower end of Harris Neck in Liberty County (McIntosh not becoming a separate county from Liberty until December 1793). It is unclear whether this was newly-purchased land by Levett, possibly on counsel from his late father's friend, Henry Laurens, or whether it had been obtained by his father before the Revolution, and retained through Levett's Loyalist claims on his father's estate. If the latter was the case, it was fortunate for Levett that he was able to retain the Harris Neck land.

In 1787 Francis Levett, Jr. and his family thus established themselves on the lower end of Harris Neck, Liberty County, Georgia (McIntosh after 1793) on the plantation he called Julianton, after his mother, Juliana Levett, who had been with him in East Florida. "Julianton" has been spelled several ways over the years of its existence. *Julianton* is the name given by Francis Levett, a spelling supported by Levett himself in his will and the fact that it was also the name of his father's Florida plantation Another nineteenth century spelling, incorrect, is Julington. The spelling which appears on many maps, also incorrect, is Julienton. The latter spelling is noted on the 1859 U.S. Coast Survey chart for Sapelo Sound and subsequent editions of the chart until the early twentieth century.

One of the earliest documented instances regarding Francis Levett, Jr.'s activities in Georgia occurred in a Savannah newspaper in the summer of 1790. Levett is listed as being among those "Defaulters in the several Districts within the County of Chatham

---

[43] Ibid., 228-37.

who have made no return to the Taxable Property for the Year of our Lord 1790."[44]

Two years later, the Grand Jury Presentments for Liberty County makes reference to Levett and Julianton in a development noted earlier in this chapter regarding the Harris Neck road:

"We recommend on a petition from a number of inhabitants praying that a road be cut from the south point of Harris Neck [Julianton], through Eagle's Neck, up to South Newport river, intersecting the main road near South Newport bridge, and that John Bradford, David Delegal, Francis Levett, William Thomas Harris and William Myddleton be appointed commissioners for the same."[45]

Several years later Levett found himself in the midst of a debate waged through the Savannah press as to which Georgia planters introduced sea island cotton to the region. In the fall of 1799, an anonymous "Inhabitant of Chatham County" averred in a letter to the *Columbian Museum and Savannah Advertiser*:

"[Sea island cotton] gave the [early planters] at once a supply of that article from their own territory, and completely foiled the making of indigo in the United States; but thanks to our climate, tho' the planters were compelled to turn their attention to something else, they recollected that cotton could be cultivated on lands that produced indigo, and included their thoughts to that article, and to this most were encouraged by a crop of black seed cotton from seed procured for Major Barnard on Wilmington Island which was raised on the Island of Skidaway, 10,000 lbs. of which crop was shipped to England in the spring of 1791 by Messrs. Johnston and Robertson on account of Francis Levett, Esq. which established the character of Georgia sea island cotton; being the first shipment of any

---

[44] *Georgia Gazette*, August 20, 1790.
[45] Ibid., August 30, 1792. Harris Neck and the South Newport River district were a part of Liberty County until December 1793 when the Georgia legislature created McIntosh County from Liberty.

consequence; and to him [Levett] the state is indebted for having it entered as an article of commerce in the British prices current."[46]

Several weeks later, another Chatham County planter, Nicholas Turnbull, made a rather scathing retort with a letter to the *Georgia Gazette*. Turnbull took issue with Levett receiving so much of the credit for the early effort to grow cotton on the Georgia coast. He said, among other things, that John Earle planted sea island cotton on Skidaway Island in 1767, and that he, Turnbull, successfully grew cotton on Whitemarsh Island in 1787 with a shipment to England the same year. Turnbull noted:

"I conceive Mr. Levett is not entitled to any merit, as previous to that time the quantity was made in this state and shipped by the Savannah merchants, and the character firmly established; besides, I do not suppose the trouble was great to Mr. Levett, or cost him anything, and which any one could have done as well as himself...The state is not the least indebted to Mr. Levett for the author's supposed extraordinary shipments or establishment of the staple; I believe the work was completed before Mr. Levett came to the state."[47]

Nicholas Turnbull (1756-1824) is an interesting character in the antebellum tidewater Georgia story. Born at Smyrna in the Levant, he was the son of Andrew Turnbull who founded the colony of New Smyrna on the East Florida coast in 1768. Andrew Turnbull recruited Greeks, Italians and other Mediterranean peoples to establish the colony in Florida. With imported slaves, these colonists grew indigo, sugar cane and other staples in fields cleared from the swamps. The New Smyrna colony was not a success, lasting less than

---

[46] *Columbian Museum and Savannah Advertiser*, October 15, 1799.
[47] *Georgia Gazette*, November 28, 1799.

ten years. It failed primarily because of lack of adequate food supplies, a heavy rate of attrition caused by disease spread by swarming mosquitoes and lack of cooperation between the New Smyrna officials and the colonial authorities at St. Augustine. By 1777, the colony had practically ceased to exist.[48] After the Revolution Nicholas Turnbull moved from Florida to Savannah where he became a planter at Skidaway and Whitemarsh islands. As early as 1787 Turnbull planted forty acres of sea island cotton on Whitemarsh Island in Chatham County.[49] By 1792, Turnbull had acquired the Deptford Hill plantation on the Savannah River below the city. Black-seed cotton, according to the Savannah newspaper articles of 1799, was being cultivated on the Chatham islands of Skidaway, Wilmington and Whitemarsh in the late 1780s and early 1790s, about the same time that Francis Levett grew his first cotton at Julianton plantation—as did other Georgia planters, i.e. Richard Leake on Jekyll Island and James Spalding on St. Simons. In an 1828 article on the history of sea island cotton in Georgia, Thomas Spalding of Sapelo Island alludes to Turnbull and early cotton cultivation at Skidaway Island in Chatham County. In a letter to Whitemarsh B. Seabrook of Edisto Island, South Carolina in 1844, Spalding disputes Levett's claim to be the first to grow sea island cotton in Georgia.[50]

---

[48] Carita Doggett Corse, *Dr. Andrew Turnbull and the New Smyrna Colony of Florida*, (Jacksonville, Fla.: Drew Press, 1919).

[49] Savannah Writers Project, *Savannah River Plantations*, Mary Granger, ed., (Savannah, Ga.: Georgia Historical Society, 1947), 33.

[50] Buddy Sullivan, *Thomas Spalding, Antebellum Planter of Sapelo* (privately published, 2019); Sullivan, *Sapelo: People and Place on a Georgia Sea Island* (Athens: University of Georgia Press, 2017).

Levett was certainly among the first to cultivate sea island cotton in the Georgia-South Carolina lowcountry. Julianton plantation was, from all accounts, one of the most efficient on the coast, and Levett was a large slave owner. Levett's own correspondence indicates that he grew cotton at Julianton as early as 1787. Siebert notes that Levett "received some Pernambuco cottonseed, which he cultivated with a success, he declared in 1789, beyond his 'most sanguine expectations.' It has been said that he was probably the first to grow the sea island cotton in the South."[51] It is well documented that others also cultivated sea island cotton in 1786-87, including James Spalding and Richard Leake. Lewis Cecil Gray composed an account of the controversy over the claims to being the first in *History of Agriculture in the Southern United States*, noting:

"Various accounts attribute the beginnings of the sea-island cotton industry to the year 1786-87, but there has been considerable controversy as to what persons deserve the credit. Levett, a Tory rice planter in Georgia, fled to the Bahamas, but returned to Georgia. In 1786 he received from Patrick Walsh, a seed collector then travelling in South America, three large bags of cotton seed from Pernambuco. Apparently the value of the gift was not appreciated, for Levett, finding need for the sacks in gathering provisions, shook the seeds out on the dunghill. They sprouted, and in the spring a multitude of plants covered the place. These he transplanted the next year and continued their cultivation subsequently. This claim was also set forth in a letter written by Walsh in 1805 to John Couper of St. Simons Island. William W. Parrott, a merchant of Massachusetts, obtained the story in 1807 from Levett's widow. Levett's claim, at least that he was the first to grow the crop on a large scale for export i.e. the 1791 shipment of 10,000 pounds to England from the crop raised on Skidaway Island was further supported by the writer who signed himself 'an Inhabitant of Chatham county'. Levett's claim was vigorously disputed by Thomas Spalding who claimed that "in the winter of '86 several persons on the Georgia coast, including Alexander Bisset, Governor Tattnall and Mr. James Spalding, received parcels of cotton seed from friends in the

---

[51] Siebert, *Loyalists in East Florida*, 328.

Bahamas. This seed had been sent thither by the Board of Trade from Anguilla as a means of aiding Loyalist refugees. Spalding asserted that Levett did not receive the Pernambuco seed until 1794 or 1795, and that although the Pernambuco cotton bore well and was easily separated from the seed, it was inferior to the Bahama variety and was soon displaced by the latter. Spalding's account has been accepted by many writers; but in addition to its conflict with the Levett claim there are other conflicting claims made by Richard Leake and by Nicholas Turnbull. These conflicting statements appear to suggest that in the same year a number of persons on the Georgia coast received samples of sea-island cotton from the Bahamas and that this circumstance was connected with the settlement of Georgia and South Carolina Loyalist refugees in those islands. There was also a connection between the starting of the new industry and earlier experiments in the New Smyrna colony."[52]

A 1796 survey map by John McKinnon contains revealing details about Julianton plantation. The survey delineates "Julianton River," salt marsh on the west side of the plantation, salt marsh on the east, "David Delegal's Land" to the north (Delta plantation), extensive cotton fields, and provision crops astride the marsh on both sides of the plantation; also, a number of buildings on the lower end of the plantation, including a main house, several outbuildings, and a long single row of slave dwellings. The survey noted that the "Plantation called Julianton, situate on Harris Neck in McIntosh County, State of Georgia [contains] thirteen hundred and sixty-acres, exclusive of marsh."[53]

---

[52] Lewis Cecil Gray, *History of Agriculture in the Southern United States to 1860* (Washington, D.C.: Carnegie Institution, 1933), 730-31. Spalding's comments, Thomas Spalding to Whitemarsh B. Seabrook, January 20, 1844, *Southern Agriculturist*, new series IV, 107.
[53] Survey of March 25, 1796 by John McKinnon, Surveyor, Chatham County, Superior Court Records, Chatham County, Savannah.

McKinnon also rendered a drawing of the plantation to supplement his survey.[54] The house is shown in detail, appearing to be an impressive two-story frame structure with dormer windows on an upper third level. Based on archaeological investigations by Larry Babits of Armstrong State College from 1983-85, the Julianton house was in reality not nearly as large as it appears to be depicted by McKinnon. It was about sixteen feet by thirty-six feet, with two stories. McKinnon depicts a tidal slough running near the house flowing to its convergence with the main river. Also shown are several dependencies near the main house, including a barn, a dock, and a row of twenty-three slave dwellings east of the Levett house.

The painting A Slave Wedding, rendered in the late eighteenth century might well represent a scene from Julianton plantation. The colors are similar to those used by McKinnon in his sketch of the plantation house and dwellings. The Julianton sketch depicts the layout of the buildings much as they are represented in A Slave Wedding. The main house and the slave houses shown in the background of A Slave Wedding are identical to those shown in McKinnon's drawing. It is thus possible that McKinnon rendered the wedding scene based on his observations while surveying Julianton for Levett, for the buildings are arranged in the same manner in both the drawing and in the wedding painting depicting the slave dancers. Babits is convinced McKinnon did this painting, which artistically dates to the late eighteenth century.[55] There were about 200 slaves on

[54] John McKinnon, "A South View of Julianton Plantation in Georgia, the Property of Francis Levett, Esq.," 1796.

[55] Conversation by the author with Larry Babits, Savannah, Ga., June 14, 1994.

McKinnon sketch of Julianton plantation, 1796.

Julianton plantation in 1796—a sizeable aggregation by any standard.

The 1859 U.S. Coast Survey chart of Sapelo Sound (p. 66) delineates Julianton, and depicts buildings and a row of slave dwellings aligned almost exactly as those shown in the McKinnon sketch of more than a half century earlier. William Bennett, Levett's grandson who came from England to assume management of the plantation in the mid-1840s, may have added some of the buildings shown on the 1859 chart. Foundation remains show the buildings to have been about sixteen by twenty feet in size. Levett's dock is not shown on the 1859 map, although a few traces of it, or a subsequent dock built on the same site, may be seen at low tide in the Julianton River. Archaeological field work uncovered buttons of all types on the grounds from the late eighteenth and early nineteenth centuries, including coat buttons and those from knee breeches. Foundations of some type of tabby were found on the site, including in the area of the slave dwellings. Levett might have employed some tabby in his buildings as he would have been familiar with its use during his years in East Florida.

Two notices in the *Columbian Museum* allude to Levett in 1802, the year of his death:

"NOTICE—All persons to whom the estate of Francis Levett, Esq., late of Julianton, is indebted are requested to furnish their accounts, or statement of their demands, duly attested...." and, "Twenty Dollars Reward—Will be paid apprehending a young negro man named Damon, the property of the estate of Francis Levett, Esq., dec.—he is about 22 years of age, 5 feet 1 to 3 inches, rather yellow cast, round face, speaks low and thick, downcast look, had on a pair of white negro cloth trousers, red shirt and blue jacket. The above reward will be paid by the Executors for lodging him in gaol or delivering him at Julianton, in M'Intosh county, and all reasonable expenses paid."[56]

The circumstances of Levett's death on September 13, 1802 at an early age, forty-eight, are not known, although it was by some unfortunate illness, according to his obituary in the *Columbian Museum and Savannah Advertiser*, which noted: "Died, after a lingering illness, on the 13th instant, at Julianton, McIntosh County, Francis Levett, Esq. This gentleman, after the peace in 1783, removed from East Florida to this state, pursued the culture of cotton. His family is now in England. His remains were interred by his express directions at Julianton." Levett's grave is one of two at Julianton, the other being that of his son, John Levett, who died in 1808 at the age of twenty-one. There was likely a slave burial ground at Julianton, as was typical for most of the coastal plantations, but no marked graves remain.

In December 1809, Levett's widow, Charlotte Levett, married William Stephens of Savannah. Stephens (1752-1819) was the grandson and namesake of the first president of the Georgia colony under the Trustees. Stephens was a federal judge in Savannah for the last sixteen years of his life. In *The Letters of Robert Mackay to His Wife* there is an intriguing snippet from a letter by Robert Mackay dated January 27, 1810: "Judge Stephens & Mrs. Levett are actually married—cursed fools—I have no other Georgia news."[57]

Unfortunately, this odd remark goes unexplained by both

---

[56] *Columbian Museum and Savannah Advertiser*, December 7, 1802 and April 15, 1803.
[57] Walter C. Hartridge, ed., *The Letters of Robert Mackay to His Wife* (Athens: University of Georgia Press, 1949), 205.

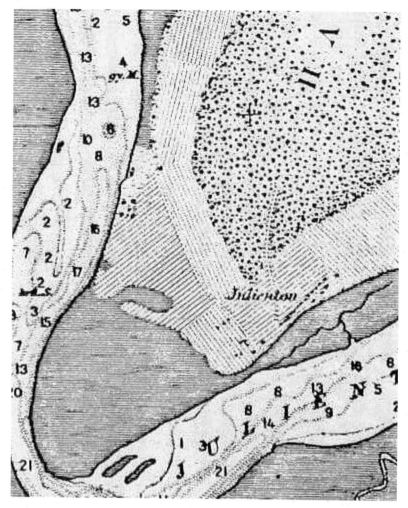

Julianton plantation in 1859. The chart delineates cultivated fields, slave dwellings, outbuildings, forested woods and salt marsh.

Mackay and the editor of his letters, Walter C. Hartridge.

After Levett's death, management of Julianton fell largely upon his widow with likely involvement from her second husband. Two children of Francis and Charlotte Levett had connections to the plantation, albeit peripherally. John Levett was born in 1787, possibly at Julianton soon after his parents arrived there from East Florida. Apparently the younger Levett was sent to England for his education for he died of unknown causes at Julianton in October 1808 within months of his return from London. In 1819, William Stephens died at the age of sixty-seven, leaving Charlotte Levett Stephens a widow for the second time. The same year, Charlotte Stephens, Christina Levett (widow of John Levett), and Rev. Thomas Bennett and his wife Charlotte Julia (Levett) Bennett, equally divided Julianton's 195 slaves. The daughter of Francis and Charlotte Levett, Charlotte Julia, was born in 1783. She married Thomas Bennett (d. 1824) in England. The last of the Bennett's six children was William Holtham Bennett, born in January 1825 after his father's death. William H. Bennett came to Georgia from England in 1846 to manage Julianton for his family; he divided his residence between Julianton and Savannah where he married Jane S. McDonald in 1853. The 1860 Chatham County census lists Bennett's occupation as "Overseer", his age as twenty-five, and his place of birth as Kent, England. In 1858, a son, William, Jr., was born to the Bennetts in Savannah. Bennett remained in Savannah during the Civil War and was affiliated in various capacities with the British consulate in that city. He was the Acting British Consul at Savannah in 1868-69, with records on file of several instances of his intercession on behalf of British shipping interests.[58]

The 1837 McIntosh County tax digest lists Charlotte Stephens as being taxed on ninety slaves and 1,150 acres of land at Julianton plantation. The 1840 census lists Charlotte Stephens in the 22nd G.M. District of McIntosh County, although her primary home was in England at this later period in her life. Charlotte Levett Stephens died in November 1841 at the age of seventy-five. She is buried at

---

[58] Papers of the British Consulate in Savannah, Keith Read Collection, Collection 648, GHS.

Canterbury Cathedral. The 1850 census reveals that William H. Bennett held eighty-five slaves working 800 acres of "improved" land at Julianton. The 1859 Coast Survey chart, *Sapelo Sound, Georgia* shows Julianton plantation on the lower end of Harris Neck as being under full cultivation in cotton and farm staples. A number of dwellings and outbuildings are also indicated on the chart at the site of Julianton.

In 1866, W.H. Bennett sold Julianton plantation to Edward W. Delegal of neighboring Delta plantation to Julianton's north, giving Delegal possession of a sizeable amount of acreage comprising the lower half of Harris Neck. Julianton's sale marked the end of nearly a century of ownership of that tract by Francis Levett and his descendants. The deed of sale was dated July 5, 1866 in Chatham County, being

"Between William H. Bennett of Chatham County and Edward W. Delegal of McIntosh County. Witnesseth that the said William H. Bennett, for the sum of two thousand dollars... hath granted, sold and conveyed unto the said Edward W. Delegal those two tracts or parcels of land lying and being on Harris Neck and Eagle Neck in McIntosh County, [the first] known as Julianton plantation bounded on the north by lands of said Delegal and on the east, west and south by the eastern branch of Sapelo river [Julianton River], containing 1,160 acres more or less, originally granted to Francis Levett; the other tract on Eagle Neck bounded north by Mrs. Harris' Belvedere Plantation and east, west and south by lands of William J. King and the estate of Jonathan Thomas."[59]

An 1894 indenture documents the Delegal family's connection with the Julianton and Delta tracts. This agreement was between

"Edward H. Delegal of the first part and Thomas W. Delegal as trustee of Eleanor M. Delegal, wife of the said Edward H. Delegal...said Edward Delegal in consideration of the natural love and affection he has for his wife and his children does hereby grant and convey to Thomas W. Delegal, trustee all of a certain interest in a tract known as Julington plantation containing 1,500

---

[59] Deed Book C (1866, re-recorded 1886), 615-16, RMCG.

acres bounded on its North by Delta plantation, on the East, South and West by eastern branch of Sapelo River. Also a certain interest in that plantation known as the Delta plantation containing 1,000 acres, bounded on the North by lands of John W. Muller, South by Julington plantation, on the East and West by salt marsh and eastern branch of Sapelo River."[60]

An 1899 indenture recorded the sale by the Delegal family, for "seven thousand dollars cash," of the Julianton tract of 1,355 acres to Irvin Davis of McIntosh County. Five years later, Julianton was sold from the Estate of Irvin Davis to Georgiana Davis, widow of Irvin Davis, and Young Davis "as the highest and best bidder" at public auction for $6,500. In 1908, the tract was sold by the Davis family to L.R Youmans of Emanuel County, Georgia.[61] Irvin Davis, and his heirs, including his widow, Georgiana Davis, had also acquired the "Muller Place" tract just north and east of Delta in the early 1890s, that being the former William J. King plantation later held by his son-in-law, John Muller (see ff.)..A "Plat of Julienton Plantation Surveyed for E.M. Thorpe, Esq., Located in Harris Neck, McIntosh County, Ga." surveyed in March 1917 by Ravenel Gignilliat, Civil Engineer, of Savannah, reported an aggregate of 3,345 acres within the boundaries of Julianton, 1,295 acres of that figure being high land. The survey plat delineates Julianton on the southern end of Harris Neck with the Julianton River flowing south and west of the tract and Little Mud River on the east. On the southeast tip of Julianton's marshes, the survey delineated scattered ballast deposits abutting the Julianton River. This was a 250-acre tract amid the marsh, separated from the Julianton upland by Shell Creek and "The Swash" as indicated on Gignilliat's survey.[62] This area was formerly owned by the Hilton and Dodge

---

[60] Deed Book F (1894), 234-35, RMCG.
[61] Deed Book G (1899), 432; Book H (1904), 474; Book I (1908), 509, RMCG.
[62] Deed Book O (1917), 319-21; Plat Cabinet A (1917), slide 119, RMCG.

Lumber Company and was used by that firm as a loading ground for ships taking on lumber in Sapelo Sound in the 1890s. On May 26, 1917, L.R Youmans sold the Julianton tract to Elisha M. Thorpe of McIntosh County.

The Delegal Family & Delta Plantation

North of Julianton was Delta plantation, a 1771 Crown grant to David Delegal (ca. 1745-1790) who lived and planted there with his wife Abigail (Green) Delegal before and after the Revolution. A son, Edward Delegal (1787-1823), was born at Harris Neck, and managed Delta until his death at the age of thirty-six in 1823. In 1809, Edward Delegal married his first cousin, Jane Delegal (1777-1857), she being the daughter of Philip and Sarah Delegal. Philip Delegal (d. 1781), brother of David Delegal, planted cotton at Skidaway Island and at other Savannah-area properties before and after the Revolution. Three sons, Edward Wentworth Delegal (1811-1876), Thomas Philip Delegal (1814-1879) and Henry H. Delegal (1816-1863), were born to Edward and Jane Delegal at Delta plantation.

The McIntosh County tax digest of 1825, two years after the death of Edward Delegal, shows Thomas E. Delegal, possibly a brother of Jane Delegal who was managing the estate after the death of Edward, being taxed on fifty slaves and 800 acres of upland at Delta plantation. The 1850 McIntosh County census lists Edward W. Delegal, then age thirty-nine, and his mother, Jane Delegal, age seventy-two, as residents of Delta. The agricultural census that year shows Delegal in possession of sixty-five slaves working 700 acres of improved land at Delta. The Delegal holdings at Harris Neck had expanded by the Civil War. The 1862 county tax digest shows a return by E.W. Delegal on thirty-three slaves and 2,070 acres of property on which he produced twenty bales of cotton and 800 bushels of corn according to the 1860 agricultural census. In 1866, as noted, Delegal acquired Julianton plantation, contiguous to Delta, and giving him ownership of most of the southern half of Harris Neck. Delegal married later in life. His wife Julia Delegal Palmer (1841-1938) was thirty years his junior and remarried twice after Delegal's death in 1876. Julia Delegal Palmer died in Miami, Florida in 1938 at the age of ninety-seven. The Delegals had three daughters, Julia Delegal Quarterman (1861-1918), Katherine Delegal King (1866-1959), and Isabelle Delegal Franks (1872-1960).

Pursuant to the Gignilliat survey noted above, L. P. Youmans sold Julianton to E.M. Thorpe in 1917.[63] Thorpe's acquisition was related to the expansion of his naval stores and cattle operations based at Townsend in the western part of McIntosh County. The same year Thorpe acquired the Muller tract north of Delta.[64] In 1936, Delta was sold by Julia F. Delegal Palmer to her daughter, Isabelle Delegal Franks (1872-1960) of Miami, Florida, the latter's father being Edward W. Delegal who had died when his daughter was four years of age. Delta at that time was described as having 600 acres, bounded north by Spring Cove, east by Barbour Island River, south by Julianton, and west by Julianton River.[65] An October 1934 series of deeds between brothers Courtney Thorpe, Jr. and E.M. Thorpe resulted in the latter acquiring lands contiguous to the King-Muller tract he had bought in 1917, referenced in the deeds as the "Muller Place." The transaction gave E.M. Thorpe the "Gould Place" (former Bahama plantation) and the "Bresnan Place" (former Margaret Harris tract). Thorpe named the whole three-property tract "Spring Cove." Combined, the tracts totaled 1,219 acres.[66] Thorpe and his

---

[63] Deed Book O (1917), 319-21, RMCG.
[64] Mealing, *Charles Thorpe of Georgia*, op cit., 37-38.
[65] Deed Book 7 (1936), 272, RMCG.
[66] Deed Book 6 (1934), 595-96, RMCG.

wife Maude Davis Thorpe moved permanently to Spring Cove from Townsend in 1936, residing in the refurbished King-Muller house originally built by antebellum planter William J. King on the tract. The house was moved to Julianton overlooking the river in the mid-1980s and refurbished once again as the residence of Julianton owner Gene Slivka.

Leading 22nd G.M.D. Planters in 1837[67]

22[nd]District. Edward Baker, 26 and 645; Jane Brailsford, 65 and 1,200; William Cooke, 55 and 600; John Calder, 26 and 717; Francis Durant, 10 and 56; William Dunham estate, 13 slaves; Thomas K. Gould, 21 and 268; John Harris, Sr., 32 and 500; John Harris, Jr., 22 and 350; Samuel King, 26 and 350; William J. King, 43 and 1,335; William J. McIntosh, 71 and 2,523; Edward Postell estate, 44 and 1,350; Charlotte Stephens, 90 and 1,150.

Upper Harris Neck: Harris & Thomas Families

A revealing, although biased, glimpse of contemporary antebellum plantation life and conditions emerges from an account of Peru plantation, on the upper end of Harris Neck, by Edward Jonathan Thomas (1840-1929), grandson of the plantation's proprietor, Jonathan Thomas (d. ca. 1849). This memoir, written in 1912, recalled the younger Thomas's early life at Harris Neck in the 1840s and 1850s. Several extracts from this document are worth noting:

"I was born at Savannah, Georgia, March 25, 1840, but a few years after we moved to the old homestead in McIntosh County, some forty miles from this city. My first recollection was of this

---

[67] Extracted from McIntosh County Tax Digest, 1837, GDAH.

plantation. It was called 'Peru' on account of its fertility—the legend of Pizarro's gold find being not yet forgotten—situated on South Newport River, a bold and wide salt water stream emptying into Black-Beard [Sapelo] Sound. My grandfather lived at one end of this plantation of three thousand acres, and my father lived at the other...Grandfather Jonathan Thomas died a few years later, leaving his many plantations—Peru, Belvedere, Baker, and Stark, comprising some fifteen thousand acres and about one hundred and twenty five slaves. His remains are buried by a large oak in our private burying ground on the banks of South Newport River.

"There was on the plantation a trusted and intelligent slave called the Driver, who was directly in charge of all field work, Sea-Island cotton, corn, peas, sweet potatoes, sugar cane, melons, and all garden stuff...The slaves were housed in two-room lumber cabins. There was a chimney to each house, and they were allowed a garden. No work was permitted on Sunday, and the slaves attended church services. They could raise as many chickens as they pleased, and they had boats and went anywhere fishing so long as they came home by daybreak to begin work. They were given two blankets, a suit of wool clothing, and a pair of shoes each winter. They were given a suit of cotton clothing in the summer but no shoes since they went barefooted during the hot months. The older slave men were allowed to keep guns given them by my father. Many had horses and cows which ran in a large free pasture. The pasture extended over thousands of acres of salt marsh. The horses were reared there and therefore were known as 'marsh tackies...' The young Negro men, getting tired of cultivating the fields, would at times run away; that is, they would leave their cabins and seek shelter in the neighboring woods or some isolated hammock which so abundantly are found about plantations on that seaboard."[68]

Peru plantation was shaped as an inverted "L" encompassing the upper part of the present Harris Neck Wildlife Refuge along the South Newport River, then taking in the land on the east side of the Neck along tributaries of the Barbour Island River southward almost to Gould's Landing. Belvedere plantation was west of Peru on the

[68] Edward J. Thomas, *Memoirs of a Southerner* (Savannah, Ga.: privately printed, 1923).

South Newport, separated from Harris Neck by a creek and marsh. The Baker tract was about two miles west of Harris Neck between Lebanon and Belvedere, with the Stark tract east of Baker. Another mainland plantation in the area, and related to the story of Peru, was Marengo, being southwest of Peru and owned by the Houstoun family, which had other acreage in the section. Some of the Houstoun lands were added to Thomas's holdings after his marriage to Mary Ann Houstoun in 1827. Peru included portions of earlier Harris-Demetre lands on the South Newport River as a result of intermarriages between the Harris and Baker families, and between the Baker and Thomas families. The antebellum Harris lands on the upper end of the Neck were south and east of Peru, fronting on the Barbour Island River and its marshes, and not within the present wildlife refuge. The Harris family tracts adjoined the Thomas and William J. King holdings. Much of the Harris family's original acreage on the Neck had earlier devolved to new owners through marriages.

As noted earlier, William Thomas Harris, an early grantee of land on the upper end of the Neck, farmed at Bethany plantation, with interaction with his Harris Neck neighbors, David and Philip Delegal, at Delta plantation to the south. Harris held about 1,100 acres when he died in 1786. His will, devised in 1785 a year before his death, stated that it was his intent that his "real estate be divided equally between my three sons William Thomas, John, and James Harris, each of the younger sons to enjoy the same at the age of 21 years...and bequeath to my beloved wife Mary Harris, my sons William Thomas Harris, my daughters, Ann, Mary, Jane and Sabra [and] my sons John & James, my personal estate after an appraisement of the whole it may be made into equal lots, divided to each equal share, to them and their heirs forever..." As noted earlier, William Thomas Harris and his wife, Mary (Landree) Harris, had three sons, two of whom lived and planted at Harris Neck. These were William Thomas Harris, Jr. (1759-1818) and John Harris, Sr. (ca. 1770-1839). However, their brother, James Harris, is the only Harris listed in the 1820 census. The census is apparently in error (not unusual for those times) and "James" was likely John Harris, Jr. as James Harris's death occurred on January 7, 1804. A newspaper legal notice of January 6, 1818 notes that John Harris, probably John, Jr., of McIntosh County applied for administration of the estate of John Neason, which suggests that John, Jr. was living at Harris Neck at that time.[69]

William T. Harris, Jr.'s wife was Mary Margaret Harper Harris (ca. 1772-1866). Their three children were John Harris, Jr. (1790-1847), Jane Elizabeth Harris (1801-1864) and Bright Baker Harris (1808-1875). Evidence points to John Harris, Sr., John Jr.'s uncle, being married to his sister-in-law, Mary Margaret, sometime after the death of his brother in 1818. Meanwhile, the connections among the Harris, Baker, Thomas and Thorpe families began after the Revolution and were often convoluted. Jane Harris, sister of William T. Harris, Jr. and John Harris, Sr., married Bright Baker (b. ca. 1760). Their daughter, Mary Jane Baker (d. 1816), was the first wife of Jonathan Thomas. The daughter of William Thomas, Jr. and Mary

---

[69] "Land Grants to William Thomas Harris, the First," in Allen D. Candler, comp., unpublished Colonial Records of the State of Georgia, 27:361, GDAH; Grant Book A, 646, in idem., 380; Will of William Thomas Harris, Sr., August 15, 1785, Liberty County Probate Records, Hinesville, Georgia; McIntosh County Tax Digest, 1825, 1837, GDAH; U.S. Census, McIntosh County, 1820, 1830, 1840; Mealing, *Charles Thorpe of Georgia*, 187.

Harper Harris, Jane Elizabeth Harris, married Charles J.W. Thorpe. The only Harris in McIntosh County listed with taxable property in the 1825 county digest was John Harris, probably Jr., with twenty-six slaves and 330 acres of improved land inherited from his late father; the 1837 digest lists John Harris, Sr. with thirty-two slaves and 500 acres, and his nephew John Jr. with twenty-two slaves and 350 acres, suggesting that John, Sr. was by then married to the widow of his brother, who had inherited part of her first husband's estate. Both John Sr. and Jr. are listed in the 1830 census. In the 1840 census only one Harris is listed, presumably John Harris, Jr. as John Harris, Sr. died in July 1839, with Margaret M. Harris and William J. King serving as administrators of his estate.[70]

A Savannah newspaper notice in June 1818 listed Benjamin Baker and William Dunham as administrators of the William T. Harris, Jr. estate. The 1837 tax records show John Harris, Sr., brother of the late William Thomas Harris, Jr., and his nephew, John Harris, Jr., living and planting at Harris Neck. John Harris, Sr. died in 1839 at the age of about sixty-nine, with Margaret M. Harris and William J. King administrators of his estate. Harris, Sr. was a fairly substantial planter on the upper end of the Neck. The antebellum Harris family lands were south of, and not within, the present Wildlife Refuge with an eastern boundary on the Barbour Island River marshes and contiguous to the plantations of William J. King and Jonathan Thomas. In 1837, as noted, both John Harris, Sr. and

---

[70] *Savannah Daily Georgian*, February 27, 1841. John Harris, Jr. died in 1847 at Harris Neck. His second wife, Jane M. Thorpe Harris, age 46, is listed in the population and agricultural census of 1850, presumably with her late husband's land and slaves. In 1854, her son, James M. Harris (1822-1861) requested dismission of guardianship of Jane Harris's younger children. *Savannah Daily Georgian*, October 15, 1854.

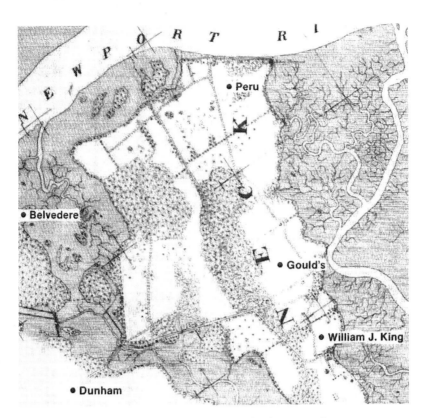

Upper Harris Neck, 1850s, with Peru and adjoining plantations.

his nephew, John, Jr., held slaves and acreage on the Neck.[71] In 1850,

Jane M. Thorpe Harris, widow of John Harris, Jr., is listed in the

agricultural census, presumably with her late husband's holdings.

Meanwhile, Margaret Harper Harris, widow of William T. Harris, Jr.,

and possibly by then the widow of John Harris, Sr., held fifty-nine

slaves, and 1,500 improved and unimproved acres. By 1860,

Margaret Harris reported ownership of sixty-six slaves and 300 acres

of improved land on which were produced nine bales of cotton and

---

[71] *Savannah Daily Republican*, June 22, 1818; McIntosh County Tax Digest,
1825, 1837, GDAH.

550 bushels of corn.[72] These numbers concur with those of two years later when the "John Harris, Sr. estate" was taxed on seventy-three slaves and 1,910 acres of improved and unimproved land.[73] The reference to "estate" in the 1862 digest supports the likelihood of Margaret Harris being the widow of John Harris, Sr. in her second marriage.

East of the Harris lands and south of Peru was the Gould tract on the Barbour River, Bahama plantation, amid which is the present Gould's Cemetery and Gould's Landing. The 1825 tax digest lists William Gould and Richard W. Gould as living at Harris Neck, presumably at Bahama, while the 1837 digest shows Thomas K. Gould there, but not the other two Goulds. Thomas Gould appears to be the most successful of his family to farm at Bahama plantation. South of Bahama was the plantation of William John King. He acquired his Harris Neck acreage at an early age as he is listed as an officer in the McIntosh County militia in 1812 and, with Jonathan Thomas, was executor in 1825 of the estate of Thomas Delegal of nearby Delta. King (see ff.) eventually turned over his plantation to his son, William J. King, Jr. and son-in-law, John Muller.

The only two surviving tax digests for antebellum McIntosh County, 1825 and 1837, and a wartime digest from 1862, provide clues to land use patterns on the upper end of Harris Neck. Twentieth century maps identify the landing on the Barbour Island River in the southeast corner of the present-day Wildlife Refuge as "Gould's Landing." Also identified is a nearby burial ground, "Gould Cemetery." Gould Cemetery is post-Civil War, as no identifiable graves in the lot relate to members of the Gould family. It was

---

[72] U.S. Census, McIntosh County, Georgia, Slave and Agricultural Schedules, 1850, 1860.
[73] McIntosh County Tax Digest, 1862, GDAH.

used by the Harris Neck freedmen and their descendants. A short distance southwest of the cemetery and landing is an older graveyard used by whites, and known locally as the William J. King Cemetery. This antebellum burial ground has long since been obliterated by agricultural and other disturbances, particularly government construction of an airfield on that section of Harris Neck in the 1930s.

For about three decades Jonathan Thomas, who died about 1849, held over 10,000 acres of upland and marsh along the South Newport River. Thomas acquired his earliest holdings though his marriage to Mary Jane Baker, who died about 1816, possibly in childbirth when her son John Abbott Thomas was born. The Baker lands included the section of upper Harris Neck that became Peru, the Baker tract west of Harris Neck near Marengo and Mosquito, and the large Stark tract south of the Harris Neck road that extended almost to South Newport. Listed as a justice of the McIntosh County inferior court in 1816, Thomas acquired additional lands later, including the Belvedere and Mosquito tracts (see the material on Belvedere following, and on Mosquito, Stark and Baker later in this chapter).

Belvedere Island was one of the properties acquired by James Gignilliat, Sr. upon his arrival in McIntosh County from South Carolina after the Revolution (see Gignilliat coverage earlier). In 1794, Belvedere was inherited by James Gignilliat, Jr. His daughter, Sarah Catherine Gignilliat (1799-1873), married Edward Perry Postell (1797-1835) of Savannah. In 1806, Postell's father, James Postell (1766-1826) had acquired a 250-acre rice tract on the northern end of Onslow Island on the Savannah River. In 1822, the *Savannah Georgian* reported the marriage "at Col. [James] Postell's in Abbeville, on the 17th ult., Edward Postell, Esq. of Coosawhatchie, to Miss Sarah

Gignilliat, of M'Intosh county, Ga."[74]

Before the marriage of Edward and Sarah Gignilliat Postell, the Gignilliat family apparently had intentions of selling Belvedere. In 1820, a public notice advertised for sale "That well known Cotton Plantation called 'Belvedere' on the South Newport river in McIntosh county." The notice indicated that Belvedere was a 1,500-acre tract of oak, hickory and low swamp land, sixty acres of the latter being under cultivation, a "sufficient proportion of pine barren attached" which produced an excellent quality of cotton. Pine land was considered an attractive quality for a coastal plantation for it afforded good cattle range and was conducive to good health for its residents. According to the notice, Belvedere was admirably suited for a force of from twenty to fifty slaves.[75] The 1825 tax digest lists Postell with forty-eight slaves and 1,400 acres at Belvedere plantation. In the late 1820s Postell apparently encountered financial stresses, as evidenced in the following notice in the *Savannah Georgian*:

"McIntosh Superior Court, April Term, 1830. On petition of Andrew Low, James Taylor and John Low, merchants under the firm of Low, Taylor & Co. stating that Edward P. Postell, by his certain promissory note in writing, bearing date on the first day of January, 1827, promised on the first day of January next from the date thereof, to pay to Messrs. Bulloch & Dunwoody, the sum of $1,211 and that for securing the payment of said sum of money the said Edward P. Postell by his certain deed of mortgage dated 26th day of February 1827, had mortgaged to said Bulloch & Dunwoody all that tract or parcel of land situate, lying and being on the waters of the South New Port River, McIntosh County, called Belvidere [sic], containing fourteen hundred acres, more or less, bounded on the east by lands belonging to Jonathan Thomas, south by lands belonging to said Thomas and W.T. and T. [Thomas] King and on the west by lands of the estate of Wm. Myddleton..."[76]

---

[74] *Savannah Georgian*, September 3, 1822.

[75] *Darien Gazette*, November 4, 1820.

[76] *Savannah Georgian*, April 24, 1830.

Postell's father died in 1826 and his Onslow Island rice lands passed into a trusteeship held by his widow, Jane Eliza Postell of Savannah and her son, Edward P. Postell. The sale of the Onslow tract may have enabled Edward Postell to meet some, if not all, of his financial obligations. In early 1832 E.P. Postell advertised for sale 120 acres of "prime tide swamp" on Onslow Island; a year later, Postell sold the Savannah River holdings to Thomas F. Potter.[77] In the fall of 1835, Postell died at Belvedere in the prime of his life, from what cause we do not know, his obituary simply noting, "Died at his residence in McIntosh County on the night of the 7th inst. Edward P. Postell, in the 38th year of his age."[78] Postell's estate is listed in the 1837 tax digest as comprising forty-four slaves and 1,350 acres at Belvedere.[79]

The same year, the acreage and slaves were advertised for sale, and were purchased by Jonathan Thomas of nearby Peru plantation.[80]

Southwest of Belvedere, and just south of the South Newport River, the Marengo tract was a Crown grant to Sir Patrick Houstoun (1698-1762), an officer of the Georgia colony and a man of considerable wealth and land holdings. Houstoun also had a claim to a 1,000-acre grant on Cathead Creek near Darien, and land in other parishes. Sir Patrick had five sons, all of whom became well-known and established in the colony, as did his son-in-law George McIntosh of Rice Hope plantation in St. Andrew Parish.[81] Marengo was located about a mile south of the South Newport River, below Lebanon plantation. and about halfway along the road connecting South Newport and Harris Neck. The chain of title to Marengo is murky after 1762. The tract

---

[77] Granger, ed., *Savannah River Plantations*, 214.
[78] *Savannah Georgian*, October 19, 1835.
[79] McIntosh County Tax Digest, 1837, GDAH.
[80] *Savannah Georgian*, February 4, 1837.
[81] Edith Duncan Johnston, *The Houstouns of Georgia* (Athens: University of Georgia Press, 1950).

could have gone to the next Sir Patrick Houstoun who died in 1785 at the age of forty-three. What seems more likely is that Marengo was inherited by another of the five sons, Dr. James Houstoun, who died in 1793. The second Sir Patrick Houstoun left no heir.

James Edmund Houstoun (1778-1819), son of Dr. James Houstoun, married Mary Ann Williamson (1786-1860) in 1806. Their children were Eliza V. Houstoun (1810-1836), Mary Williamson Houstoun (1815-1871), John W. Houstoun (1817-1861), and James E. Houstoun, Jr. (1819-1852). Eliza Houstoun was the first wife of Charles H. Spalding. She died in 1836, two years after their marriage. James E. Houstoun, Sr. died at Marengo plantation September 15, 1819. His obituary described him as "possessing fine talents, great energy of mind and unshaken integrity — he represented Chatham County and McIntosh County in the Legislature ... he filled several honorary offices, civil and military, and justly acquired the confidence of the state and of all who knew him."[82]

In 1827, Mary Ann Williamson Houstoun of Marengo plantation, widow of James Edmund Houstoun, married Jonathan Thomas of Peru plantation. Thomas was also a widower, his first wife, Mary Jane Baker Thomas, dying prior to 1820. Mary Ann Houstoun Thomas, who had been left her late husband's lands at Marengo and other nearby tracts, merged her considerable acreage with the holdings of Jonathan Thomas. The 1850 census shows the Houstoun children still living at Harris Neck, excepting the deceased Eliza Houstoun Spalding. Mary Ann Houstoun Thomas, age sixty-four, and by then the widow of Jonathan Thomas, was in a household with her daughter Mary W. Houstoun, age thirty-four and son, John W. Houston, age thirty-three, presumably at Marengo, while her other son, James E. Houston, Jr., was

---

[82] *Savannah Georgian*, September 21, 1819.

listed as the only occupant of another household, likely at Mosquito.[83] James E. Houstoun, Jr. planted cotton and provision crops at Mosquito near Marengo, and was the victim in a brutal murder at the hands of several of his slaves. On the evening of June 14, 1852, Houstoun "left his residence alone in a small canoe to visit an island near Harris Neck upon which he had negroes at work . . . the negroes returned, reporting that their master had not arrived on the island." An investigation revealed that Houstoun had been murdered in his sleep on a marsh hammock east of Harris Neck, Wahoo Island, and buried there by the twelve slaves involved in the plot. The murderers were convicted in McIntosh County court and five were hanged.[84]

The antebellum conveyances of land and slaves in the Harris Neck section are often convoluted, confused and jumbled due to the loss of most of McIntosh County's pre-Civil War public records in courthouse fires. Examples of the fluidity of these transactions are revealed in the records of the Thomas and Houstoun families contained among the Mary Williamson Houstoun Papers on deposit at the Georgia Historical Society.[85] Extracts from these documents relevant to the activities of the two families in the Harris Neck area aid in developing chains of title to the properties under discussion here. A deed dated January 7, 1802 between Richard Leake of Belleville plantation, McIntosh County, and James E. Houstoun of Chatham County conveyed a plantation of 700 acres on Bruro Neck, "Known by the name of Leake land," from Leake to Houstoun for $300. It is unclear as to the precise location of this land, but it was likely the tract later known as Priester, a section of upper Bruro Neck bounded on the north by the Julianton River. The tract adjoins

---

[83] U.S. Census, McIntosh County, 1850, Population Schedules.
[84] *Savannah Georgian*, July 21, 1852.
[85] Mary Williamson Houstoun Papers, Collection 398, GHS.

Marengo, being separated from it by salt marsh and Woodruff Creek. It appears the land was either an annex of, or otherwise connected with, Marengo. The 700 acres of "Leake land" probably acquired the Priester designation sometime after 1885.

A bill of sale of March 7, 1827, just before her marriage to Jonathan Thomas, documents the sale (or proposed sale) by Mary Ann W. Houstoun of thirteen slaves, "to wit, Tena, William, Caroline, Joseph, Alexander, Rose, Maria, Juno, Barrack, Hannah, Tom, Grace and Tenah, with the future issue and increase of the female slaves," and 1,300 acres at Marengo to Crawford Davidson of Chatham County for $3,100.[86] This transaction was apparently not consummated since the property remained in the possession of the Houstoun-Thomas family as validated by a deed conveyance of Marengo from Mary Ann Thomas to Jonathan Thomas four years later in 1831.[87] A deed of September 2, 1828 certifies the conveyance at a sheriff's sale of the 488-acre Mosquito tract just west of Belvedere Island on the South Newport River "bounded east by land of E.P. Postell, south by land of the Estate of Bright Baker, west by the land of Mrs. Myddleton and north by salt marsh" to Jonathan Thomas, the highest bidder. This acquisition evolved from the previous owners of Mosquito, William and Mary Myddleton, the tract previously being among the holdings of Bright Baker who, parenthetically, was the father-in-law of Jonathan Thomas from his first marriage. Bright Baker also held lands immediately south of Mosquito between Marengo and the Baker tract, including the Stark

---

[86] Ibid.
[87] *Savannah Georgian*, July 6, 1831.

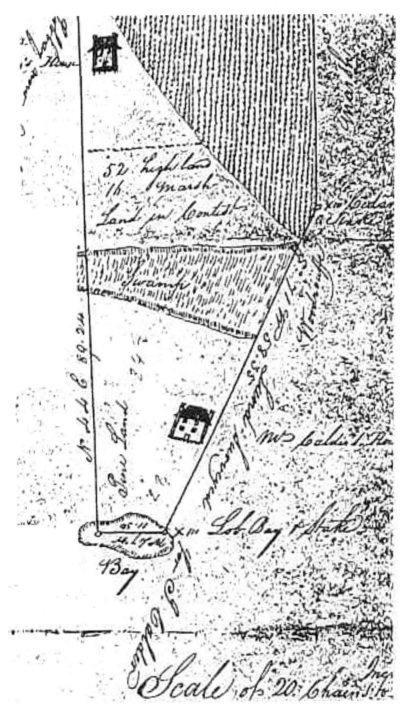

An 1829 survey for Jonathan Thomas of land at Marengo. The area at the top of the plat to the right of the structure is salt marsh.

tract, all properties that devolved upon Jonathan Thomas upon the death of Baker (see ff.).

A subsequent indenture, dated December 31, 1836, conveyed from Thomas in trust to his wife, Mary Ann Thomas, Mosquito and "400 acres of pine barren land adjoining Marengo, originally part of the Stark tract." Soon thereafter, Thomas placed in trust for his wife "the tract of land known by the name of Maringo [sic] and also eight negroes and their issue and increase." The 1827 sale of slaves by Mary Ann Houstoun cited above was apparently never finalized as they are referred to again in an indenture of April 13, 1839 in which Thomas conveyed to John W. Houstoun, son of James E. and Mary Ann Houstoun, Marengo and twenty-nine slaves. The same document records the bequest by Mary Ann Thomas to her daughter, Mary Williamson Houstoun, the slaves William, Caroline, Joseph, Alexander, Rose, Lucy, Affy, Titus and Betsy, "and that the following Negro Slaves be equally divided between my sons John W. Houstoun and James E. Houstoun, viz: old Maria, Barrack, Juno, Hannah, Maria, Tom, Grace, Tena, Isaac, Phoebe, Cyrus, Bob, Little Maria and Little Barrack."[88]

In 1837, Thomas purchased the 1,350 acres and forty-four slaves of Belvedere from the estate of Edward P. Postell.[89] In 1845 Mary Ann Thomas willed her slaves to her three children, Mary, John and James Houstoun and also "for Mary W. Houstoun and John W. Houstoun Marengo Plantation with Calders Tract, Mosquitoe Tract and 400 acres Pine Land Mr. Thomas gave me, Furniture and everything in my house, one fourth of my cattle and sheep to J.E.

---

[88] Mary Williamson Houstoun Papers, GHS.
[89] *Savannah Georgian*, February 4, 1837.

Wahoo Island in the 1850s, showing areas under cultivation.

Houstoun." A later will of February 1, 1847, witnessed by John A.
Thomas and William J. King, gave her children eighty-seven slaves
valued at $29,650.[90] Extract of a letter of July 29, 1850 from James E.
Houstoun, Jr. to his brother, John W. Houstoun , posted from South
Newport: "I am perfectly willing that you should take Hector at $500 on
condition of his not being brought back to this part of the
country...Everything is going on as usual these days since we had the only rain
that has been of any service to the crops for two months past. The early corn is
entirely lost. About a fourth of a crop of cotton will be made."[91] James
Houstoun, Jr. was likely planting all, or a portion, of his cotton at
Mosquito and Wahoo Island by 1850. The murder of Houstoun in the
summer of 1852 by his slaves probably occurred at Wahoo, a marsh
hammock on the Wahoo River , a tidal tributary of the lower South Newport
River, and three miles across the marsh from the east side of Harris Neck.
Although owned at the time by Harris Neck planter William J. King, Wahoo

---

[90] Mary Williamson Houstoun Papers, GHS.
[91] Ibid.

was either being leased by Houstoun for cotton cultivation, or Houstoun was an overseer in King's employ supervising the islands King owned east of Harris Neck. The following information about Harris Neck, Wahoo and the Houstoun incident was recorded years later by Maude Thorpe, wife of Harris Neck landowner E.M. Thorpe:

"As given [me] by Joe Sallins: His mother was Sarah; his father was Jack Sallins, a house servant. He knew Mr. William J. King & wife Martha who owned a big house on the Spring Cove tract [bought by E.M. Thorpe in 1917]. Jack's grandmother, Teena, was house servant for Mrs. Martha King. Mr. King owned Barbours Island, Oldnors and Wahoo. A gunboat fired on the house [in the Civil War] from the "New Cut." Mr. King had six-oar boats. The overseers carried the hands to farm on the islands. All hands, except two men, were women. Jim Houston [sic], who farmed Wahoo, was killed by the slaves at Houston Creek, and buried in the creek. He was a nice looking man, but was bad. His people did not love him. Julia Tice was little and was the only one who was not hanged. The Harris's owned Belvedere, Statesfield, Johnsfield, Dunham and Dillon. Mrs. Margaret M. Harris was loved by her slaves..."[92]

Across from Wahoo on the upper end of the Neck between Peru (north) and King's plantation (south), was the Bahama plantation of Thomas K. Gould. Now known as Gould's Landing, this site would have been the likely departure point by boat for James. E. Houstoun and others managing the farm operations at Barbour, Oldnor and Wahoo islands. Bahama plantation prospered in the 1830s and 1840s. The 1837 tax digest shows Thomas K. Gould with twenty-one slaves and 268 upland acres at Bahama; the 1840 census listed Gould as possessing twenty-seven slaves. The 1850 census has the "estate of Thomas K. Gould" with twenty-three slaves. Nineteenth century artifacts recovered at the site, such as English-manufactured refined

---

[92] Extracted from the private papers of E.M. Thorpe, courtesy of Isabel Thorpe Mealing, Darien, Ga., 1992.

earthenwares, attest to activity associated with the Gould house at Gould's Landing overlooking the marshes toward Wahoo and Barbour islands. Other evidence of antebellum activity is established by faunal material, including fragments of cattle and pig bones, and domestic artifacts which indicate the possible presence of Gould's plantation kitchen near the present cemetery site. Indian activity has also been investigated on the north end of Harris Neck, from Gould's Landing northward to Thomas Landing on the South Newport River. Upper Harris Neck, from all indications, was a settlement in the Espogache-Tupiqui kingdom.[93]

Mary Williamson Houstoun Thomas's new will in December 1853 contained the same provisions regarding Marengo and her slaves as her wills of 1845 and 1847, but does not mention Mosquito, which by that time had apparently been conveyed to Mary Ann's son, James E. Houstoun, Jr., since it is known that he had been planting cotton there at the time of his death the year before in 1852.[94] In the mid-to-late 1850s, Mary Ann Thomas, or her heirs, sold Marengo and Mosquito to Charles A. Stebbins. This transaction presumably occurred before Mary Ann's death in 1860; it was certainly after the death of her husband, Jonathan Thomas. The exact year of Thomas' death remains a mystery. He clearly died prior to 1850 as he is not listed in the federal census of that year. His wife Mary Ann Thomas is listed with two of her adult children as members of one household, presumably at Marengo. In the household at Peru in 1850 are John Abbott Thomas (1816-1859), son of the late Jonathan and Mary Jane (Baker) Thomas, his wife Malvina (Huguenin)

---

[93] "Archaeological Investigations at 9McI41, Harris Neck National Wildlife Refuge," Chad O. Braley, Principal Investigator, for U.S. Fish and Wildlife Service (Athens, 1986), 70, 98,140.

[94] Mary Williamson Houstoun Papers, GHS.

Thomas (1816-1890) and their five children, all aged ten years or under. The 1850 agricultural census does not list Jonathan Thomas with slave or land holdings, but does list Mary Ann Thomas with 114 slaves and 200 acres of improved land, and John A. Thomas with 104 slaves and 800 acres. Mary Ann's bondsmen presumably included slaves willed her by her husband and those attached to Marengo. Jonathan Thomas probably died ca. 1849, by then having turned over the management and holdings of Peru plantation to his son and his wife. Jonathan Thomas is not listed in the 1850 census.

Charles Austin Stebbins (1806-1877) was born in Massachusetts and moved to the South as a young man, establishing residence in Savannah, and later in Riceborough in lower Liberty County where he operated a general store. About 1860, perhaps earlier, Stebbins acquired the 1,350-acre Marengo plantation, not far from Riceborough. Prior to 1850, William Bryan Nelson (1814-1899) and his family moved to north McIntosh County from North Carolina. The 1850 census lists William B. Nelson and his wife Nancy as residents of the 22nd G.M. District. Stebbins hired Nelson as his overseer at Marengo and the Nelson family settled there. Nelson also obtained lease rights from Stebbins to process turpentine in Marengo's pine lands. One of the Nelson daughters, Wilhelmina, subsequently married a Stebbins' son, Charles A. Stebbins, Jr. (1838-1914). Two other sons were John S. Stebbins (b. 1846), and King Benjamin Stebbins (1848-1892). The 1870 census lists Charles A. Stebbins, Sr. and his wife Margaret as McIntosh County residents, thus it appears that the elder Stebbins was living at Marengo after the Civil War because of the loss of his business interests in Savannah and Riceborough. Like many coastal planters, Stebbins manufactured salt during the Civil War. His salt-works at Marengo was at the headwaters of Carter's Creek, a tributary of the Julianton River. The 1870 census also lists Charles A. Stebbins, Jr. and his wife Wilhelmina, and John S. Stebbins and his wife

90

Catherine. Stebbins, Sr. died in 1877 in Liberty County and is buried at Nelson (Marengo) cemetery, located on the site of the old Marengo plantation on Young Man's Road connecting Harris Neck Road and the road to Shellman Bluff.[95] The Stebbins family has an interesting genealogy. The son of King B. Stebbins was Charles C. Stebbins, Sr. (1885-1976) of Darien whose son, C.C. Stebbins, Jr. (1917-1997), was a well-known Darien attorney. The son of Charles Austin Stebbins, Jr. was James Lachlison Stebbins (1878-1945), who was the father of Charles Austin Stebbins (1902-2004), prominent businessman and civic leader of Darien, and James Robert Stebbins (1907-1978), a Darien merchant.

According to a deed filed shortly after the Civil War, Marengo was recorded in the name of one of Charles A. Stebbins's sons, John S. Stebbins, at the time of the elder Stebbins' death in 1877: "This indenture made by Charles Austin Stebbins, Sen. on the one part and John S. Stebbins of the other part, that Charles A. Stebbins in consideration of the sum of $1,800 to him in hand paid by the said John S. Stebbins, all that tract of land formerly belonging to J.E. Houstoun and Mary Houstoun and known as the Marengo plantation containing 1,350 acres, bounded as described in plat and titles conveyed from Jonathan Thomas and John W. Houstoun and Mary Houstoun."[96]

Another Harris property was the Dunham tract, part of a grant apparently acquired by William Thomas Harris before the Revolution. It may have evolved as a Dunham tract for a time through two marriages between the Harris and Dunham families. One connection is seen through an 1824 legal notice stating that

[95] U.S. Census, McIntosh and Liberty counties, Population Schedules, 1860, 1870; Mattie Gladstone, et al., eds., *Cemeteries of McIntosh County, Georgia* (Darien, Ga.: Lower Altamaha Historical Society, 2000), 195-96.
[96] Deed Book B (1870), 151, RMCG.

William Dunham and Charles J.W. Thorpe, son-in-law of William T. Harris, Jr. (died 1818), had been appointed administrators of the estate of Elizabeth Harris, she possibly being the widow of James Harris, brother of William T. Harris, Jr. and John Harris.[97] William Dunham is listed as a McIntosh County resident in the 1820 census. Dunham, which then included the Springfield tract, was west of the upper end of Harris Neck, the two tracts separated by marsh and a tidal creek. William Dunham was accepted for membership in the Harris Neck branch of the Darien Presbyterian Church in 1825.[98] The same year, he was taxed on ownership of fifteen slaves and 317 acres, evidence that Dunham was producing cotton and provision crops at Dunham.[99] Dunham and Springfield were on lower Eagle Neck between the Harris Neck road and the upper Julianton River. Springfield abutted Dunham to its south and west. Dunham is referenced as a family tract in the 1865 will of Margaret M. Harris (see ff.). The loss of deed records prior to 1873 due to courthouse fires makes specific, and accurate, chains of title difficult to determine for many of the antebellum tracts. While listed in the 1825 tax digest with slaves and land, Dunham is not recorded as a county resident in either the census of 1830 or 1840, thus he may have farmed the tract for only several years. The original Harris family possession of Dunham before the Revolution and its later use by William Dunham may be validated by two marriages: that of John Harris, Jr. to Sarah Dunham of Liberty County in 1814 (she died a year later), and, in 1834, that of cousins Ann Harris (1815-1854)

---

[97] *Darien Gazette*, February 6, 1824; Mealing, *Charles Thorpe of Georgia*, 8, 77, 187.
[98] Sessional records, Darien Presbyterian Church, v. 1, 1821-1869.
[99] McIntosh County Tax Digest, 1825, GDAH.

daughter of John Harris, Jr. and Sarah Dunham Harris, to Thomas J. Dunham (1810-1885) of Liberty County, son of Rev. Jacob H. Dunham, brother of Sarah Dunham Harris, and Mary Baisden Dunham. William Dunham (1786-1856), born and died in Liberty, and planted for several years at Dunham near Harris Neck, was married to Ann Todd Dunham (b. ca. 1795).[100] Another Dunham, James Harris Dunham (1819-1885) was born in Liberty County, possibly as the son of William and Ann Todd Dunham, and named for the brother of William T. Harris and John Harris, Sr. Coincidentally, Thomas J. Dunham and his wife Ann lived at Dunham plantation in Liberty County and—again coincidentally—it being adjacent to Springfield plantation in Liberty.[101] Thomas Dunham's plantation was near Sunbury west of Colonels Island. Thomas Dunham and Ann Harris Dunham are buried in Sunbury Cemetery.[102]

In 1855, 600 acres on the South Newport River were sold from the estate of James Victor L. Corker of the 22nd G.M. District, McIntosh County, to Thomas J. Dunham of Liberty County. The 1850 census lists the widow of J.V.L. Corker, Anne J. Corker and her son, James A.M. Corker in the 22nd G.M.D. The 600-acre tract, Log Island, west of South Newport settlement, was acquired by Corker in 1840 from Samuel King, and was near the headwaters of South Newport River.[103] One of the children of Charles Thorpe and his wife Anne Jurdine Thorpe was Anne Jurdine Thorpe (1794-

---

[100] Robert Manson Myers, ed., *The Children of Pride: A True Story of Georgia and the Civil War* (New Haven, CT: Yale University Press, 1972), 1509-10.
[101] Springfield was one of the more common plantation names in the Georgia-South Carolina low country.
[102] Myers, ed., *Children of Pride*, 1509; Liberty County Tax Digest, 1851.
[103] U.S. Census, McIntosh County, Population Schedules, 1840, 1850; Agricultural Schedules, 1850.

1871), wife of James V.L. Corker.[104]

James and Anne Corker also had a daughter, Margaret (1829-1871) who married George Dunham (b. 1825). George Dunham was probably related to the Dunhams already discussed; he and his wife are listed in the 1850 census as residents of Darien. From this discussion, it is clear that the genealogical connections between the Harris, Dunham, Thorpe and Corker families of Liberty and McIntosh counties are extensive and often quite convoluted.

In 1875, the Dunham tract was included as one of the Harris family parcels in the estate of Bright Baker Harris, son of William T. Harris, Jr. and Margaret M. Harris. In 1881, Donald R. McIntosh (1844-1929) acquired Dunham from his father, Lachlan McIntosh (of Donald, 1799-1886) of South Newport. A 1927 timber lease provides further validation of the William T. Harris, Sr. connection to the tract by noting that Dunham was bounded north by the Harris Neck road, south and east by the Julianton River, and west by Springfield, containing approximately 600 acres, being granted by King George II of England to Harris. The lease noted that Dunham was

"bounded on the north by the Harris Neck public road and a creek, south and east by Julienton, or Sapeloe, River, and west by lands of Morison [Springfield] and lands of Travis and Travis, said Tract being known as the old Dunham plantation. Said tract of land herein described being the same granted by King George II of England to Harris, and later on 16th May 1881 conveyed by Lachlan McIntosh to D.R. McIntosh and in said deed and grant described as containing 350 acres, but by later survey and measurement shown to contain approximately 600 acres."[105]

---

[104] Mealing, *Charles Thorpe of Georgia*, 5-9.
[105] Deed Book 1 (1927), 172, RMCG.

Across the Julianton River from Springfield is the Priester tract. Priester is bounded on the north and east by marshes and the Julianton River, and to the west by the marshes of Woodruff Creek, the latter named for Joseph Woodruff, whose son-in-law was Ferdinand O'Neal, both being late eighteenth century land owners in the section. Priester is defined by a high bluff overlooking the Julianton River and Springfield. At one time it may have been a part of Marengo plantation, which was to its west. It is not clear how Priester got its name. However, a clue, and hence its possible tie to Marengo, comes in local cemetery records. The death of Emma Stebbins Priester in childbirth is recorded in 1887.[106] She was born in 1866, probably at Marengo plantation as the daughter of Charles A. Stebbins, Jr. and Wilhelmina Stebbins. The 1870 census shows that family as residents of the 22nd G.M.D. However, no Priester surname is listed in the census of 1870 or 1880, nor is any Priester cited in the deed records. Nonetheless, it seems reasonable to assume based on the available evidence that the unidentified Priester and his new wife, Emma Stebbins from nearby Marengo, settled on the tract about 1885 or 1886. The Priester tract was among the later holdings of E.M. Thorpe and the Georgia Land and Livestock Company in the 1920s. In the 1930s, a section of Priester was acquired by J.H. Hawthorne of McIntosh County. The rest of Priester was largely apportioned to the Union Camp Corporation's 1,724-acre holdings in that section known as the Miller No. 1 tract. Tract No. 1 of the Miller No. 1 tract encompassed Priester lands and entailed "All that certain tract or parcel of land containing 546 acres of upland and 33.5 acres of marshland and being generally bounded on the North by the low water mark of the Julienton River and by marsh hereinafter conveyed, on the East by lands now or formerly of J.H. Hawthorne, on the south by the centerline of

---

[106] Gladstone, et al., eds., *Cemeteries of McIntosh County*, 241. Emma Priester and her infant are buried in the Stebbins family plot, St. Andrew Cemetery, Darien.

Hawthorne Road, and on the West by the eastern right of way line of [Old] Shellman Road."[107] On the other side of Woodruff Creek and its marshes, west of Priester and east of Marengo, was a tract of highland described as "containing 169.6 acres bounded on the northeast and southeast by marshlands, on the south by the northern right of way line of [Old] Shellman Road and on the northwest by the eastern right of way line of Young Man's Road and by lands of the Nelson Family [Marengo] Cemetery." This was Union Camp's Tract No. 2 of the Miller No. 1 tract.

* * *

An 1853 deed, concluded after the death of Jonathan Thomas, gives a picture of the inter-relationships of the planters on the upper end of Harris Neck. Three of these, Thomas, John Harris, Sr., and William J. King, as we have seen, had substantial land holdings at Harris Neck and its environs, many of the properties being contiguous to each other. There were connections by marriage between the Thomas, Baker and Harris families dating from the late eighteenth century. For example, as noted earlier, Bright Baker married Jane Harris, daughter of William Thomas Harris, Sr. and Mary Harris.[108] Baker was the father-in-law of Jonathan Thomas whose first wife was Mary Jane Baker. The deed relates the conveyance of Belvedere plantation from the Thomas holdings to those of Margaret Harris:

"This Indenture made the 12th day of December 1853 between William J. King, Executor of the will of Jonathan Thomas, deceased of the first part, and Margaret M. Harris, Administratrix upon the estate of John Harris, Senior, deceased, of the second part. Whereas

[107] Deed Book 67 (1974), 443, RMCG.
[108] Lucy C. Peel, ed., *Historical Collections of the Joseph Habersham Chapter of the Daughters of the American Revolution* (Atlanta, 1902), 2:329.

by a decree rendered in the spring term 1852 of the McIntosh Superior Court it was ordered that the party of the first part should be authorized and empowered to sell and dispose of certain lands forming part of the Estate of Jonathan Thomas and whereas Margaret M. Harris hath become the purchaser of the land as hereinafter described for a full and adequate consideration and price, now therefore William J. King, as acting trustee, hath conveyed unto Margaret M. Harris all that certain tract of land containing 1,200 acres bounded on the north by South Newport River, east by the lands of the estate of Jonathan Thomas [Peru], south by lands of W.J. King, estate of Bennett, and the estate of Jonathan Thomas, and west by lands of Mrs. M.A. Thomas [Mosquito], reserving only the spot of land used as a burying ground..."[109]

Additional documentation is provided in the will of Margaret Ann Harris, recorded in 1865, and included among McIntosh County records that were re-recorded after the 1873 courthouse fire. The will refers to tracts at Harris Neck, Dunham, Belvedere and Dillon as being in possession of Margaret Harris, likely the widow of John Harris, Sr. Margaret Harris died in early 1866, leaving her estate to her son Bright Baker Harris, land that included the tracts of his parents at Harris Neck, Belvedere, Dunham and Dillon. A decade later, in an October 1875 indenture between the estate of Bright Baker Harris and Charles O. Fulton, with W.J. Wallace acting as administrator of Harris' estate, the 1,200 acres of highland and marsh at Belvedere Island were sold to Fulton for $410.[110]

Edward J. Thomas's recollections of antebellum life at Peru plantation included details on structures and people at Harris Neck. For example: "Negro slave cabins" about a mile from one of the "big houses." Church—"Several miles away in some shady grove used by blacks and whites together." Cotton gin—"Great big cotton house."

---

[109] Deed Book A (1853, re-recorded 1874), 275-76, RMCG.
[110] Deed Book B (1865, re-recorded 1875), 76; Deed Book B (1875), 39, RMCG.

Big house—Two dwellings for the Thomas family, one on the upper and the other on the lower section of the plantation. Family cemetery—Near the South Newport River. Buried there is Jonathan Thomas. No trace of this cemetery remains, it likely being disturbed, perhaps eradicated, by land-clearing equipment during the Harris Neck airfield construction. Nearby—"Old lady, Aunt Peggy Harris' plantation," and "Mrs. Anderson, a neighbor." "Aunt Peggy" is Margaret Ann Harris, widow of John Harris, Sr. Ann Susan King Anderson, daughter of William John and Martha C. King of Harris Neck, was the widow of Dr. William J. Anderson (d. 1841). She subsequently married John Muller in 1861. The 1850 census lists Margaret Harris as head of household in the 22nd G.M. District. Her age is given as eighty-three. Also in her household was her son, Bright Baker Harris, age forty-three. The 1860 census lists Margaret Harris as being seventy-nine years of age and Bright B. Harris as age fifty-two. Age and name-spelling discrepancies are common in census data for the antebellum period; the 1860 ages given for the Harrises are more plausible. Edward Thomas recalled: "To make my story complete, I must tell of an old lady, Aunt Peggy Harris, as everybody called her, who owned a plantation and some twenty-five or thirty slaves, all being raised by her during a long life, from a few negro women inherited in her youth. She did not keep her plantation in very good discipline, and hence father, her nearest neighbor, did not like to have his Negroes companionable with hers."[111]

A partial list of the Peru slaves in the late 1850s included Mama Chaney (the Thomas children's nurse), Mama Martha, (head servant), Fanny (servant to Martha Thomas), Phillis (cook), Mamma

[111] Thomas, *Memoirs of a Southerner.*

Peggy (housekeeper), Ann (seamstress), Lizzie (seamstress), Little Lucie (maid), Zelieau (maid), Nancy (washerwoman), Old Lucy (keeper of the chickens), Nellie, Daniel Butler, Daddy Phil (coachman), Joe (servant to Edward J. Thomas), Daddy John (driver), William (hostler), Bony (fisherman, husband of Mama Peggy), and Henry (gardener, husband of Nancy).

In the 1850 agricultural census, John A. Thomas reported holdings of 800 acres of "improved" land and 2,200 acres of "unimproved" land at Harris Neck and its environs. He cultivated cotton and provision crops, and raised cattle. Other long-established families in the section are present, including Delegal, Todd, King, Baker, Harris, Thorpe and Caldwell. Life in the South Newport River-Harris Neck area in the 1850s reflected similar economic and social patterns as that of the previous two decades. The younger generations were assuming management of the plantations, and census records attest to a large slave population in the Harris Neck area. No Thomas is shown residing in McIntosh County in the 1860 census, but Peru plantation reported production of twenty bales of cotton and 600 bushels of corn on 600 acres of improved land with seventy-six slaves. In comparison, William Cooke produced fifty-two bales of cotton and 1,200 bushels of corn on 800 acres with ninety-six slaves on Bruro Neck and Creighton Island; William J. King produced forty-five bales of cotton and 1,200 bushels of corn with sixty-seven slaves on 310 acres at Harris Neck; Daniel McDonald reported sixty bales of cotton and 1,500 bushels of corn with sixty-three slaves on 600 acres at Fair Hope; Margaret Ann Harris had nine bales of cotton and 550 bushels of corn with sixty-six slaves on 300 acres; and Edward W. Delegal had twenty bales of cotton and

800 bushels of corn with thirty-five slaves on 1,400 acres at Delta plantation. By far the largest cotton producer based on the 1860 census was Randolph Spalding of Sapelo Island with 200 bales.[112] Two years later, the 1862 wartime tax digest reflects changing conditions in the status of the plantations. The estate of John A. Thomas held 4,000 acres and forty-five slaves; Margaret Harris had 1,910 acres and seventy-three slaves; E.W. Delegal had 2,070 acres and thirty-three slaves; John Muller (William J. King's son-in-law and overseer of his plantation) had 1,475 acres and forty-four slaves; and Charles C. Thorpe had 494 acres (Lebanon plantation) and sixteen slaves.[113]

Near the end of the antebellum period during which Edward Thomas was attending the University of Georgia, his father, John Abbott Thomas, died at Walthourville, Liberty County: "Father died in the year 1859 in his forty-third year; was buried beside my grandfather in the old graveyard on South Newport River. He was not a church man; a man of good deeds, rather than of faith, and goodness and sympathy beamed from him as naturally as light from the glowworm."[114] Rev. Charles C. Jones of Maybank plantation on nearby Colonels Island, was not as charitable in his assessment of Thomas. In November 1859, Jones noted, "What an unexpected and afflicting death is that of Mr. John A. Thomas! Buried on Monday. About forty-five. Leaves a wife and six or seven fine children. What

---

[112] U.S. Census, McIntosh County, 1860, Agricultural Schedules. The Thomas family had a second home in Walthourville, Liberty County, and resided there in 1860.
[113] McIntosh County Tax Digest, 1862, GDAH. See a summary of this digest in the Civil War chapter following.
[114] Thomas, *Memoirs of a Southerner.*

warnings we have had in this [section]. My son, touch not, taste not, handle not. Another awful warning of the use of spirituous liquors. A man of many excellent traits of character. What a melancholy end!"[115]

The Thomas family was not in residence at Peru at the time of Thomas's death. He and his wife, Malvina H. Thomas, a native of Charleston, had a home in Walthourville, where one or more of their children attended school. Thomas died there, apparently quite suddenly. His widow remained at Walthourville, later moving to Savannah where she died in 1890, being buried at Bonaventure Cemetery. Her husband's remains were moved from the family plot at Peru and reburied by her side. Edward Thomas completed degree requirements at Athens in the summer of 1860 amid a backdrop of change:

"On my route home, at most every station, a liberty pole was erected from which flags of various designs were hung, always expressing something defiant of the Yankee. Father's death made it necessary for me to take charge of our plantation, and this, with the unsettled condition of our country, made me forget my individual interest. The first of January 1861, I assumed charge, and with the assistance of our old driver, 'Daddy John,' prepared to plant the usual crops. Our family lived in Walthourville, Liberty County, twenty miles away, in order that the younger members of the family might have school privileges. I kept bachelor's quarters on the plantation...[Later] Federal gunboats could be seen out in the sound, and the neighboring planters became uneasy."

Thomas served in the Confederate army; after the conflict, he was compelled to settle the disorganized affairs of the family's holdings, a

---

[115] Charles C. Jones to Charles C. Jones, Jr., November 6, 1859 and November 10, 1859, in Myers, ed., *Children of Pride*, 531, 1701.

circumstance not uncommon among planter families during the post-war turmoil. In 1862, Thomas married Alice Gertrude Walthour (1843-1927), daughter of prominent Liberty County planter George Washington Walthour (1799-1859). Thomas settled in Savannah after the war where he was a railroad agent, supervisor of Chatham County, and engineer of the Savannah streetcar system. When he died in 1929, he was the oldest living alumnus of the University of Georgia.[116]

Cotton Cultivation on the Low Country Coast

Because both long staple and short-staple cotton were the most profitable crop commodities for the antebellum planters of Harris Neck and northern McIntosh County, it will be useful to assess the staples from the perspective of the ecological characteristics of the section. Sea island cotton was first introduced into the United States by several coastal Georgia planters shortly after the American Revolution. The soils of the barrier islands and the immediate coastal mainland were ideal as they were well-drained and nutrient-rich for long staple cotton on pine lands and cleared oak hammocks. Up to about 1840, sea island and short staple cotton were also occasionally cultivated as a rotation crop in the fertile bottomlands of the Altamaha delta south of Harris Neck. With the adoption of sea island cotton in Georgia in 1786-87 it became apparent that the black-seed staple was a superior variety over that cultivated in the interior. Coastal planters were impressed by the plant's adaptability to the tidewater environment, and they began large-scale cotton production. By 1798, sea island cotton had replaced indigo as the tidewater's primary cash crop. Cotton brought top prices on the English market, and

---

[116] Thomas, *Memoirs of a Southerner*; Myers, ed., *Children of Pride*, 1700-01.

South Carolina and Georgia planters realized great profits. In 1828, extra fine sea island cotton was selling at two dollars a pound, the highest price ever obtained for the staple.[117]

Sea island cotton cultivation was limited to the immediate coast, particularly the barrier islands where the plant thrived in the porous sandy soils and saline atmosphere up to about thirty miles inland. Seed was planted in early spring, then hoed frequently until it began to sprout in early July. The crop was harvested and processed from September until early December. The picking of cotton was tedious. A hand rarely averaged more than seventy-five to 100 pounds picked per day, compared to upland fields in which hands picked 200 or more pounds in a day's work. G.G. Johnson notes:

"The preparation of the staple for market was the most tedious part of the growth of sea-island cotton. Before 1820 sea-island cotton was suited primarily only for coarse fabrics. As the demand for the long staple became greater for making fine laces and muslins planters were forced to use more painstaking methods. The gin house, although only a simple barn, had separate rooms for the different processes. Upon being dried, it was taken to the whipper which extracted the sand and imperfect fibers, and then sent to the assorters. From the sorters, the staple went to the gins, and from there to the moting tables. The lint was then packed into round bags of about three hundred pounds each, 1,500 pounds of seed cotton being required for a bale of this size.

"Whitemarsh B. Seabrook of Edisto Island estimated in 1844 that fifty-four laborers were required to prepare the seed cotton for market. On the average plantation it required from fifty to sixty days of labor to cultivate and gin a bale of fine cotton. The routine of labor on a sea-island cotton plantation from planting time until the crops were laid is illustrated by that on John Fripp's Bluff plantation. In 1856 when John E. Fripp of St. Helena Island bought the Chechessee Bluff plantation of about 560 acres he equipped it as follows: a saddle, or sulkey, horse and a pair of carriage horses; four mules; eighty-eight stock cattle; six oxen; a large flat boat and two small ones; four good and three

---

[117] Although dated, an especially insightful technical overview of antebellum sea island cotton cultivation is Guion Griffis Johnson, *A Social History of the Sea Islands with Special Reference to St. Helena Island, South Carolina* (Chapel Hill: University of North Carolina Press, 1930), 23-30, 46-73.

'indifferent' plows; three mule or horse carts, two ox carts, plow line chains; collars; one small corn mill, a small sugar mill; spades, axes, and hoes."[118]

One of the techniques by which many coastal planters enhanced the potential of their sea island cotton yield was the use of *Spartina* marsh and marsh mud to fertilize their crops. This manuring method was utilized both for its convenience and the accessibility of the resource—another excellent example by which local ecological conditions could be adapted to provide sustainability and profitability for an agricultural enterprise; by the late 1820s the system of manuring with marsh and mud was in widespread use. Saltmarsh mud was within easy reach of the cotton fields on most of the local plantations. The usual method of application began with slaves going out in boats to the nearby marshes in the creeks and rivers, loading them with marsh mud, then returning to the fields and applying it at the rate of about forty ox cart loads to the acre. According to prominent rice grower Robert F.W. Allston of Georgetown District, South Carolina, some planters made a compost of the marsh mud by mixing it with "farm-yard, cow pen and stable litter, salt marsh and even salt, applied to the land in winter at the rate of forty, fifty and seventy cart loads."[119]

The value of employing marsh mud as a fertilizer for sea island cotton cultivation lay in its content of saline and organic matter. Marsh mud has a low lime content, however, thus cotton planters such as Thomas Spalding, John Couper, and others, addressed the lime deficiency by applying crushed oyster shell over their cotton fields beneath layers of *Spartina* and marsh mud. Spalding disdained the use of chemical fertilizers for his cotton and sugar cane, preferring instead to utilize natural animal manures, marsh mud and

---

[118] Ibid., 29-30, 47, 49.
[119] R.F.W. Allston, "Essay on Sea Coast Crops; read before the Agricultural Association of the Planting States," Charleston, S.C., 1854.

Spartina on his fields. In 1837, the *Southern Agriculturist* reported that the use of marsh grass was a suitable substitute for the marsh mud as a fertilizer:

"[Marsh] may be gathered in the summer, and put up in heaps, for use in the following spring. Putting in the marsh at so early a period gives it abundant time to rot by the ensuing spring ... the marsh must be put in heaps to rot during the summer, for the field is then occupied with the cotton. With a good scythe ... one fellow will do six times as much at cutting marsh as in digging mud: and when it is considered that six cartloads of marsh will manure a task better than 21 loads of mud, the balance is greatly in favor of marsh ... Some planters object to marsh, and say that it produces 'blue' in cotton; but no one need apprehend this, if the marsh has been put into the land so as to give it sufficient time to rot, before the cotton-plant reaches it."[120]

William John King of Harris Neck

William John King (1790-1861), as we have seen, was a planter with substantial acreage at Harris Neck. His son-in-law, John Muller (b. 1833), acquired many of the properties through his marriage into the family ca. 1861. King's wife was Martha Cooper King (1795-1860). There is early evidence of King's activities in McIntosh County: in 1818 he and Thomas King applied for administration of the estate of Solomon Harper.[121] In October 1823, a public notice reported the application of William J. and Thomas King for leave to sell the estate of Solomon Harper. In early 1825, a notice reported that "Jonathan Thomas and William J. King, Executors of Thomas Delegal, dec'd., give notice to debtors and creditors."[122] William J. King is listed in every census from 1820 to 1860. His son was William John King, Jr. (1823-1885). The 1850 census includes in the King household his wife, daughters Ann (King) Anderson and Mary E. King, and son, William

---

[120] *Southern Agriculturist* X (1837): 175; Thomas Spalding, "Brief Notes," *Southern Agriculturist* I (1828): 59.

[121] *Columbian Museum and Savannah Daily Gazette*, May 4, 1818.

[122] *Darien Gazette*, March 1825.

King, Jr., who was noted as "plantation manager." The 1860 census identifies a household comprised of King, age sixty-nine, Martha King, sixty-five, and daughter, Ann (King) Anderson, age forty. In 1862, the estate of William J. King included forty-four slaves and 1,475 acres.[123] The 1870 census lists no Kings in the Harris Neck area but does show a household comprising John Muller, age thirty-seven of Switzerland, and his wife, Ann Susan (King) (Anderson) Muller, age forty-five. Susan Muller is listed in the 1880 census as being sixty-one years old and in a household with her seventeen-year-old grandson, Edward LeGriel; oddly, John Muller is not listed in the 1880 census but is known to be alive in the 1890s and early 1900s based on land transactions made by him in the Harris Neck section during that period.[124]

An antebellum deed reflects the survey of a 640-acre tract on the South Newport River for Samuel King in 1833, a tract bounded by lands of William McDonald, Lachlan McIntosh (of Donald, b. 1799) and Hugh Ross. Samuel King is listed in the censuses of 1830 and 1840 as being a resident of the 22nd G.M. District, but does not turn up thereafter. He was possibly a relation of William J. King, as was Thomas King, who also had land holdings in the region. Thomas King moved to Bibb County ca 1840 or 1841.[125] Before his relocation to middle Georgia he may also have leased cotton land at Bourbon Field, Sapelo Island.[126]

---

[123] McIntosh County Tax Digest, 1862, GDAH.

[124] U.S. Census, McIntosh County, 1820 through 1880. John Muller (b. 1833) would have been about seventy a few years into the twentieth century. Census data in antebellum America was often confusing and inaccurate. The author encountered numerous contradictions in census records for names, ages and relationships for residents while researching the antebellum and postbellum history of McIntosh County.

[125] Not to be confused with Thomas Edward King (1829-1863), son of Barrington and Catherine Nephew King of McIntosh and Liberty counties. Myers, ed., *Children of Pride*, 1585.

[126] Sullivan, *Sapelo, People and Place on a Georgia Sea Island*, op. cit., 140.

The King plantation and homeplace was contiguous to the south end of Peru as validated in the memoir of Edward Thomas. Of Ann King Anderson Muller, Thomas noted, "One of our neighbors, Mrs. Anderson, had a son about my age, a nervous and eccentric chap, and a very interesting daughter. I frequently rode or drove to their home, and was always welcome. They were distant relatives."[127] Following her first husband's death in 1841, Ann Susan Anderson lived with her parents and continued to after her marriage to the family's overseer, John Muller, in 1861. William John King, Jr. became a co-partner of Edward J. Delegal (1815-1892) in the Liberty County firm of King & Delegal, salt-boilers at Half Moon Bluff on the North Newport River.[128] King, Jr. enlisted in the 29th Regiment, Georgia Cavalry, in December 1863 and lived in Liberty County after the Civil War.

According to the records of the Darien Presbyterian Church, William J. King, Sr. was an elder in that church in the late 1850s. These records aid in knowing some of the activities of the King family of Harris Neck in the 1850s and early 1860s. For example, the church records report a meeting of session in March 1838, with Rev. N.A. Pratt and elders Henry Atwood and E.S. Rees in attendance, when approval was made for the dismission of Mrs. Julia King, wife of Roswell King, Jr., "from this church to unite herself to the church in Midway of Liberty County. Also Mrs. Susan M. Anderson, late Miss King, having removed to Macon, applied to be dismissed."[129] The records also note that Ann Susan Anderson had married Dr. William J. Anderson in 1838. He died three years later. An entry in the summer of 1858 shows that the Session convened at Harris Neck with Rev. F.R. Goulding and elder William J. King in attendance. The minutes state:

---

[127] Thomas, *Memoirs of a Southerner.*

[128] Myers, ed., *Children of Pride*, 1062, 1072-73.

[129] Minutes of Session, Darien Presbyterian Church, March 17, 1838, v. 1 (1821-1869).

"Mary, a servant of Mrs. W.J. King, & Lydia, a servant of Mrs. Susan Anderson, being charged with irregularity of life, appeared before Session, made confession of all that was charged against them, but professing a sincere penitence for the same, were suspended from church privileges, indefinitely, until their lives gave proof of their penitence. In the case of Lydia there were some decidedly ameliorating circumstances. They were both earnestly exhorted to cleave to the Lord with greater circumspection than before. The Sacrament of the Lord's Supper was administered to about fifteen whites & about 25 blacks."[130]

A Presbyterian meeting in early 1861 notes that "Session met at the home of Mr. Wm. J. King, who was confined to his bed by sickness." A note at the bottom of the page of the original record notes: "Wm. King died 8 days afterwards" on February 4, 1861.[131] A final mention of the King family occurred in the spring of 1876 when it was noted that "Mrs. Susan A. Muller was received into the membership of the church by certificate from Midway Congregational Church."[132]

In the 1840s and 1850s, William J. King owned outright, or shared interests in, property that included a portion of Springfield plantation west of Harris Neck, and the nearby islands of Barbour, Oldnor and Wahoo. The topography delineated in the 1859 Coast Survey chart of Sapelo Sound shows that Barbour and Wahoo islands were under cultivation, probably in cotton but possibly in provision crops as well. There is documentation of land transactions relating to the King family in the Harris Neck region during the antebellum period and after. An October 1818 survey for King is among the county records "for 100 acres "on head branch of South Newport River."[133] An 1838 deed links King and the Durant family, which was also engaged in

---

[130] Ibid., August 29, 1858.
[131] Ibid., January 27, 1861.
[132] Ibid., April 2, 1876, v. 3 (1876-1912).
[133] Land Plat No. 89 (1818), Plat Records, RMCG.

agricultural activities in the 22nd District. This deed, dated May 1, 1838, was the instrument by which Francis Durant

"Planter, for and in consideration of the natural love and affection which I have and do bear unto my beloved son, Joseph C.S. Durant and of ten dollars to me in hand paid by William J. King as Trustee have granted unto the said William J. King ... the following property to wit: a negro boy named Ned, and a negro girl named Kate, both slaves. Also, the plantation and improvements on Eagle Neck containing 56 acres, adjoining Springfield, and formerly occupied by Mr. Abernathy, but now occupied and owned by me, the said Francis Durant..."[134]

Another deed, dated January 15, 1853, establishes a connection between King and the Thomas and Houstoun families:

"[This indenture] between Mary A. Thomas, Mary W. Houstoun and Johnson W. Houstoun of Chatham County, and William J. King of McIntosh County. Witnesseth that for the sum of $600, the parties of the first part confirm unto the said William J. King all that plantation on the waters of South Newport River and on both sides of the road leading to Harris Neck, now belonging to heirs of James E. Houstoun late of McIntosh County, deceased, and which were in possession of said James at the time of his death, purchased by the said Mary A. Thomas from George Rentz and conveyed by him to the said Mary A. Thomas on February 8, 1847."[135]

The inference of the deed is that this unnamed tract sold to King by the Houstouns is Mosquito, land that had been in possession of the Thomas and Houstoun families since 1828 (see earlier discussion). It fronted the South Newport River immediately west of Belvedere and extended to the Harris Neck road. James E. Houstoun was farming Mosquito at the time of his death in 1852. George Rentz (1792-1851) is listed in the 1820 and 1830 McIntosh County censuses as living in the Harris Neck area. Rentz was a Trustee of the South Newport Baptist Church when it relocated from Harris Neck seven

---

[134] Deed Book A (1838, re-recorded 1873), RMCG.
[135] Deed Book E (1853, re-recorded 1893), 567, RMCG.

miles west to South Newport in 1831. He would have been in the Harris Neck area at the time Jonathan Thomas acquired Mosquito in 1828. Rentz and his family removed to Houston County, Georgia before 1840, which makes his owning Mosquito in the 1830s even more problematic. Nor is there a record extant of Jonathan or Mary Ann Thomas selling Mosquito to Rentz, or buying it back in 1847. The land in the deed just cited is likely another tract nearby, probably the Rentz tract itself bought by Mary Ann Thomas then awarded to her son, James Houstoun. Additionally, for the selling price of only $600 it could not have been a very large piece of land, likely 100 acres or less, and Mosquito was much larger than that.

King had a part-interest in Springfield, an 840-acre tract across the marsh west of Harris Neck. Springfield was a combination of smaller tracts originally granted to John Houstoun (200 acres), John Barnaby (100 acres), Josiah McLean (200 acres), William McIntosh (100 acres), Robert Houstoun (forty acres), and John Law (200 acres). It was bounded on the north by Harris Neck Road, east by Dunham and Harris Neck Creek, and south by Julianton River. North of Springfield was Belvedere. An 1809 advertisement likely refers to Springfield: "Alexander Currie and Joseph Miller, Admrs. of estate of John Currie, advertise for sale 380 acres of land on Eagle Neck in McIntosh County, Georgia, with neat dwelling house and other buildings, situated on high bluff with a bold creek in front, &c. and a fine spring of water within 100 yards of the house. About 50 acres cleared and under fence."[136] This suggests Springfield. Its "high bluff" on the upper Julianton River is a prominent part of Eagle Neck. Additional records attest to the sale to John Muller by Edward D. Thomson of Liberty County his one-third interest in Springfield, and Barbour, Oldnor and Wahoo islands. This indenture of August 11, 1876 nots that

---

[136] *Columbian Museum & Savannah Advertiser,* May 22, 1809.

"Edward D. Thomson has conveyed unto John Muller his undivided one third interest in the islands known as Barbour's, Wahoo, Oldnor's, or Norse, islands, bounded as follows: Barbour's and adjacent marsh lands by Barbour's Island river, Sapelo Sound and creek, Wahoo Island by South Newport river and by South Newport Sound and creek, Oldnor's, or Norse, Island by Sapelo Sound and creek, also his undivided one third interest in the following tracts of land on the main in McIntosh County, the Baker, or Home tract, containing 350 acres bounded east by creeks and lands of the Estate of Harris, north by lands of the Estate of Harris, south by lands of the Estate of E.W Delegal; also the Gould tract bounded east by Swain's river [Barbour Island River], north by lands of the Estate of Thomas, south and west by lands of the Estate of Harris containing 130 acres; also the Lowe [Law], Springfield and other tracts on Eagle Neck containing 1,200 acres, bounded east by the Dunham tract and creek, south by a creek, west by lands of the Estate of Thomas, and north by lands of the Estate of Thomas and the places Belvedere and Bennett... the said one third interest of the said Edward D. Thomson in the Estate and under the last Will and Testament of William J. King, late of McIntosh County, and deceased."[137]

In 1890, Muller sold to Elijah P. Butts of McIntosh County Barbour, Oldnor and Wahoo islands, plus 100 acres at Springfield. In 1891, Butts sold the three islands to Robert S. Morison of Chicago. The islands subsequently went, in 1914, to George A. Morison who held them until 1936. A deed recorded February 29, 1892 in Jacksonville, Florida documented the sale to Muller the interests of his wife's grandson, Edward C. LeGriel, in Springfield and other tracts around Harris Neck. LeGriel affirmed to Muller "all the right, title and interest I have under the Will of William J. King, Sr., and as an heir at law of Mrs. Ann S. Muller, formerly Mrs. Ann S. Anderson, my grandmother." The chain of title for Springfield takes another turn in 1911. An indenture in August of that year confirmed the transfer of Springfield from Mrs. E.C. Hewett to Charles C. Stebbins, it being a tract "bounded north by lands of McIntosh, east by a creek and river, south by lands bargained to

---

[137] Deed Book C (1876), 290-91, RMCG.

Sallins and others, and containing 410 acres and being all of the lands purchased by [Hewett] from John Muller by deed dated May 22, 1907. Meanwhile, an 1892 deed certified the sale to Muller the interests of his wife's grandson, Edward C. LeGriel, in Springfield and other tracts. The chain of title for Springfield takes another turn in 1911 as an indenture that year confirmed the transfer of Springfield from Mrs. E.C. Hewett to Charles C. Stebbins, the tract then described as "containing 410 acres and being all of the lands purchased by E.C. Hewett from John Muller by deed dated May 22, 1907." In 1904, Muller sold the 765 acres of the King-Muller family tract at Harris Neck to Georgiana Davis, et al., the deed citing the land as the "Muller Home Place" of 362 acres of high land and 403 acres of marsh bounded east by the Barbour Island river marshes, west and south by Delta plantation, and north and northwest by the former plantation lands of Thomas and Harris. The sale included the two-story frame dwelling house, "15 head of cattle, a buggy, wagon and skiff, and certain household furnishings." A survey plat accompanying the deed shows the house near the marsh on the east, with the road and forested woodland to the west.[138] Georgiana Davis (1855-1911) of the northwestern part of McIntosh County was likely completing a transaction with her children begun by her late husband, Irvin Davis (1853-1904). In 1904, Muller sold the "Muller Place" tract (former King plantation) to Irvin Davis and his wife Georgiana Davis.[139]

---

[138] Deed Book H (1904), 400-02, RMCG.
[139] Ibid. See also other records, mortgage records, plat books, 1890-1914, RMCG.

1904 survey of the King-Muller tract on Harris Neck.

Eagle Neck Tracts: Lebanon & Baker

Charles Thorpe (b. 1760) lived at Sunbury, Liberty County, after the Revolution, and was later active in the South Newport River area. In 1789, Thorpe married Anne Jurdine, daughter of Leonard and Elizabeth Jurdine of Liberty County. In 1792, their son, Charles Joseph Washington Thorpe (1792-1874), was born at Sunbury. In 1815, C.J.W. Thorpe, who had by then established himself in north McIntosh County, married Jane Elizabeth Harris (1801-1864), daughter of William Thomas Harris, Jr. and Mary (Harper) Thomas of Harris Neck. The Thorpes lived at Rice Hope plantation near present Eulonia where he was probably an overseer. The eldest son of C.J.W. and Jane Harris Thorpe was Charles Courtney Thorpe (1816-1901). Other children included William Thomas Thorpe (1819-1882), Samuel Randolph J. Thorpe (1825-1890), and John Harris Thorpe (1826-1895). Before the Civil War, C.J.W. and his son, Charles C. Thorpe lived at Lebanon plantation. Charles C. Thorpe married first, Margaret S. Williams, and second, Harriet Elizabeth McDonald. These two generations of the Thorpe family are buried in the Baker Cemetery on the South Newport River west of Lebanon plantation.

Lebanon was on the South Newport River at the upper end of Eagle Neck about halfway between Harris Neck and South Newport. This section was a Crown grant to Edward Baker in May 1773. Lebanon was developed on a peninsula, bounded on its north by marsh and the river, on its west side by Baker's Creek, south and east by Marengo, and east by marsh. The next two tracts east were Mosquito and Belvedere. The Thorpes grew cotton at Lebanon and had a house overlooking the marsh and nearby river. Across the South Newport was Liberty County and Colonels Island. A partial description of Lebanon:

"This indenture made the 20th day of July, 1891 between Charles C. Thorpe and Edwin W. Thorpe, Charles C. Thorpe, Jr., Mary C. Thorpe, David G. Thorpe, Elisha M. Thorpe, Daniel L. Thorpe, Julie E. Thorpe and Sarah J. Thorpe. The said Charles C. Thorpe, for and in consideration of the natural love and affection of his children grants and conveys unto [his children] all that tract of land consisting of two or more small tracts of land located on Eagles Neck and known as Lebanon Homeplace of the said Charles C. Thorpe, bounded on the north by South Newport River, and on the South and East by lands of C.O. Fulton [Marengo tract], and on the West by lands of Mrs. A.I. Pease, containing 445 acres, more or less."[140]

West of Lebanon and Baker's Creek was Stark, a large tract originally among the Baker holdings and acquired by Jonathan Thomas through his marriage ca. 1814 to his first wife, Mary Jane Baker. Stark's north end fronted the South Newport River and extended as far west as the junction of the Harris Neck and Shellman-South Newport Road, about a mile east of the South Newport settlement. James J. Garrison surveyed Stark in 1841 for Thomas and determined that the tract comprised 3,015 acres and extended from the South Newport River south about four miles to Minton Swamp.[141] Only a small portion of Stark was cultivated by Thomas, likely for provision crops. After the death of Thomas ca. 1849, Stark was sold off in smaller tracts, sections being acquired by the Thorpes. After 1870, Stark was sold in lots, one example coming in 1881 when William Thomas Thorpe purchased from H.H. Thomas of Savannah Lot No. 2 of 326 acres fronting on the South Newport River less than two miles east of South Newport. W.T. Thorpe (b. 1822), the son of Charles J.W. Thorpe, was a younger brother of Charles C. Thorpe. A June 1889 transaction shows that part of Stark was still in possession of the Thomas family as 350 acres, "The estate of Jonathan

---

[140] Deed Book E (1891), 368-69, RMCG.
[141] Plat Book 1, page 421, folio 843, survey dated October 28, 1841, RMCG.

Thomas," was leased by Thomas' daughter-in-law, Malvina H. Thomas, and granddaughter, Mattie Thomas, to Edwin W. Thorpe for turpentining.[142] About two miles east of South Newport was Limerick, the home of Samuel R.J. Thorpe, another brother of Charles Courtney Thorpe. According to a 1904 deed, Limerick comprised 225 acres fronting the South Newport River.

Across Baker's Creek and west of Lebanon overlooking the marshes is the Baker-Thorpe Cemetery, identified on some later maps as "Lebanon Cemetery." Nearly all the graves are post-Civil War, and most are from the early 1900s. The earliest tombstone identified in the Baker-Thorpe plot is that of Benjamin Bright Baker, Jr. who died in 1855. Also buried there are Charles J.W. Thorpe and his wife Jane Elizabeth Harris Thorpe, William T. Thorpe, Charles C. Thorpe, Samuel Thorpe, John H. Thorpe, Richard S. Baker, and King Stebbins, as well as their families. Baker-Thorpe Cemetery is probably on land that was once part of the Baker-Thomas family's Stark tract. The 1841 Garrison plat referred to above delineates Stark as extending to the west side of Baker's Creek, which would include the land where the cemetery was started in 1855. The land may have been bequeathed by Jonathan Thomas for family use, or sold by his estate after his death ca. 1849.

South and east of Lebanon, near Marengo and Mosquito, were more of the Baker family lands, a smaller farm tract that came into the Thomas holdings about 1820. As noted earlier, the Bakers also had holdings on upper Harris Neck, land that became Jonathan Thomas's Peru plantation upon his marriage to Mary Jane Baker who died ca. 1816.[143] A December 1876 indenture between Edward J. Thomas and Edwin W. Thorpe records the sale by Thomas of a portion of Baker plantation "bounded as follows: North by

[142] Deed Book C (1881), 159, Book D (1889), 469, RMCG.

[143] Gladstone, et al. eds., *Cemeteries of McIntosh County, Georgia*, 216. See discussion of the Thomas-Baker connection earlier in this chapter.

the Mosquito Tract, South by Carter's Creek, East by Lot No. 7 and West by C.C. Thorpe."[144] This indicates the Baker tract adjoined both Lebanon and Mosquito. Carter's Creek, a small tidal stream extending westward from Julianton River, lay just south of the Harris Neck public road. A later deed involving the children of Charles C. Thorpe provides additional context into the land that encompassed Lebanon. The May 1917 indenture between brothers Edwin W. Thorpe of Florida and Elisha M. Thorpe of McIntosh County, et al., provided that the former "in consideration of the love and affection he bears his brothers and sisters does grant, give and convey to his brothers and sisters all his right, title and interest in all that parcel of land known as Lebanon or 'The Home Place' containing 604 acres bounded north by the South Newport River, on the east by a tract of land known as Mosquito, on the south by Carter's Creek, and a tract of land known as Marengo, and on the west by said South Newport River and Baker's Creek.."[145]

In the 1850 census, Charles J.W. Thorpe is listed as fifty-seven years old and his wife Jane Harris Thorpe as forty-nine. This correlates with their respective birthdates of 1792 and 1801. However, the 1860 census lists Thorpe as being of seventy-nine years, obviously an error; as he would have been only sixty-seven at the time. Thorpe died in 1874 at the age of eighty-two. The 1860 census shows C.J.W. Thorpe as the postmaster of an unnamed post office, probably South Newport. At one time, Thorpe's son, Charles C. Thorpe, owned both Lebanon and Mosquito. On the former, he had two cotton gins, both destroyed by raiding federal forces in the Civil War. He also had a store at the Sandy Run Crossroads in Liberty County at its intersection with the Stage Road. During the war, Charles C. Thorpe manufactured salt at

---

[144] Deed Book E (1876, recorded 1892), 336-37, RMCG.
[145] Deed Book O (1917), 262-63, RMCG.

117

Lebanon, the kind of operation that encouraged several Union raids in the South Newport River area. According to Isabel Thorpe Mealing, granddaughter of C.C. Thorpe, one of these raids resulted in the burning of the Lebanon house. After the war, the home was rebuilt on the same site, and it survived into the twentieth century. In 1914, one of C.C. Thorpe's sons, David G. Thorpe, compiled a list of family-owned property lost in the Union raid: "List of Houses, Barns, Gin & supplys [sic] burnt by Union forces at Lebanon 5 miles east of South Newport, Ga. in year 1865. Property of Charles C. Thorpe. 1 dwelling house, 8 rooms; 1 kitchen & dining room, 1 meat & sugar house, 1 2-story barn, 3 tenant houses, 1 gin house, 1 cotton gin, 10,000 pounds of cotton, 1,000 bushels of rice, 200 bushels of peas, 500 bushels of corn, 1 ½ miles fence rails, 1 dairy house, 800 pounds ham &. Bacon."[146]

C.C. Thorpe experienced additional difficulty in the war according to a story told by Isabel Thorpe Mealing. Thorpe was captured by Union soldiers at Lebanon following a trip to St. Catherines Island to negotiate with Union authorities. He was imprisoned at Fort Pulaski. The Thorpe family collected $300 in gold which had been hidden in a well, and used the money to bribe a jailer to allow Thorpe to escape. Rufus Lester (later a senator) drove Thorpe by horse and buggy to the Savannah railroad depot to catch the train to McIntosh Station in Liberty County. Weak from eight months in prison, it took Thorpe three days to walk from McIntosh Station to meet his family at Jonesville where it had taken refuge. Thorpe's brother Samuel Thorpe was among those McIntosh County men captured by federal forces at Ebenezer Church in August 1864. He was imprisoned for the rest of the war (see chapter 3 in the present study for an account of the Ebenezer incident).

---

[146] Thorpe family private papers, courtesy of Isabel Thorpe Mealing, Darien, Ga., 1992.

Charles C. and Harriet McDonald Thorpe's sons were Edwin White Thorpe (1867-1928), Charles Courtney Thorpe, Jr. (1869-1937), David G. Thorpe (1875-1961), and Elisha McDonald Thorpe (1878-1966), all born at Lebanon. In the early twentieth century, Courtney Thorpe, Jr. became a prominent Savannah banker, businessman and civic leader. He was president of the Savannah Bank and Trust Company, and owned a large amount of land. His brother Elisha Thorpe, as we have seen earlier in this chapter, became a prominent businessman and the largest landowner in McIntosh County in the early twentieth century. After the Civil War Lebanon was divided among family members with the tract primarily utilized for livestock and naval stores operations.[147]

Concomitant to this discussion is the Baker family of north McIntosh County, already mentioned several times in this chapter. Edward Bright Baker (b. 1792) was a planter on the Baker family's land west of Harris Neck. He apparently was a son of Bright Baker of the Harris Neck section, and probably a grandson of Edward Baker who had been granted Lebanon and contiguous lands ca. 1773. Bright Baker and his brother, Benjamin Baker, grew up on family lands in the Harris Neck section before the Revolution. As noted earlier, Bright Baker married Jane Harris, sister of William Thomas Harris, Jr. and John Harris, and was the father-in-law of Jonathan Thomas of Peru plantation; he was a McIntosh County grand juror in 1806 and held considerable land in northern McIntosh County. Edward B. Baker and Mary Jane Baker were likely the children of Bright and Jane Harris Baker. Bright Baker is not in the 1820 census, apparently being deceased by then. As the son of Bright Baker, Edward Baker would be the brother-in-law of Jonathan Thomas who married Mary Jane Baker about 1814, and in so doing acquired

---

[147] *Savannah Morning News*, December 10, 1937 (obituary of Charles Courtney Thorpe, Jr.); Mealing, *Charles Thorpe of Georgia*, 21-23, 155-60.

Baker land on the north end of Harris Neck that became Peru plantation. Mary Jane Baker died ca. 1816, possibly in childbirth.

In December 1820, Edward Bright Baker married Frances Leonard Jurdine (b. ca. 1805). Baker was an elder in the Darien Presbyterian Church in the 1830s and is listed in the McIntosh County census from 1820 through 1850. The first son of Edward B. and Frances Baker was Benjamin Bright Baker (1824-1855). A second son, John St. Leonard Baker (1829-1861), married Mary Georgia Dunham (1836-1904), daughter of George C. Dunham (1798-1881). John S. Baker was a Darien druggist and, like his older brother, died young—succumbing to yellow fever in Darien on August 26, 1861. The 1837 tax digest shows Edward Baker as owning twenty-six slaves and 645 upland acres. The 1850 census lists him as age fifty-eight and his wife Frances as age forty. Also in this household was Benjamin Bright Baker, then aged twenty-five, and John, twenty-one. They probably lived on the Baker family tract west of Harris Neck, near Lebanon. Parts of the Baker lands west of Peru, as noted earlier, were at one time among the Jonathan Thomas holdings through his first wife, Mary Jane Baker. While the familial relationship between Edward B. Baker and Mary Jane Baker has not been established with certitude, the possibility is very good that they were brother and sister. If so, it could have been that each were left separate tracts by their father Bright Baker—Mary Jane's on the land that became Peru plantation and Edward on the Baker lands west of Harris Neck. In the 1850s, Edward and Frances Baker left McIntosh County as they are listed in the 1860 Duval County, Florida, census.[148]

---

[148] U.S. Census, 1820, 1850, McIntosh County; McIntosh County Tax Digest, 1837, GDAH; Myers, ed., *Children of Pride*, 1459.

Leading 22nd G.M.D. Planters in 1850[149]

First figure is slaves owned; second figure is improved land owned; third figure is unimproved land

22nd G.M. District. Mary A. Thomas, 114 slaves and 200 improved acres (including slaves from Jonathan Thomas estate and those at Marengo plantation); John A. Thomas, 104 slaves, 800, 220 (from Jonathan Thomas estate); William Cooke; 86, 850, 1000; William H. Bennett, 85, 800, 350; William J. King, 75, 460, 400; Edward W. Delegal, 65, 700, 3800; Margaret M. Harris, 59, 150, 1340; William Brailsford, 50, 800, 800; Reuben King, 42, 200, 1793; James E. Houstoun, 35, 80, 200; Margery Forbes, 24, 100, 150; Thomas K. Gould estate, 23 slaves.

Leading 22nd G.M.D. Planters in 1860[150]

Delineating plantation, slaves owned, acreage cultivated, and crop production for year

22nd G.M. District. William Cooke (Creighton Island and Shellman), 96 slaves, 800 improved acres, 52 bales cotton, 1,200 bushels corn; William H. Bennett (Julianton), 85 slaves, 800 improved acres, cotton yield not listed; Alexander B. Kell (Rushland), 80 slaves, 70 improved acres, 16 bales cotton; John A. Thomas estate (Peru), 76 slaves, 600 improved acres, 20 bales cotton, 600 bushels corn; William J. King (Harris Neck), 67 slaves, 310 improved acres, 45 bales cotton, 1,200 bushels corn; Margaret M. Harris (Harris Neck), 66 slaves, 300 improved acres, 9 bales cotton, 550 bushels corn; Daniel McDonald (Fair Hope), 63 slaves, 600 improved acres, 60 bales cotton, 1,500 bushels corn; Reuben King (Mallow), 58 slaves, 120 improved acres, 14 bales cotton, 600 bushels corn; John M. McIntosh, 46 slaves; Gideon B. Dean (Sapelo River headwaters), 45 slaves, 150 improved acres, 7 bales cotton; William J. Anderson estate, 39 slaves; Edward W. Delegal (Delta), 35 slaves, 1,400 improved acres, 20 bales cotton, 800 bushels corn; Ann J. & Margery Forbes (White Chimney), 28 slaves, 100 improved acres, 3 bales cotton; William M. McDonald (South Newport River), 19 slaves, 88 improved acres, 20 bales cotton; Charles C. Thorpe (Lebanon), 14 slaves, 100 improved acres, 10 bales cotton, 500 bushels corn.

---

[149] Extracted from data in U.S. Census, McIntosh County, 1850, Slave and Agricultural Schedules.
[150] Extracted from data in U.S. Census, McIntosh County, 1860, Slave and Agricultural Schedules.

3

Other North McIntosh Plantations

The 1860 census identifies other families of the 22nd G.M.D including those of planter William R. Townsend (1806-1874), William Todd (b. 1802), George W. Todd (b. 1812) and members of the Wallace family, including William J. Wallace (1812-1881) and Thomas Wallace (b. 1821). Also in the area were Francis B. Williams (b. 1812), Gideon B. Dean (b. 1798), Margaret R. Forbes (b. 1803), and Francis D. Durant (b. 1833), and his sons, Francis E. Durant (1861-1910) and Joseph Durant. Francis Durant was active in local business and civic affairs in the postbellum period, was treasurer of McIntosh County from the 1880s to the early 1900s, and ca. 1890 built a home at the new settlement of Meridian seven miles northeast of Darien on the Cow Horn Road.[151]

Contentment–John Calder (1761-1845) came to McIntosh County from South Carolina after the Revolution and cultivated Contentment plantation on the Bruro River after acquiring it from the Gignilliat family. He married (second) Winnewood F. Richey (1776-1854) in 1803. He died in 1845 with

---

[151] For Francis E. Durant, see *Darien Timber Gazette*, September 29, 1888; *Darien Gazette*, August 17, 1895, December 14, 1901; for the Durant family see Sullivan, *Early Days on the Georgia Tidewater*, all editions; Gladstone, ed., *Cemeteries of McIntosh County, Georgia*, various references.

his son-in-law, James J. Garrison, as executor of his estate. According to the 1825 tax digest, John Calder had seventeen slaves and 793 acres of upland at Contentment plantation. In 1837, he had twenty-six slaves.

Fair Hope and Mallow—Fair Hope plantation on the Sapelo River was a prominent enterprise in the antebellum era. Planting there was William J. McIntosh (1782-1863), the son of John McIntosh (1748-1826) of Fair Hope, and Sarah (Swinton) McIntosh. John McIntosh, grandson of John Mohr, inherited Fair Hope from his father, William McIntosh. William J. McIntosh was educated at Sunbury Academy under the tutelage of William McWhir, and served as a midshipman and lieutenant in the U.S. Navy. After resigning from the navy in 1808, McIntosh married Maria Hillary (1788-1862) of South Carolina in 1810. He was a planter in McIntosh and Liberty counties until the mid-1840s. He assumed the management of Fair Hope upon his father's death in 1826. The 1837 tax digest lists W.J. McIntosh with seventy-one slaves and 2,523 acres in the Sapelo River area, much of it at Fair Hope plantation before its acquisition by Daniel McDonald. McIntosh moved to Savannah in 1846. He was a supporter of secession and offered his services to Josiah Tattnall's Georgia navy when the war began. His son, Thomas Spalding McIntosh, died at the battle of Sharpsburg in 1862.[152] In 1849, McIntosh sold Fair Hope to Daniel McDonald, one of the preeminent overseers of tidewater Georgia. McDonald (1811-1893) was born in McIntosh County, the son of William McDonald (1772-1844) and his first wife Pheriba Farrow (1776-1811) who died at childbirth. William McDonald's plantation was on the South Newport River, likely one of the tracts just east of South Newport. In 1846, during service as the highly-efficient overseer for Hopeton plantation, Daniel McDonald married Matilda Powell (1821-1898), daughter of Allen

---

[152] McIntosh County Tax Digest, 1837, GDAH; Myers, ed., *Children of Pride*, 1609.

Beverly Powell and Mary (Calder) Powell of Darien. McDonald left the employ of James H. Couper at Hopeton in 1849 upon acquiring Fair Hope from McIntosh. McDonald prospered at Fair Hope in the 1850s. On the eve of the Civil War he owned sixty-three slaves and had one of the most profitable plantations in the county as evidenced by the production of sixty bales of cotton in 1860. The 1862 tax digest listed McDonald with sixty-one slaves and 1,600 acres.[153] In the November 1862 raid by federal naval forces on the Sapelo River, Fair Hope plantation was attacked and Daniel McDonald, then fifty-one, was taken away as a prisoner. His family took refuge at Jonesville. McDonald was eventually released and he resumed planting at Fair Hope after the war. He was the uncle of Elisha McDonald, also an overseer before the Civil War for the Couper and Jones families of Glynn and Liberty counties.

The adjoining plantation to Fair Hope was Mallow, the present site of the Pine Harbor residential community. Pine Harbor and Fairhope are contiguous communities separated by a swath of salt marsh and a pronounced "bend" of the tidal Sapelo River. The histories of the two places have been intertwined since the Georgia colonial era. There is often confusion about Fairhope, however. Fair Hope (two words) plantation was situated on the site of the present Fairhope (one word) community. Meanwhile, the original name of the Pine Harbor community in the early twentieth century was "Fairhope." The short-lived Fairhope township was developed on the former site of Mallow plantation on the bluff overlooking the Sapelo River. Both the Mallow and Fair Hope plantations had their origins in the colonial era well before the American Revolution. With these

---

[153] U.S. Census, 1860, McIntosh County, Agricultural Schedules; McIntosh County Tax Digest, 1862, GDAH; Myers, ed., *Children of Pride*, 1605-06.

facts in mind, the reader is therefore cautioned and forewarned about the provenance and use of these place names as their interchangeability has occasionally led to confusion on the part of historical and genealogical researchers, as well as cartographers.

Guale Indians first traversed these areas in the pre-Columbian period. Native American artifacts have been discovered in and around present-day Pine Harbor through archaeological field investigations by academics, as well as being found in quantities by local residents over several generations. The origins of European occupation of the Sapelo River bend at Pine Harbor may go back to the seventeenth century. By 1660, there were five principal Spanish missions in Guale Province administered from the Florida capital at St. Augustine. While most were on the larger barrier islands, the mainland Spanish mission and Guale settlement of Santa Clara de Tupiqui is thought by some archaeologists and historians to have been on the Sapelo River at or near present-day Pine Harbor. This mission was relocated to Sapelo Island about 1674, and ten years later all the missions in what became Georgia were moved to northern Florida.

Three McIntoshes

John McIntosh (1748-1826). Aside from Lachlan McIntosh, John McIntosh was the best-known of the Georgia McIntoshes. The son of William and Mary Jane McIntosh, John McIntosh lived at his father's plantation on the Sapelo River, Fair Hope. John McIntosh acquired fame in the Revolution when, as a colonel in the colonial forces, he commanded Fort Morris on the Medway River at Sunbury.

During a British attack attached to the Savannah campaign in November 1778, McIntosh received a demand to surrender the fort from the British commander, Colonel L.V. Fuser. McIntosh, in refusing to surrender, made a well-known reply with his defiant words, "Come and take it!" Fuser obliged and the British attackers were repulsed with heavy losses. Fort Morris finally fell several months later when the British forces invested Savannah. After the Revolution, John McIntosh became a planter and prominent citizen of the newly-created McIntosh County while residing at Fair Hope. McIntosh also spent time in Spanish East Florida where he was accused of being an American spy, and imprisoned in Cuba before his release was arranged by U.S. officials. McIntosh was commissioned a general in the War of 1812. He was an influential businessman, planter and ruling elder of the Darien Presbyterian Church at the time of his death in 1826. Like his well-known uncle, General Lachlan McIntosh, John McIntosh is regarded by state historians as being one of Georgia's leading figures during and after the Revolution.

John McIntosh of Benjamin, a different branch of the McIntosh family from that of Mohr. Captain John McIntosh served with distinction with the British forces in Florida during War of Jenkins Ear, and was awarded several Crown grants. One of these was a tract "on the second bluff of the river Sapolla" which became Belleville plantation. John McIntosh had another land grant further up the Sapelo River on the present site of Pine Harbor. This was Mallow, a tract abutting the Fair Hope tract on the same river just to the southwest. Later residing at Belleville was John McIntosh's daughter, Catherine, who married a British naval officer, Captain George

Troup. Two of their sons became prominent Georgians in the first half of the nineteenth century: George Michael Troup (1780-1856), who served as Governor of Georgia from 1823-27, then served in the United States Senate, 1829-33; and James McGillivray Troup, who became a prominent planter and acquired substantial amounts of land in the Georgia lowcountry during the antebellum era. James M. Troup (1786-1849) served in the state senate, was mayor of Darien and managed the Broadfield rice plantation on the Altamaha River (later named Hofwyl) through his marriage to Camilla Brailsford.

Roderick McIntosh. When Captain John McIntosh went to live in the Indian country ca. 1760, his plantation at Mallow was occupied and managed by his brother Captain Roderick (Rory) McIntosh, and their sister, Miss Winnewood McIntosh. They lived in a house at Mallow built in the 1760s on the Sapelo River bluff at present-day Pine Harbor. Roderick McIntosh was a Loyalist, and served with the British forces during the Revolution; in the operations at Fort Morris he opposed his kinsman, Colonel John McIntosh of neighboring Fair Hope plantation. Roderick was wounded in action at Fort Morris. After sojourning in British East Florida (as did many Loyalists of South Carolina and Georgia), he died in England in 1782; Miss Winnewood died in 1786, and was buried at Mallow. Later, Mallow was acquired by Reuben King, a transplanted New Englander who came to McIntosh County in 1801. Roderick is one of the more interesting figures in the history of St. Andrew Parish.

In 1801, Reuben King (1779-1867) of Windsor, Connecticut joined his older brother Roswell King in Darien, and in 1812 married Abigail Austin (1783-1863). In 1839 the Kings moved to Mallow plantation where King became a planter with a real and

127

personal estate valued at over $40,000 in 1860. Reuben and Abigail Austin King had two daughters: Sarah Amanda King (1817-1876) who in 1839 married her cousin, James Walker of Homer, New York; and Elizabeth Aurelia King (1824-1892) who married Octavius C. Hopkins, son of Francis Hopkins of Belleville plantation, McIntosh County. James and Sarah King Walker are buried in Darien's Upper Mill cemetery, and Octavius and Elizabeth King Hopkins are interred in the Hopkins Cemetery at Crescent.

The plantation journal of Reuben's nephew, Roswell King, Jr., who managed the Butler estates at Butler's and St. Simons islands, and had his own plantations in lower Liberty County, noted in an entry of December 8, 1845: "Damp & cloudy this morning. Went to see Mr Reuben King at Mallow, returned to So Hampton. This suggests that the King family had interaction between their plantations in Liberty and McIntosh counties. Reuben King had 58 slaves working 120 improved acres at Mallow, producing 14 bales of cotton, and 600 bushels of corn, according to the 1860 agricultural census.

Strawlathlan–Another farm tract was Strawlathlan near South Newport, and part of the original McIntosh family Crown grant lands. An 1853 will noted that "Whereas Lachlan McIntosh, late of McIntosh County, Known while living as Lachlan McIntosh B by his last will and testament bequeaths to Margaret his daughter, now Margaret Mann, the one third and middle part of a tract of land containing 750 acres, bounded on the east by the Darien road and lying but a short distance from South Newport bridge and known as Straw Lathlan.[154]

Liberty-McIntosh Connections–James Dunwody Jones (1842-1904) was the eldest son of Rev. John Jones (1815-1893) and Jane Dunwody Jones (1820-

---

[154] Deed Book A (1853, re-recorded 1873), 511, RMCG.

1884). He was born at Hopestill, the McIntosh County rice plantation of his maternal grandfather, James Dunwody. His father was a Presbyterian clergyman who served congregations at Darien (1843-47), Marietta (1847-53), Savannah (1854-55), Walthourville (1855) and Rome (1857-63). James D. Jones was a nephew of Rev. Charles Colcock Jones of Maybank and Montevideo plantations in Liberty County; in his adolescence the younger Jones spent time both there and at Hopestill. He saw service as an officer in the Confederate army in Virginia and Georgia. After the war Jones planted for several years in Liberty County before removing to Atlanta where he lived until his death in 1904.[155]

Elisha McDonald (1826-1893) was a plantation overseer during the antebellum period. Born in McIntosh County as the eldest son of William M. McDonald (1800-1879) and Mary Walker McDonald (1805-1876), William M. McDonald was a South Newport River area planter where Elisha McDonald learned his craft. From 1848-58 he managed Cannon's Point, the cotton plantation of the Couper family at St. Simons Island. His uncle, Daniel McDonald, was also an overseer in the employ of the Coupers, at Hopeton plantation on the Altamaha River. After departing Cannon's Point in 1858, Elisha McDonald served as overseer for Charles C. Jones at Maybank and Montevideo plantations in Liberty County until 1861. During the Civil War, Elisha McDonald served in Company K of the McIntosh County Cavalry. After the war he was a planter and merchant in McIntosh County. He is buried in the McDonald-Davis cemetery off the Jones Road about two miles west of South Newport.[156]

---

[155] Myers, ed., *Children of Pride*, 1571.
[156] Ibid., 1606; Gladstone, ed., *Cemeteries of McIntosh County, Georgia*, 184.

Lower Bruro Neck Tracts

Bruro Neck was a large section extending from the Sapelo River on the south and the Julianton River on the north, bordered on the east by the Bruro River, west by the White Chimney River marshes, and north by Contentment and Priester. Patrick Sutherland, one of the heroes of Bloody Marsh in the War of Jenkins Ear, was among the first of the British regiment to receive a Crown grant. Acreage on Bruro Neck, on the "first bluff of the River Sapolla" still bears his name though there is no evidence that the English officer ever lived at Sutherland's Bluff. The origin of the place-name "Bruro" is not difficult to establish, although technically "Bruro" is incorrect. County historian Bessie M. Lewis, commenting in 1973 on the many variations of this name, noted that "since the property near this neck was granted to Patrick Sutherland and to this day is known as Sutherland's Bluff, and *Brora* is part of the Sutherland holdings in Scotland, why should not this be Brora?" Miss Lewis's argument for the proper spelling of "Brora" is perfectly reasonable and certainly correct. The name has been mispronounced and misspelled on maps and in documents since the eighteenth century, known variously as Brora, Broro, Bruna, Brewer, Bruner and Bruro, among others.[157]

On the southern end of Bruro Neck was Sutherland's Bluff.

In 1776, colonial authorities laid out a naval shipyard at Sutherland's Bluff. Men from the colonial Maritime Committee had inspected the high point of land at Sutherland's Bluff near the entrance to Sapelo Sound and the inland waterway, and determined

[157] The author, throughout his writings on the history of McIntosh County, has chosen to follow the path of least resistance, opting for the most common and locally familiar "Bruro" Neck.

130

that the site was ideal for shipbuilding. The bluff was endowed with prolific stands of live oak timber for constructing wooden warships. Moulds were made in Philadelphia and sent southward to Sutherland's Bluff, accompanied by instructions which called for the construction of a 74-gun ship of the line, four frigates and several gunboats. However, the construction did not get very far, as the project was abandoned in 1778 when the British naval blockade of the coast made local shipbuilding too risky. A 1781 report states that some of the timbers still lay at Sutherland's Bluff, useless on the ground.

By the early 1820s, Sutherland's Bluff had become a plantation profitably cultivated by Daniel Heyward Brailsford, the son of William Brailsford. Daniel H. Brailsford (1797-1833) graduated from Harvard College in 1817; served in the Georgia legislature as McIntosh County representative in 1824, 1825 and 1827; and as a state senator in 1829.[158] Brailsford was the brother-in-law of James McGillivray Troup who, in 1814, had married Camilla Brailsford and had plantation properties on the Sapelo River near Sapelo Bridge. In 1821, D.H. Brailsford married Thomas and Sarah Spalding's oldest child, Jane Martin Leake Spalding (1796-1861). Spalding had owned Sutherland's Bluff since 1810. Two references in *Letters of Robert Mackay to his Wife* indicate that in the first decade of the nineteenth century Sutherland's Bluff was owned by either Robert Mackay or William Mein or by them jointly. They were Savannah merchants of the firm of Mein & Mackay. Sutherland's Bluff was under cultivation as seen in a letter by Mackay in 1807: "The [rice] crop looks famously at Coleraine & the Overseers letters from Sutherlands Bluff are very flattering, I hope this good appearance may

---

[158] Myers, ed., *Children of Pride*, 1471; Gladstone, ed., *Cemeteries of McIntosh County, Georgia*, 261.

continue, for a thousand Barrels of Rice and One hundred &. fifty Bales Cotton will help to reduce our debts in England very much."[159] A Mackay letter in February 1810 indicates that Sutherland's Bluff had been sold for $50,000 to Spalding, the Sapelo Island planter with whom Mackay and Mein had business dealings. Spalding gave Sutherland's Bluff to his daughter and her husband, Daniel H. Brailsford as a wedding gift.

On August 22, 1833, Daniel Brailsford was murdered by his former overseer, John Forbes, ostensibly because of the latter's dismissal by his employer. The *Savannah Georgian* reported:

"Homicide — With feelings of deepest regret for the victim, we are called upon to announce the untimely death of one of Georgia's most favoured sons. Col. Daniel H. Brailsford of McIntosh County. We were appalled by the awful intelligence that the virtuous and intelligent Brailsford had met with a sudden and violent fate. On Thursday last, in the afternoon, he was shot down with a fowling piece by a man named Forbes who had for nine years been his Overseer, but who is now in another employ. The lead entered the abdomen, and there was one second between Time and Eternity. Forbes was then knocked down and secured, and carried to jail immediately. Thus was taken an individual whose upright conduct, whose chivalrous character, and whose manly deportment commanded esteem. It was murder at the hands of one to whom he had been a benefactor, and whose hands now reek with his blood. Our late respected friend was cruelly shot down while exercising his duties as a Commissioner of the Roads near Darien, without we are informed of the shadow of a provocation. Leaving a sick and distressed family to perform his public duties, unarmed and defenseless, as we learn, he encountered death upon the highway at hands of one from whom he had a right to expect any other fate..."[160]

The incident occurred just off the Stage Road near Sapelo Bridge. Brailsford died about a hundred yards north of the Sapelo River bridge above present Eulonia. A week after its initial report, the *Georgian* provided an

---

[159] Hartridge, ed., *Letters of Robert Mackay to His Wife*, op. cit., 73.
[160] *Savannah Georgian*, August 27, 1833.

update, with additional insights into an incident that had created a sensation throughout coastal Georgia:

"It was the misfortune of the deceased that the individual who killed him was associated with him as a Commissioner of the Public Roads, and some difference in regard to the disposition of the hands was made the pretext for the assault which terminated his existence. The real cause is to be sought, in the fact, that about two years ago, Forbes was in the employment of the deceased as an overseer, as he had been for years before, but in consequence of a removal of a portion of the negroes from the plantation [Sutherland's Bluff] it was found inexpedient to continue his services any longer, and he [Forbes] was notified accordingly. This notification was conveyed in the most friendly terms accompanied with expressions of regret at parting with him, and a complimentary tribute to his services as a manager ... From that moment [Forbes] conceived the most rancorous and deadly hate, which nothing but the blood of his victim could appease. Accordingly, on the morning of the 22nd of August, while the deceased was on the road superintending the public work, Forbes rode up, and after some violent abuse, which was unprovoked, made an assault on the deceased with the muzzle of a double barreled gun, inflicting two severe wounds on the lower jaw, and but for the interposition of armed men, one of whom was a commissioner, it is supposed [Forbes] would then have carried into effect his vengeful purpose. On the evening of the same day, and nearly on the same spot, while the deceased was giving his orders for the next day, Forbes again rode up, and dismounting from his horse, shot the deceased with a double barreled gun, the contents of which entered a little below the groin and instantly deprived him [Brailsford] of life. Thus perished Col. D.H. Brailsford, in the prime of life, aged 36 years."[161]

A local jury convicted Forbes of murder in a two-day trial in November. The jury deliberated only fifteen minutes. Forbes was sentenced to death by the judge and, not long thereafter, he was executed by hanging at Darien. Forbes' dismissal as overseer by Brailsford may only have been an ancillary cause of the unfortunate incident near Sapelo Bridge. There may have been another more immediate factor which motivated Forbes. Robert Manson Myers notes in *Children of Pride* that the murder occurred "allegedly in

---

[161] Ibid., September 3, 1833.

response to Brailsford's attentions to Forbes's wife."[162] Support for this theory is provided by C.S. Wylly, a nephew of Brailsford, who somewhat delicately notes that Brailsford was widely known as a "charmer among the ladies."[163]

Virginia Steele Wood notes that "a memorial marker to Brailsford was placed at the site where he was killed, about eleven miles north of Darien, off U.S. Highway 17 [close to the Sapelo River headwaters]. Near an old section of the road, it is no longer visible from the highway. In 1962 the editor [Wood] located this marker, on its side and half buried in mud, surrounded by a broken iron fence."[164] In 1990, the author found a portion of the stone foundation and the rusting remains of a few pieces of the iron fence, all nearly covered by soil and needle-marsh. They were found in a small live oak grove about fifty yards east of the highway and about 100 yards north of the river, actually a tidal creek at that point. There was no trace of the monument itself. The monument's inscription was found among surviving Spalding papers: "This Pillar is erected to mark the spot where Daniel Heyward Brailsford, One of the Noblest of Men, Fell under the Hand of an Assassin 22nd August 1833. Spare this sacred Monument All ye that pass by. For my God will punish the Sacrilegious hand that violates the sad Memorial set up by a widowed heart."[165]

Sutherland's Bluff plantation remained in Brailsford family possession for more than thirty years after Brailsford's death. He and Jane Spalding Brailsford had two children, Sarah Spalding Brailsford (1824-1856) who married Darien rice planter R.L. Morris, and William Brailsford (1826-1887). William continued the operations of his father when he was older, and had

---

[162] Myers, ed., *Children of Pride*, 1471.

[163] Charles Spalding Wylly, *These Memories* (Brunswick, Ga., 1916).

[164] Wood, ed., *McIntosh County Academy*, op. cit., 181 (n45).

[165] Spalding Family Papers, Collection 750, series 8, box 2, GHS. The monument was commissioned by Brailsford's widow, Jane Spalding Brailsford. Both Brailsford and his wife are buried in the Spalding family plot, St. Andrew Cemetery.

about sixty slaves at 1,200-acre Sutherland's Bluff plantation. A notice in the Savannah press in the spring of 1859 amplified William Brailsford's agricultural activities: "Adv. 2/2 — I have this day associated with me Wm. Brailsford in the Factorage and Commission business and will continue under the name of Jno. C. Fraser & Co."[166]

Brailsford was an enthusiastic sportsman, and apparently a quite carefree sort. He often associated with his uncle, Randolph Spalding, only four years his senior, James H. Couper and Charles A.L. Lamar in hunting and other outdoor pursuits. Brailsford and Lamar were members of the exclusive Savannah Jockey Club. Both had the reputation of being high-spirited and big spenders. Some evidence is provided by a handwritten note found among the Spalding papers. Dated October 26, 1859, in Savannah, and written in a barely legible scribble, the paper reads: "The undersigned agree to run a Race Mile Heat over the Tenbroeck Course — Race to be run on the last day of the Races in January next. Two hundred & fifty dollars entrance each — play or pay — Randolph Spalding enters a Roan Filly by Chester out of Phillis three years old — William Brailsford enters a gray mare by — out of Alice Gray six years old & is to ride his boy William. Jack Bryan enters Chestnut Gelding by Chester out of Sapello three years old. Randolph Spalding & Jack Bryan bind themselves not to ride less than eighty pounds."[167] The paper was signed by Spalding, Brailsford and Bryan. There is no word on the outcome of the bet. Brailsford reputedly had a violent temper, and was quite given to drink, characteristics that contributed to the frequent disputes he had with many people. He had a second plantation, Retreat, in Bryan County, south of Savannah. Retreat was on the lower end of Bryan Neck overlooking St. Catherines Sound. Brailsford had part of his workforce at Retreat in the late

---

[166] *Savannah Daily Morning News*, May 11, 1859.
[167] Spalding Family Papers, series 3, box 1, GHS.

1850s, and was cultivating cotton there and at Sutherland's Bluff when the Civil War began.

Brailsford succeeded Lamar as captain of the Savannah Mounted Rifles in September 1861, and utilized Sutherland's Bluff as a Confederate picket station to track down runaway slaves from the coastal islands. Sutherland's Bluff was burned by Union forces in November 1862, among which were several former Brailsford slaves. In September 1864, Brailsford was captured in Tennessee and was imprisoned at Johnson's Island, Ohio. Several weeks after Brailsford's capture, Thomas Clay Arnold, at Bryan Neck attending his family's rice plantation, wrote to his father, Richard James Arnold, in Rhode Island requesting that his parents provide Brailsford with money "and some comforts; I would be glad as he has been kind to me." Richard Arnold biographers Charles and Tess Hoffmann are not unaware of the irony in all this—"for William Brailsford, one of the wealthiest cotton planters in coastal Georgia before the war, was the opposite of Richard Arnold in his lifestyle." Apparently, whatever assistance the Arnolds provided Brailsford did not extend to his early release from prison as he was not freed until May 1865. Brailsford returned to Retreat where he continued to live an "outrageous" lifestyle. When he died in 1887 his obituary noted that "he was probably the last of his class in Georgia. Money with him was made only to spend, not in his own enjoyment but in contributing to the enjoyment of others. Ready at all times to serve a friend, even at the risk of his life, he was often identified with affairs of honor in the days when men were called upon by public sentiment to recognize the code *duello*." Brailsford was survived by his natural daughter, Catherine Brailsford, a mulatto servant to whom he bequeathed his property. He was buried in the family cemetery at Retreat.[168]

---

[168] Thomas C. Arnold to Richard J. Arnold, November 23, 1864, Arnold-Screven Papers, SHC, cited in Charles Hoffmann and Tess Hoffman, *North by South, the Two*

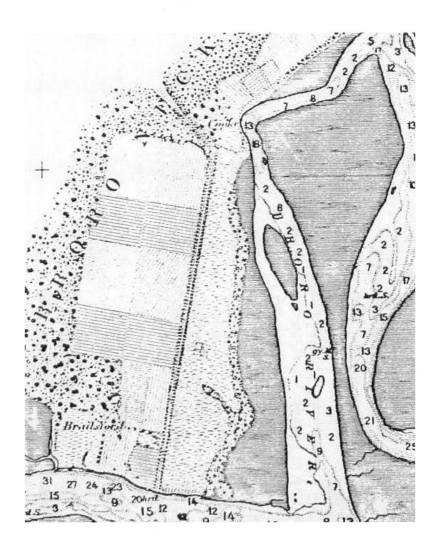

Sutherland's Bluff ("Brailsford," lower) and Shellman ("Cooke," top) 1859.

The 1859 Coast Survey chart of Sapelo Sound has detail relevant to the agricultural activities in the Bruro Neck region. The chart (above) delineates a dirt road running the length of lower Bruro Neck from Shellman plantation

Lives of Richard James Arnold (Athens: University of Georgia Press, 1988), 246; *Savannah Morning News*, July 2, 1887; Buddy Sullivan, *From Beautiful Zion to Red Bird Creek, A History of Bryan County, Georgia* (Pembroke, Ga.: Bryan County Commission, 2000), 95-96; Myers, ed., *Children of Pride*, 1471.

to the Sapelo River at Sutherland's Bluff. Shown are fields under cultivation from the Brailsford plantation northward to William Cooke's plantation at Shellman, and John Calder's Contentment plantation north of that. Across the marsh to the east the chart shows Julianton plantation under cultivation on the lower end of Harris Neck, and the north end of Creighton Island across the Sapelo River from Sutherland's Bluff.

Among the Spalding Papers is a November 1857 deed to a grant of 500 acres to Charles H. Spalding, being a tract east of Bruro Neck, almost all of it salt marsh and known as Fourmile Island, surveyed for Spalding by James J. Garrison in March 1843. A crudely-sketched plat shows the marsh tract bounded west by Sapelo River, northeast by Julianton River, south by a creek and northwest by "Montford's Creek" (Bruro River). Delineated on the plat a short distance northeast of Spalding's marshland is "Julianton house." Shown a little further to the northwest, is "Mr. Wm. Cooke's house" at Shellman, and a short distance from that, "Contentment, or Mr. J[ohn] Calder's house."[169]

William Cooke (1796-1861), a native Englishman, was another Thomas Spalding son-in-law, having married Hester Margery Spalding (1801-1824). Cooke was engaged in agriculture on Bruro Neck; his plantation, Shellman, was on the present site of Shellman Bluff. Cooke also owned Creighton (see ff.), and is known for his close association with both his father-in-law, Thomas Spalding, and brother-in-law, Charles. When Cooke died in 1861, he willed his properties to Charles Spalding, executor of his estate. In the 1860s, Joseph Durant was the overseer for Spalding at Shellman and Creighton plantations, and possibly for Cooke before that.

The Sapelo River and adjoining Sapelo Sound, waters contiguous to Sutherland's Bluff, received the attention of the federal government as a

---

[169] Spalding Family Papers, series 8, box 2, GHS.

potential site for a U.S. naval base due to the desirability of the natural harbor:

"LETTER FROM THE SECRETARY OF THE NAVY

"Transmitting a copy of a report of Lieutenant James Glynn of his survey of Sapelo harbor, in the State of Georgia. March 26, 1842:

"Washington, May 18, 1841. Sir: In obedience to orders from the Secretary of the Navy I have surveyed Sapelo inlet. Sapelo bar lies four miles from the nearest land, and divides the main channel into two branches. The southern branch of the channel is more intricate and less wide but, if carefully buoyed and marked, would probably afford two more feet of water. The entrance to the harbor is about a mile across and is formed by St. Catherine's island on the north and Blackbeard's island on the south. The islands are of the salt-marsh formation which, towards the sea, has been drifted by the wind into hillocks and ridges. The high ground is covered with a growth of live oak, and the low land with a species of palm and a rank grass. Blackbeard's island belongs to the Government, and at different times has furnished ship timber for naval purposes. Up the harbor, about ten miles from its entrance, on the north side of the inlet, is a plateau of land known as Southerland's bluff, which offers every convenience for the location of a commercial emporium. A draught of sixteen feet or more water can be carried up as far as this. Abreast of Southerland's bluff, vessels may lie in from 18 to 24 feet of water, and with their own tackles, load from a natural quay twenty feet above their decks, and an abundant supply of the purest fresh water may be led from natural springs in the sand banks into the holds of the vessels. Vessels would find in Sapelo inlet a convenient, healthy and safe retreat from a superior force, or a sickly or hurricane season in more southern latitudes. A regular communication might be maintained, even during a war from Charleston to the St. John's river, by means of steamboats operating through the inland passages."[170]

Another Bruro Neck plantation was Travellers Rest. It was an 1,831-acre plantation comprising much of Bruro Neck west and north of Sutherland's Bluff and Shellman plantations. The combined Travellers Rest and Sutherland's Bluff tracts, an aggregate of 4,000 acres, comprised almost all the lower half of Bruro Neck. Sutherland's Bluff's south end was on the Sapelo River; the tract stretched northward along the Bruro River, abutting Shellman plantation. Travellers Rest, the larger of the two tracts, ran parallel north and

---

[170] 27th Congress, 2d Session. Document No. 159, House of Representatives.

south to the west of Sutherland's Bluff, extending from the lower White Chimney River marshes on the south northward to the middle of Bruro Neck.[171]

Travellers Rest had considerable agricultural activity during the late antebellum period, as indicated in Joseph Durant's journal. Evidence suggests that the tract was cultivated by William Cooke. The 1850 agricultural census show Cooke with eighty-six slaves and 850 improved acres under cultivation or cleared for cultivation, with an additional 1,000 "unimproved" acres. He had ninety-six slaves and a similar amount of land ten years later in 1860. These figures are fairly consistent with the acreages encompassed by Travellers Rest, and Cooke's known properties, Creighton Island and Shellman, not including the marsh associated with the tracts. Due to the loss of deed records it is unclear if Cooke actually owned Travellers Rest, but it is likely he did. In his 1862 journal, Joseph Durant indicates he is in the employ of Charles Spalding and is serving as overseer at Shellman, Travellers Rest and Creighton. Upon his death in 1861, as noted above, Cooke left all his holdings to Spalding.[172]

After the war, most of the coastal planters were financially destitute. Their only real asset was their land. To acquire capital, therefore, many planters sold tracts of land to those who did have money—northerners in most cases. Large amounts of local acreage came under the ownership of northern interests. Ruined by the war, William Brailsford sold Sutherland's Bluff to Henry Center of New York City in 1867. In addition to Sutherland's Bluff, Center

---

[171] *Soil Survey of McIntosh County, Georgia*, Series 1929 (Washington, D.C.: Bureau of Chemistry and Soils, U.S. Department of Agriculture, 1932), county soil map accompanying report.

[172] Will of William Cooke, recorded November 4, 1861, Probate Records, Court of Ordinary, RMCG; Joseph S. Durant journal, 1862, excerpts, included in the following chapter.

also acquired the adjacent Travellers Rest tract. While there are no surviving deeds for the sale of the two tracts to Center due to the loss of county records in the 1873 courthouse fire, there is extant documentation relating to Shellman, which was contiguous to Sutherland's Bluff and Travellers Rest. In March 1879 Charles Spalding sold a seventy-acre section of the Shellman tract to Andrew J. Harris, land "bounded to the westward by Mrs. Center's lands [Travellers Rest], to the northward by unknown lands [Contentment], to the eastward by lands originally part of the Shellman tract, and southward by lands of William Morse."[173] Morse had acquired a forty-acre tract fronting the Bruro River from Spalding in 1875, acreage was bounded south and west by lands of T.P. Pease and others, and west by other Spalding land.[174] An 1886 deed lends clarity to Sutherland's Bluff and Travellers Rest. The indenture in September 1886 was

"between Elizabeth Mary Ludlow, formerly Elizabeth Mary Center, party of the first part, and Robert Center, party of the second part. Witnesseth that the said party of the first part has conveyed unto the said party all that of her undivided half-interest of that certain plantation known as Sutherland's Bluff on Bruro Neck, and bounded on the north by lands of T.P Pease and Forbes and by the tract of land called Travellers [sic] Rest, and lands of Charles Spalding, formerly William Cooke, on the east by lands of Pease and Charles Spalding, formerly William Cooke, and Bruro River, on the south by Sapelo River and a branch thereof, and on the west by said branch of Sapelo River and the lands of Pease and Forbes, and containing 1,420 acres of high land and 750 acres of salt marsh, according to a plan or plat of said plantation made by John McKinnon on the 10th day of March 1808. Also her half-interest of that other plantation near Bruro Neck and known as Travellers Rest, bounded and described as follows: North by lands of Hope and unknown lands commonly called lands of B. McIntosh and lands of Charles Stebbins, east by lands of Charles Spalding, McDonald and the road from South Newport to Sutherland's Bluff, south by lands of McDonald, Sutherland's Bluff plantation and the lands of Pease and Forbes, and west by

[173] Deed Book D (1879), 327, RMCG.
[174] Deed Book B (1875), 92, RMCG.

the lands of Pease and Forbes and lands of Hope, containing 1,831 acres of land, according to a plat and survey of said plantation made by James J. Garrison on the 5th day of March, 1867."[175]

McIntosh County deed records in the next six years attest to the acquisition of these tracts by Darien businessmen Reuben K. Walker and Joseph Hilton, with their subsequent acquisition by Norman W. Dodge of New York. A series of transactions from 1916 to 1921 between the Newport Company of McIntosh County, a local land investment firm, and representatives of the Dodge interests in New York, resulted in the two tracts being transferred to the Newport Company and, finally, to its successor firm, the Georgia Land and Livestock Company. The arrangement by which these transactions developed is an indenture of February 28, 1921

"by and between Newport Company of the first part, and Georgia Land & Livestock Company of the second part. Witnesseth that said party of the first part does convey unto the party of the second part an undivided one-eighth interest in all those certain tracts known as Sutherland's Bluff tract containing 1,420 acres of high land and 750 acres of marsh ... Also all that tract known as Travellers Rest containing 1,831 acres, said two tracts being adjacent to each other and containing in the aggregate 4,001 acres, and being the same property described in deeds from E.C. and H.L. Center to R.K. Walker dated September 13, 1888 ... Deed from Margaret M. Center to R.K. Walker dated September 13, 1888 ... Deed from Robert Center et al. to R.K. Walker dated September 13, 1888 ... Said one-eighth interest being the same conveyed by H. Stuart Dodge et al. to the Newport Company, deed dated April 1, 1920 ... being the same and all the interest formerly owned in rent lands by Norman W. Dodge, deceased."[176]

---

[175] Deed Book C (1886), 619-20. The Center family resided in New York at the time.

[176] Deed Book D (1888), 445; Book E (1892), 362; Book R (1920), 157; Book R (1921), 115-17, RMCG. The land investment corporation known as Georgia Land & Livestock Company held large tracts of McIntosh County acreage in the early twentieth century. See chapter 7 of the present study.

Also of interest is a small twenty-six acre tract on Bruro Neck owned by T.P Pease of the Thicket called Pokalego. Pease died in 1878; in 1882, his widow, Augusta I. Pease, sold Pokalego to Charles Bacon.[177]

White Chimney River Tracts

Both before and after the Civil War, Marsden C. Mints (b. 1820) of North Carolina purchased acreage in McIntosh County, much of it in the White Chimney River region. In 1871, Mints acquired 170 acres at White Chimney formerly owned by the Cannon family. In 1875, he bought the north half of Creighton Island, as well as Black Island, both from Charles Spalding. The Mints influence in this section is validated by a bridge over the upper White Chimney River, on the road to Shellman Bluff, noted on an 1882 map of McIntosh County as "Mints bridge." Marsden Mints came to McIntosh County in the mid-to-late 1850s; he and his wife Lenora (Young) Mints (1840-1883) are listed in the 1860 census as residents of the 22nd G.M. District, Mints shown as age thirty-five and his wife age twenty. Both are in the 1870 census. Mints had a store at White Chimney in the 1860s and 1870s, near the bridge over the White Chimney River, the crossing then known as Mints bridge, on the site of the present span. Lenora Mints died in 1883 at the age of forty-three and was buried in the Mints cemetery off the road leading to Shellman Bluff. Marsden Mints is not listed as a McIntosh resident in the 1880 census.[178]

The White Chimney River area before and after the Civil War was influenced by the farming activities of the Cannon and Forbes families. The

---

[177] Deed Book C (1882), 428, RMCG.
[178] Survey map of McIntosh County by Alexander C. Wylly, 1882, Surveyor General Department, GDAH, copy in Buddy Sullivan Papers, Collection 2433, GHS; Gladstone, ed., *Cemeteries of McIntosh County, Georgia,* 199; U.S. Census, McIntosh County, 1860, 1870, 1880.

1850 census lists a household headed by Margaret (Margery) R. Forbes (b. 1803), age forty-seven, widow of John Forbes who had been executed in 1833 for the murder of Daniel H. Brailsford. The Forbes land was at White Chimney with the Forbes cemetery just off the road to Shellman near White Chimney River.

West of Travellers Rest, abutting the White Chimney River and its marshes, was the small Forbes plantation, alluded to above where Joseph Durant was apparently the overseer for the tract's owner, Margery R. Forbes, widow of John Forbes. An 1848 plat delineates the Forbes, Wallace and Shaw families on contiguous tracts on the east side of the White Chimney River, which flows into the Sapelo River west of Sutherland's Bluff. The 1850 McIntosh County census lists eighteen-year old Joseph Durant residing in the household of William Todd at White Chimney. In June 1854 Durant married Susannah Elizabeth Cannon, daughter of William J. Cannon. Susannah died in childbirth in 1855 at the age of sixteen and was buried in the small Forbes cemetery just off the Shellman road near the White Chimney River. In 1862 Margery R. Forbes (born 1803) was taxed on seven slaves and 350 acres. She apparently had divested herself of many of her bondsmen, for in 1859 she and her daughter Ann were listed with twenty-eight slaves and one hundred acres of improved land at her White Chimney plantation, producing three bales of cotton that year.[179]

Henry Cannon (1781-1850) owned three farm tracts in the White Chimney area known as Folly, Rose and Upper McCoy, one of which abutted the Forbes plantation. Cannon's other two farm tracts

[179] McIntosh County Tax Digest, 1862, GDAH; U.S. Census, McIntosh County, Population Schedules, 1850, Agricultural Schedules, 1860.

144

were at Belle's Landing on the White Chimney River, and at Cannon's Bluff. Cannon's son, William J. Cannon (1804-1865), like his father, was a farmer and salt maker at White Chimney in the years before and during the war.

In the 1830s and 1840s, Henry Cannon (1781-1850) owned three farm tracts in the White Chimney area: Folly, Rose Bluff and the Upper McCoy tract. One of these abutted part of the Forbes tract on the east side of the White Chimney close to, or contiguous to, Travellers Rest. The Cannon tracts were in proximity to each other, one on White Chimney River at Cannon's Bluff; another on the opposite side of the river adjoining Forbes, and the third at nearby Belle's Landing on the White Chimney. Cannon farmed and manufactured salt. He was also the head keeper of the Wolf Island beacon in Doboy Sound from 1845 to 1850, according to records of the U.S. Lighthouse Establishment, apparently holding the position until his death in 1850 at the age of sixty-nine. Curiously, the light keeper at Wolf Island preceding Henry Cannon was William H. Cannon, serving from 1840 to 1845. Presumably the two were related. William Cannon, age thirty-six, is listed in the 1850 census as residing in the 271st G.M.D. of McIntosh County. The 1850 census also lists a household headed by William James Cannon (1804-1865) at White Chimney, he being the son of Henry Cannon. Like his father he was a farmer and salt-maker, and was county tax collector. W.J. Cannon was one of the McIntosh County men captured at Ebenezer Church by Union forces in 1864. He was taken to a northern prison, never to see home again, expiring en route to Georgia from prison when the war ended, according to documentation obtained by Annie Fisher Gill whose ancestors were the Cannons of White Chimney.[180]

---

[180] Cannon family papers, Annie F. Gill Collection, Lower Altamaha Historical Society Archives, Darien, Ga.

The White Chimney River was the scene of considerable waterborne commerce. On the small highland bluff, near the headwaters of the river where the present bridge crosses toward Shellman Bluff, there were docks where small vessels and boats called to load cotton from the local plantations, and discharge supplies to the planters. In the late postbellum period, Edwin Thorpe had a store and turpentine still at this White Chimney landing near the Mints bridge. The point of land near the bridge continued to be a landing for small vessels coming up the White Chimney River.

The first decade of the 1900s saw land conveyances on the White Chimney River with respect to the Cannon, Forbes and Walker families. Two Cannon parcels were sold in 1901 to Joseph A. Walker, one being of 150 acres originally granted Henry Cannon **in** 1841, **a** tract "known as the White Chimneys," and the other tract of twenty-one acres "known as Cannon's Bluff" bounded by land of J.T. Wallace, east by the White Chimney River and south by land of Joseph A. Walker.[181]   Six years later, sixty-nine acres of the Forbes tract on the opposite side of the White Chimney River, as based on a January 1873 survey by Alexander C. Wylly, were sold by Robert Forbes, with a 71-acre parcel of the original Forbes plantation retained by Ann J. Forbes Walker, bounded on the north by the Shellman road, and a third Forbes parcel of seventy-one acres then owned by the estate of Stephen McIntosh and formerly of Mary Forbes. The 1873 Wylly survey noted four Forbes tracts totaling about 200 acres, bounded north by the "Road to Sutherlands Bluff,"

---

[181] Deed Book H (1901), 39, RMCG. The Annie Fisher Gill Collection, Lower Altamaha Historical Society, Darien, Georgia, contains material about the White Chimney section of McIntosh County. Mrs. Gill (1906-2007) was a Cannon family descendant.

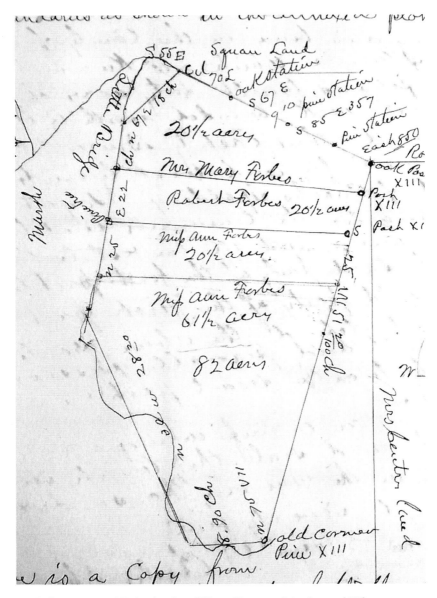

Postbellum survey of Forbes lands at White Chimney. Marshes and White Chimney River are at left.

147

west and south by White Chimney River marshes, and east by "Mrs. Center's land" (Travellers Rest).[182]

In 1907 Robert Forbes sold his half interest in

"that certain tract of land in the 22nd G.M. District commonly known as the Forbes Plantation on the Harris Neck Road, about sixteen miles from Darien, and containing 69 acres, being the tract originally containing 71 acres and owned by Robert Forbes, Sr., all of which appears from a plat and survey made by A.C. Wylly on January 24th, 1873. Said land is bounded on the north by 71 acres formerly of Miss Anne Forbes, now Walker, bought from John G. Forbes by Walker, and the Harris Neck Public Road, on the south by 71 acres formerly of Miss Mary Forbes and sold by her to Charles Pinkney and land formerly owned by Pease and on the west by land formerly owned by Pease and Forbes, but now owned by estate of Stephen McIntosh and others."[183]

Antebellum Creighton Island

Creighton Island, the upper end of which is across the Sapelo River from Bruro Neck, was advertised for sale in April 1817, a legal notice indicating that "Joseph Miller, surviving Admr. of estate of John Currie, deceased, applies for leave to sell the south part of Creighton Island in McIntosh County, containing 548 acres it being a part of the estate lands."[184] Less than a year later, the upper end of the island was advertised: "John Eppinger, U.S. Marshal for Dist. of Georgia, advertises for sale 1st Tuesday in March 1818, at courthouse in Darien, the north half of Creighton Island containing about 1,000 acres, together with 60 head of slaves on the said property; levied on and to be sold as property of the late Col. Ferdinand O'Neal dec'd..."[185]

Patrick Gibson acquired the upper half of Creighton in 1818; a decade

---

[182] Deed Book B (1873), 91; Book I (1907), 299-300, RMCG.
[183] Deed Book I (1907), 299-300, RMCG.
[184] *Columbian Museum and Savannah Daily Gazette*, April 8, 1817.
[185] Ibid., February 5, 1818.

later he had possession of the entire island. Gibson is listed in the 1820 McIntosh County census, and lived on Creighton where he had agricultural operations through the 1820s and 1830s. The 1837 tax digest shows that Gibson was taxed on 1,105 acres of upland and 110 slaves on Creighton Island.[186] In 1836, Gibson accompanied four of his slaves to New Bedford, Massachusetts, one being Betsy with whom "he had lived as man and wife," the other three being their daughters, Helen, Jane and Margaret. Gibson placed his family with a prominent New Bedford black family so that his daughters could be educated; he returned to McIntosh County where he died in 1837. His estate instructed his friend Edmund Molyneux, the British consul at Savannah, to pay the expenses of his New Bedford family. Gibson's will also stipulated that thirty-four of his slaves, including the four in his New Bedford family, and $20,000, be bequeathed to Molyneux, and that they be freed and transported to a free state or country, Jamaica being suggested by Molyneux.[187]

A deed in February 1838 recorded the sale of Creighton Island from Gibson's estate to William Cooke, being

"Between Jonathan Thomas and Richard R. Cuyler, executors of the will of Patrick Gibson, late of the county of McIntosh, Planter of the first part, and William Cooke of McIntosh County of the second part. Witness that whereas the said Patrick Gibson, by his last will and testament, gave authority to his

---

[186] McIntosh County Tax Digest, 1837, GDAH; U.S. Census, McIntosh County, 1820, 1830.
[187] Mary Bullard, *Robert Stafford of Cumberland Island: Growth of a Planter* (DeLeon Springs, Fla.: E.O. Painter, 1986), 122-24, relates Patrick Gibson's ownership of slaves in Georgia, and the relocation of four of his female slaves to New Bedford in 1836. Bullard also covers Gibson's will and his connection with Edmund Molyneux. The sources cited are Philip Purrington, unpub. ms., Old Dartmouth Historical Society, New Bedford, Mass, and news accounts from the New Bedford *Mercury*, January 30, 1840. Molyneux (1791-1864) was British Consul at Savannah from 1831 to 1864. He built his residence and consulate at Forsyth Park in 1857, a structure that later became the Oglethorpe Club.

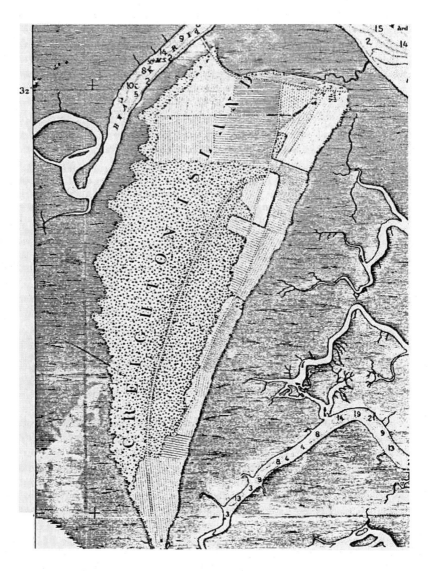

Creighton Island in 1859 with north end fields under cultivation.

executors to sell his real estate, witnesseth that the said parties of the first part, for the sum of $13,500, have sold and conveyed to William Cooke all that parcel of land being the whole of an Island well known as Creighton Island whereon the testator resided ..."[188]

---

[188] Deed Book C (1838, re-recorded 1881), 484, RMCG.

Cooke, as noted above, was a Bruro Neck planter and had been a business partner of Daniel H. Brailsford who, like Cooke, was a Thomas Spalding son-in-law. Cooke presumably resided on Creighton at least part-time to manage his plantation there while also utilizing a home at Shellman, his smaller plantation across the Sapelo River. It is possible Spalding had a financial interest in Creighton, perhaps assisting Cooke in the acquisition of the island in 1838. Spalding was involved to some degree with the agricultural affairs of Creighton Island since he always maintained a close relationship, both business and personal, with his son-in-law, Cooke, whom he looked upon as one of his own sons. Cooke cultivated the upper end of Creighton in sea island cotton and farm staples during the 1840s and 1850s, continuing to utilize cleared fields, and possibly some slaves, acquired from the estate of Gibson. The 1859 Coast Survey chart of Sapelo Sound shows fields under cultivation on the upper end of Creighton. In 1860 Cooke produced fifty-two bales of cotton and possessed ninety-six slaves working 800 acres of improved land at Creighton Island and his Bruro Neck tracts. Gibson and Cooke both resided on the north end of Creighton in a house either built by Gibson or an earlier owner such as Ferdinand O'Neal. Tabby slave dwellings were built on the north end, probably by Gibson with possibly some added later by Cooke.

Cooke died October 17, 1861. In his will written on February 9, 1857, he left all of his real estate and slaves to his brother-in-law and executor, Charles H. Spalding, including Shellman plantation, and Creighton Island.[189] This would explain Spalding's involvement in the plantation activities associated with Shellman and Creighton in the period during and just after the Civil War. In February 1868 Spalding placed Creighton in the administration of

---

[189] Will of William Cooke, recorded November 4, 1861, probate court records, RMCG.

John McIntosh Kell and Alexander Baillie Kell as a trust for his wife, and the Kells' sister, Evelyn West Kell. The deed was

"between Charles Spalding of McIntosh County, of the first part, and John Kell of the county of Spalding and Alexander Baillie Kell of the county of McIntosh of the second part. Witnesseth that Charles Spalding, for and in consideration of the natural love and affection which he has for his wife, Evelyn Spalding, formerly Evelyn Kell, and in further consideration of the sum of six thousand dollars hath granted, sold and conveyed, in trust, unto the said John Kell and Alexander B. Kell all that tract of land situate on Sapelo River known as Creighton Island containing two thousand acres [including marsh], more or less, for the sale and separate uses of the said Evelyn Spalding during her life."[190]

Seven years later, in March 1875, Charles and Evelyn Spalding sold the northern half of Creighton Island to Marsden C. Mints for $4,000. The Spaldings "forever quit claim to Marsden C. Mints a certain tract of land containing 525 acres, with the marsh attached north of the partition line, being that portion of Creighton Island formerly owned by Col. Ferdinand O'Neal which is bounded on the north by Sapelo River, on the east and west by two rivers, known as front and back river, and on the south by lands of Spalding, originally 'Currie' as defined in McCall's survey."[191] George E. Atwood of McIntosh County bought the north end of Creighton from Mints in 1891. Two separate transactions led to the acquisition of the 548 acres of high land comprising Creighton's south end by William Henry Atwood, older brother of George. In 1878 Charles Spalding sold 160 acres of Creighton's south end to W.H. Atwood then, in 1884, Evelyn Kell Spalding sold to Atwood the remaining 388 acres of the south end tract.[192]

---

[190] Deed Book B (1868, re-recorded 1876), 329-30, RMCG.
[191] Deed Book A (1875), 571, RMCG.
[192] Deed Book B (1878), 333; Book C (1884), 346; Book E (1891), 214, RMCG.

Slaves & Religion in the Antebellum Period

Religion and spiritual expression were important to the bondsmen of the Georgia coastal plantations, as it was throughout the agricultural South. Spirituality through its expression in religion and religious practices, symbolized a connection between the slaves' African spiritual heritage with their acquired Christianity in the western hemisphere. The religious music of the slaves, often embodied through their chants and spirituals handed through the generations, was the direct expression of their sorrowful plight and suffering. Black ministers provided the gospel to black congregations in churches established in Charleston and Savannah after the American Revolution. The mission of the ministers often extended to the remote plantations along the coast. They exercised great influence over the slave populations and were, in some cases, given considerable latitude by the white plantation owners. In the rural areas of coastal Georgia it was not uncommon for bondsmen to accompany their masters to Sunday services, worshiping in separate pews. The Darien Presbyterian Church, the Midway Congregational Church and the Bryan Neck Presbyterian Church are examples of this practice in the antebellum period.

At Darien's Presbyterian church, blacks and whites regularly worshiped together before the Civil War. Rev. Francis R. Goulding pastored the church from 1856 until the congregation dispersed in early 1862. In early 1858, Goulding reported, "members are thirty-five whites and fifteen colored, in all fifty," in the church membership.[193] The church apparently experienced growth over the next several years, particularly in the number of slaves attending services as Goulding reported membership as being 120 at the time of its closing because of the war. Half the total, sixty-one, were identified as being black.[194] A "List of Members Reported to Presbytery, April 1857" was compiled by Alexander Mitchel, clerk of session for the Darien church, possibly at the request of Presbytery Moderator Robert Quarterman Mallard at the meeting of Presbytery in Waynesville March 26, 1857. The list included the names of bondsmen, many of whom had the surnames of their owners. Included were slaves owned by such McIntosh County planters businessmen as Delegal, King, Young, Hopkins, Trezevant, Wylly, Townsend, Robson, Pease, Anderson and McDonald.[195]

Joseph Williams was a free black who worked with Darien's white Presbyterians in the 1850s. He brought a number of local slaves into the church membership, and served as an itinerant preacher at the plantations. "Williams' evangelical work exemplifies the expertise and valuable role of the black preacher in the control of slaves," notes Julia Floyd Smith who researched the religious aspects of slave culture in the antebellum period. "The slaves Sandy, Abram, Sarah and Edmund 'upon profession and examination, together with the recommendation of Joseph Williams, under whose teaching they had sat for the past year,' were received into the church in 1856. On

---

[193] Minutes of Session, Darien Presbyterian Church, Jan. 4, 1858, v. 1 (1821-1869).

[194] Ibid., May 14, 1861.

[195] Ibid., undated. A list of slaves and free blacks entered on the rolls of the church during 1857 and early 1858 is Appendix C in Buddy Sullivan and William G. Haynes, Jr., *History of the First Presbyterian Church of Darien, 1736-1986* (Darien, Ga.: First Presbyterian Church, 1986), 62-63.

another occasion the Presbyterian Session met at Harris Neck where Goulding baptized and extended membership to twenty slaves, one of whom, Lucy, had been expelled because of her 'cold and backsliding state.'" In 1857, the Presbyterian church began a mission branch at Ebenezer between Darien and Sapelo Bridge to minister to the black people of that section of McIntosh County. This effort was also led by Joseph Williams. "Only twice is Ebenezer Church mentioned in the sessional records," notes Presbyterian historian John G. Legare, "and from these minutes we conclude that the Darien church organized the Ebenezer church for the benefit of the colored people of the vicinity. It seems to have had no white members."[196]

There was a revealing item from the Presbyterian sessional record in 1838 relating to the salvation of a black woman, to wit: "Nothing has occurred since the meeting of Session April last to require the members to be called together until now—a state of lamentable supineness has universally prevailed within our bounds—today we have been aroused from our slumbers by the cry of one penitent sinner anxiously seeking the Salvation of her soul." The sessional minutes in 1858 reveal that "the case of Eliza, a servant of Mrs. Jane K. Young of Harris Neck was taken up—It seems she had united with the church there some ten years since, but for six years past had been living in the neglect of Christian duty & in the indulgence of sinful habits—for which she expresses deep sorrow and penitence and for

[196] Minutes of Session, Darien Presbyterian Church, Jan. 10, 1857 and December 20, 1857; John G. Legare, "Historical Sketch of Darien Presbyterian Church," 1899, copy in Buddy Sullivan Papers, GHS; Julia Floyd Smith, *Slavery and Rice Culture in Lowcountry Georgia, 1750-1860* (Knoxville: University of Tennessee Press, 1985), 156-57.

the future promises, with God's help, conformity to the laws of the Gospel. We have therefore deemed it best to restore her to the privileges of the church."[197]

It seems clear from the foregoing accounts that antebellum white churches of the coastal region, were generally very rigid in their insistence on conformance to the proper codes of spirituality of the time, and were not inclined to overlook "neglect of Christian duty." The ruling bodies of churches often governed with an unsympathetic and dispassionate approach to affairs in cases such as those of Eliza and Lucy above. "Whites and blacks alike were placed on probation or even excommunicated from the church for misconduct, such as 'back-biting,' excessive drinking, fighting, swearing or immorality."[198]

As noted by Frederick Law Olmsted in observations made during a tour of the South, religion provided the bedrock of "the southern planter's rationalization of slavery as a social institution, whatever the economic reasons."[199] The significance and the meaning attached to this seemingly innocuous statement has been examined, dissected, expounded upon and argued over by American sociologists and religious historians for generations since. In point of fact, many (if not most) of the planters of the South Carolina and Georgia rice-planting districts encouraged their slaves to embrace the Christian faith and consciously adhere to its values.

One of the great paradoxes of this era is seen in Rev. Dr. Charles Colcock Jones (1803-1863) of Maybank plantation, Liberty County.

---

[197] Minutes of Session, Darien Presbyterian Church, Jan. 13, 1838 and May 15, 1856.
[198] Smith, *Slavery and Rice Culture*, 157.
[199] Hoffman and Hoffman, *North by South*, op. cit., 49.

In 1850, Jones was simultaneously a greatly-respected, practicing Presbyterian clergyman and the possessor of 107 slaves. His position typified the attitudes of many slave-owning Southerners of the time. For antebellum adherents of the Christian faith and its virtues, the conflicting inner struggles evinced through conflating their religion with the bondage of large numbers of their fellow human beings within their midst was not inconsiderable. The ambiguity entailed by the master-slave-Christian doctrine overlap was rarely, if ever, satisfactorily resolved in the conscientiousness of the white plantation classes in the antebellum period, and for a considerable time afterwards.

Clearly, in all good conscience as evoked through his many writings on the subject, Jones strongly advocated the "Religious Instruction of the Negroes" by the tidewater planter class as an essential ingredient in providing for the well-being of the bondsmen, as well as being instrumental in fostering the moral loyalty of the slaves to their masters.[200]

The social order of the plantation and the constantly reinforced concept of slave-to-master subservience was an important element in the Christian training of the bondsmen. The church was the primary vehicle for its implementation. The idea that the slave should be blindly subservient to the plantation master was the foundation for the religious instruction of the bondsmen, a "reflection of the cosmic order of the universe."[201] The oft-repeated theme preached to the

---

[200] Charles C. Jones, *The Religious Instruction of the Negroes in the United States* (Savannah, Ga., 1842), GHS; Charles C. Jones, "The Religious Instruction of the Negroes: A Sermon Delivered Before Associations of Planters in Liberty and McIntosh Counties," Princeton, N.J., 1832, 6-17.

[201] Hoffman and Hoffman, *North by South*, 49.

slaves was that absolute obedience to the master was tantamount to obedience by the Christian to God, as all men are God's servants.

In the early 1830s several northern McIntosh County planters were active in a new movement to bring religious instruction to the enslaved people of the local plantations. In his important tract, *The Religious Instruction of the Negroes*, C.C. Jones observed:

"In the winter of 1830 and the spring of 1831, two Associations of planters were formed in Georgia for the special object of affording religious instruction to the Negroes, by their own efforts and by missionaries employed for the purpose. The first was formed by the Rev. Joseph Clay Stiles in McIntosh county, embracing the neighborhood of Harris' Neck, which continued in operation for some time, until by the withdrawment of Mr. Stiles' labors from the neighborhood and the loss of some of the inhabitants by death and removals it ceased. The second was formed in Liberty county by the Midway Congregational church, and the Baptist church under their respective pastors, the Rev. Robert Quarterman and the Rev. Samuel Spry Law."

In March 1831, twenty-nine planters from Liberty County and several from the South Newport River region of McIntosh gathered in Riceborough, the county seat of Liberty, for the organization of "The Liberty County Association for Religious Instruction of the Negroes." In his sermon before the gathering Jones noted, "We are bound to give the Negroes the Gospel. Should we continue to neglect them, our neglect might not only shut their souls out of heaven, but our own. The great object for which we would communicate religious instruction to them slaves is that their souls may be saved. To this all other objects should be subordinate." In the 1830s and 1840s Jones accomplished considerable missionary work among the slaves in the tidewater region.

Jones was known as the "Apostle of the Blacks" for his advocacy of the promulgation of Christianity among the plantation slaves. Jones, Goulding, John Winn, and other antebellum white Presbyterian clergymen, found themselves enmeshed in a crisis of

158

conscience, a moral dilemma, over the issue. The ambivalence so obviously manifested over slavery and religion by Jones and his contemporaries may have been at least partially assuaged by their retention of ownership of their slaves—for obvious reasons of economy, but in some cases, particularly in that of Jones, to devote their spiritual energy toward the religious instruction of not only their own slaves, but those of their neighbors as well. Jones encouraged local slave owners, such as his close friend, Thomas Savage Clay of Bryan County, his uncle, William Maxwell of Liberty County, and others, to strive for the well-being and comfort of their bondsmen. This approach was embraced by the majority of coastal slave owners: "It was in their own enlightened self-interest to improve the moral and social condition of their slaves."[202]

Clay embraced the theories and concepts of Jones, and made an important statement regarding the religious development of slaves when he published a layman's viewpoint for the Georgia Presbytery in 1833 in which he expressed his belief that religious instruction would provide a stabilizing factor in the lives and discipline of the slaves, "doing more for the good order and the quiet of the country than any civil or military patrol we have ever had." Slavery was sanctioned by God, Clay wrote, and "obedience by the slave was to a master who was God's temporal representative on earth."[203]

---

[202] Ibid. Myers, ed., *Children of Pride*, 1621.
[203] Thomas S. Clay, "Detail of a Plan for the Moral Improvement of Negroes on Plantations," presented before the Georgia Presbytery (1833), 7, 10.

The Jones Family Letters and McIntosh County, 1854-1864

Robert Manson Myers edited the voluminous correspondence of the Jones family in *The Children of Pride, A True Story of Georgia in the Civil War*, published by Yale University Press in 1972. While primarily focused on the planter families of lower Liberty County just before, and during, the Civil War, some of the letters pertain to families and individuals in neighboring McIntosh County with whom the Jones family had business and social interaction. Charles Colcock Jones was a Presbyterian clergyman long associated with the Midway Congregational Church, and was married to Mary Jones Jones. The family owned three plantations in lower Liberty County, making their primary residence at Maybank on Colonels Island.

Rev. Charles Colcock Jones to C.C. Jones, Jr., in Savannah, August 7, 1854.
"We have had much sorrow in our little circle since we last wrote you. Our old friend and neighbor Mr. [Roswell] King [Jr.] is no more![204] He was taken violently ill with inflammation of the stomach and after three days illness (the last of which he was in a comatose state) he died on the evening of July 1st. You may picture to yourself the distress of his family. Your brother and myself performed the last sad office of friendship, preparing him for his grave...It has created a great vacuum in our little community [Colonels Island]. I performed his funeral service at Woodville on Sabbath afternoon the 2nd and he was interred in Midway on Monday the 3rd.

---

[204] Roswell King, Jr. (1796-1854) first son of Roswell and Catherine Barrington King of McIntosh and Glynn counties. In 1825, Roswell King, Jr. married Julia Rebecca Maxwell (1808-1892) of Liberty County. He cultivated South Hampton plantation on the North Newport River and Yellow Bluff on Colonels Island where the Kings were friends and neighbors of the Jones family at nearby Maybank. He also managed the Pierce Butler interests in McIntosh and Glynn counties. Myers, ed., *Children of Pride*, 1584.

Mrs. Susan M. Cumming to Rev. C.C. Jones, March 20, 1855. "A meeting is to be held this evening to take into consideration the calling of a pastor to our church. I fear Mr. King will be the one called.[205] He has a call elsewhere and wishes to ascertain if he will be called here before he decides. The building of the lecture room has been commenced, and Mr. King has been very active in proposing plans for raising the money to pay for it. Perhaps he is the one to build it but I hardly think it will please a minister long though I may be mistaken in my judgment."

Rev. C.C. Jones to C.C. Jones, Jr., June 11, 1855. Let us have the flag at the masthead, an open sea and a fair fight. That is the best way in everything. Will you call at Mr. Lincoln's drugstore and request to send out for me to Riceboro by the Thursday stage a box of fresh Saratoga water? I wish the water for your mother. Direct care of C. Stebbins. One dozen bottles."[206]

Miss Mary Sharpe Jones to Rev. & Mrs. C.C. Jones, October 1, 1855. "Tomorrow we expect to go to Roswell. We saw Mr. Goulding a few evenings ago and he said that he felt so badly about having gone to sleep in the cars that he came very near writing us a letter of apology. Aunt Mary said she hoped he had waked up. 'Why,' he said, 'he hoped in a short time to awake to some very pleasant realities!' His marriage will take place on the 18th of this month."[207]

---

[205] Rev. Charles Barrington King (1823-1880), born at Baisden's Bluff, McIntosh County, the eldest son of Barrington and Catherine Nephew King. In 1848, C.B. King married Anna Wylly Habersham of Savannah, daughter of Dr. Joseph Clay Habersham. King, a Presbyterian minister, was pastor of the White Bluff Congregational Church near Savannah, 1856-1880. He was sent by Savannah Presbytery to assist in the reorganization of the Darien Presbyterian Church in 1870 following its loss in the burning of Darien. Myers, ed., *Children of Pride*, 1580.

[206] Charles Austin Stebbins (1806-1877), store owner at Riceborough in lower Liberty County.

[207] "Mr. Goulding", Francis R. Goulding (1810-1881), born in Liberty County and reared at Baisden's Bluff, McIntosh County. He became a Presbyterian minister in 1833 and was pastor of churches in Greensboro, Washington, Bath and Augusta, all in Georgia, and Charleston in South Carolina. He was principal of a boys school in Kingston, Georgia, north of Atlanta, 1854-56, and was pastor of the Darien Presbyterian Church, 1856-62. After the death of his first wife in 1853, Goulding married, in October 1855, Matilda Rees (b. 1820), daughter of Ebenezer Senior Rees of Darien. Goulding was a prolific journalist and author. The Rev. John Jones noted on the death of Goulding in 1881, "We have lost a man of genius, of rare attainments, of varied information, of worldwide reputation. His active

Rev. C.C. Jones to C.C. Jones, Jr., July 17, 1856. "Will you be good enough to see Messrs. Palmer & Son and get from them a coarse wire sifter of good size as masons use for sifting lime and send it out by Monday's stage, care of C. Stebbins. Also request Messrs. Palmer & Son to send me another keg of lathing nails by the first vessel. Also Mr. Brunner, corner of Jones and Barnard streets to send me by first vessel 4000 laths more, 30 bushels hair for plastering, 12 barrels stone lime, 4 barrels plaster of Paris."

C.C. Jones, Jr. to Rev. and Mrs. C.C. Jones, September 9, 1857. "Our city is now very quiet, although it is the pressure on the money market at the North that will have an unfavorable effect. You have doubtless observed in what an unfortunate condition the banks in the principal Northern cities now find themselves. Cousin Charles and Cousin Eliza are at present unwell. Nothing serious."[208]

Rev. Robert Quarterman Mallard to Mrs. Mary Sharpe Mallard, March 3, 1858. "We reached Darien after a pleasant ride early in the evening—say half past four o'clock—and went immediately to the little homeopathic doctor's residence, but not finding him at home we turned our horse's head to Mr. Mitchel's. As we rode up Father spoke to a little Negro boy. 'Howdy, John.' 'My name is Norman, sir.' 'Ah, yes—Norman.!' As we passed, someone asked Norman who we were. 'I don't know,' was his reply, 'who he is. But he know me.' Mr. and Mrs. Mitchel we found well, and we were very pleasantly entertained by them. The doctor and Mr. Goulding came over in the course of the evening and took tea with us. I walked down to the boat with Mr. Goulding, calling at his residence on our way, and thus made Mrs. Goulding's acquaintance...Our St. Marys party was rather a small one, Mr. Mitchel being the only delegate to Presbytery besides ourselves....Mr. Goulding not having been able to attend in St. Marys, would probably like an adjourned meeting in Darien to receive him into our Presbytery."[209]

---

mind ranged over a vast field with intelligence and marked originality." Myers, ed., *Children of Pride*, 1532.

[208] "Cousin Charles", Charles William West (1815-1860) born in Savannah, the son of Dr. Charles B. West of Liberty County and Sarah Evelyn Nephew West of McIntosh County. Myers, ed., *Children of Pride*, 1723.

[209] Alexander Mitchel (1797-1864), born in Scotland and settled in Darien in 1823. Mitchel was a merchant, civic leader and an elder in the Darien Presbyterian Church. He was a close friend of Rev. C.C. Jones. When the federal navy threatened the coast in early 1862, Mr. and Mrs. Mitchel moved to Macon where he died of typhoid fever in 1864. Myers, ed., *Children of Pride*, 1626.

Rev. C.C. Jones to Mrs. Mary Jones, March 24, 1858, from St. Marys. "We had a pleasant ride and reached Darien. Dr. Dunwoody was out in the country on his practice, and we drove on to Mr. Mitchel's and were received with great kindness. Brother Goulding called over to see us. In good health and spirits. Getting a little bald. His wife a most active minister's wife, making herself useful in every way. Dr. Dunwoody called also. You would scarcely know Darien. Every church newly painted. Courthouse also. And a new townhall. New hotel building. And the lots generally brushed up..."[210]

Mrs. Eliza G. Robarts to Rev. C.C. Jones, January 22, 1859. "As regards the sale of my Negroes, I have no desire to sell them on a rice plantation. My women would not suit Mr. Gignilliat's work. Of those in Savannah, Charles is the only one who would. If I sold the others I could not support my family, my income would be so small."[211]

Rev. C.C. Jones to C.C. Jones, Jr., November 10, 1859. "As years increase, my dread and abhorrence of the use of spirituous liquors and opium do also increase. Death is smiting us with a perpetual stroke with these means! What an unexpected and afflicting death is that of Mr. John A. Thomas! Buried on Monday. About forty-five. Leaves a wife and six or seven fine children! What warnings have we had in this county? My son, *obsta principiis:* touch not, taste not, handle not. Men in public life are particularly exposed and therefore require to be doubly on their guard."[212]

Miss Mary E. Robarts to Mrs. Mary Jones, March 30, 1860. "It seems that he had been taking his meals at Mrs. LaRoche's for a month before his fatal marriage, and when he told her of it, she said she had not the heart to tell him to leave her house—that she and Mr. LaRoche had promised poor Sophia to stick to him and save him from ruin. Came every day to his meals, but the girls kept their

---

[210] "Dr. Dunwoody", William Elliott Dunwoody (1823-1891), physician of Darien and later, Marietta, Georgia, born in Liberty County, the son of John and Jane Bulloch Dunwoody. In 1846, W.E. Dunwoody married Ruth Ann Atwood (1826-1899), daughter of Henry Skilton Atwood and Ann McIntosh Atwood of Cedar Point plantation in McIntosh County. Myers, ed., *Children of Pride*, 1512.
[211] "Mr. Gignilliat", William Robert Gignilliat (1814-1882), rice planter of Greenwood plantation, McIntosh County. See chapter 6 in the present study for particulars on the Gignilliat family.
[212] John Abbott Thomas (1816-1859), of Peru plantation, Harris Neck, McIntosh County, son of Jonathan and Mary Jane Baker Thomas of McIntosh County. Charles C. Jones, Jr. served one term as mayor of Savannah, 1860-61. Myers, ed., *Children of Pride*, 1701.

room, and when he left the house on Wednesday morning they
looked at his retreating form through the window and saw that he
was weeping. Poor girls. It almost broke their hearts. He said in his
letter that would be the last communication they should receive from
him unless they saw fit to answer it. Mrs. LaRoche gives this version
for this dreadful affair. For a fortnight before, he had been drinking
so much that Mr. LaRoche told him that he was a fit subject for the
lunatic asylum; and he was certainly intoxicated the night he was
married. They told the girls that the woman had said she would just
as soon have a millstone about her neck as him. He will never be to
me a brother again until he repents and forsakes those two awful sins
which caused his downfall."[213]

Mrs. Mary Jones to C.C. Jones, Jr., October 26, 1861. "Mr. McDonald
expects to leave in a short time. I have closed hurriedly for want of
time. Colonel Charles Spalding is keeping our coast guarded:
seventeen men from the troops at Riceboro, a guard at Harris Neck,
etc., etc. It is very inspiring to know we have an active officer in
command.[214]

Rev. C.C. Jones to Lt. C.C. Jones, Jr., March 14, 1862. "Last Saturday
we had an arrival of friends from McIntosh. Mrs. Dunwoody and
Miss Dunwoody, and Mrs. Dean Dunwoody and five children, and
ten servants, two carriages and one baggage wagon, and four horses
and two mules—en route for the upcountry, having broken up their
plantation on the Altamaha, leaving a small part of the Negroes

---

[213] This incident occurred at the home of James Archibald LaRoche (1811-
1889), a Savannah druggist, merchant and brick manufacturer in the 1850s
and 1860s. Joseph William Robarts' (1811-1863) "fatal marriage" was to
Ella Sommers. Mary Sophia Robarts was the niece of Mary Madeleine
Gibson, who was the wife of James Archibald LaRoche. In 1880, James A.
and Mary LaRoche settled on a farm at Baisden's Bluff. Both died before
the decade of the 1880s was over; they were buried in the Atwood family
cemetery at Shellbluff (Valona). The LaRoche's youngest daughter, Sophia
Letitia LaRoche (1851-1930) married George Elliot Atwood (1849-1914) in
Putnam County, Georgia in 1870. They later lived in McIntosh County
where George Atwood became one of the county's leading landowners and
merchants. Myers, ed., *Children of Pride*, 1589-90, 1659.
[214] "Mr. McDonald", Elisha McDonald (1826-1893), McIntosh County
native and plantation overseer for C.C. Jones, 1858 to 1861. Charles H.
Spalding (1808-1887), a prominent planter and landowner of McIntosh
County, was the son of Thomas and Sarah Leake Spalding of Sapelo Island.
See chapter 6 of the present study for particulars on Elisha McDonald and
Charles H. Spalding.

164

behind for future disposal, the bulk moving up by steamboat to Doctortown and through Liberty to No. 3 station, part going to southwest Georgia and part to the vicinity of Columbus. The river bottom of the Altamaha [delta rice plantations] has been pretty much abandoned. Negroes moved up the river and the greater part of the market crop also, the enemy having free access to every part of the river if he chooses to come up. Darien is pretty well deserted. Colonel Spalding has ordered a detachment of twenty-five men from the Liberty Independent Troop to be stationed at Fort Barrington to arrest the ascent of the enemy up the river and so to protect the bridge at Doctortown."[215]

Rev. C.C. Jones to Lt. C.C. Jones, Jr., November 10, 1862. "Our report from McIntosh County is that the abolition gunboats ran up Sapelo River, burnt Captain Brailsford's house, took off every Negro belonging to Mr. Reuben King at Mallow, and reduced the aged couple to nothing, and Mrs. Walker's tears alone prevented their carrying the old gentleman off. Captured one of the McDonalds at Fair Hope (the married one) with a squad of armed Negroes, and carried him off. His family and household and brother escaped. Burnt Colonel Charles Hopkins' place on the opposite side of the river where they were fired upon and some of them killed by Captain Octavius Hopkins' company. We much need an intelligent, brave and active commander of the cavalry corps stationed in the three counties {Bryan, Liberty, McIntosh] to effect concert of action and celerity of movement."[216]

Mrs. Mary S. Mallard to Mrs. Mary Jones, September 27, 1864. "No one gained anything by remaining in Atlanta. I should like to know how much the exiles were allowed to bring with them, the newspaper accounts are so conflicting it is difficult to get at the truth. Mr.

---

[215] "Mrs. Dean Dunwoody", Catherine McDonald Dunwody (1826-1889), wife of McIntosh County rice planter Dean Munro Dunwody (1825-1878) of Sidon plantation. She was a daughter of Charles McDonald, former governor of Georgia. Myers, ed., *Children of Pride*, 1510.

[216] "Captain Brailsford", William Brailsford (1826-1887), planter at Sutherland's Bluff on the Sapelo River, and Retreat in lower Bryan County. Reuben King (1779-1867), planter of Mallow plantation on the Sapelo River, married to Abigail Austin King. Charles H. Hopkins (1812-1886), lawyer and planter at Belleville, on the Sapelo River. His younger brother, Octavius Caesar Hopkins (1819-1881), was a McIntosh County civic leader and public servant in the years leading up to the Civil War. Daniel McDonald (1811-1893), planter of Fair Hope plantation on the Sapelo River, and uncle of Jones's former overseer, Elisha McDonald.

Mallard received a letter from Mrs. Pease yesterday in which she mentions they are now living in the female college in Macon. We have not gotten our horse as yet, as Mr. Pease has been unable to get transportation for him. The cars have been so much taken up with government transportation that it is impossible for them to take private freight. At this time everything is very quiet in the county. Last week one or two families moved away from Jonesville because the troops were temporarily withdrawn from McIntosh County and sent up to the Altamaha bridge, but they returned again and all feel safe. The militia is disbanded at present so that the planters may have an opportunity of harvesting their crops."[217]

---

[217] "Mr. Pease", Philander Pitkin Pease (1821-1900) moved to Darien from Somers, Connecticut in 1846 where his double first cousin, Theodore Pitkin Pease (1813-1878) was established in business. In 1851, Philander Pease married Emma Cornelia Powell (1829-1894), daughter of Allen Beverly and Mary (Calder) Powell of Darien, and sister of Augusta I. (Powell) Pease (1827-1909), wife of Theodore P. Pease. Philander Pease moved to Atlanta at the start of the Civil War and lived there until 1875. He engaged in a successful grocery business in Chicago until his death in 1900 from injuries sustained in a streetcar accident. Myers, ed., *Children of Pride*, 1641.

4

The Civil War in North McIntosh County

On November 7, 1862, a raid by Union forces was carried out against plantations on the Sapelo River. Comprising a portion of the force was the First South Carolina Volunteers, a recently recruited black regiment. The raid's purpose, in concert with others the same week at other points on the lower Georgia coast, was to prove that blacks would stand and fight under fire, which some Northerners at first doubted, and to destroy rebel salt-works, harass the plantations and disrupt the chain of Confederate picket stations along the coast.[218] Captain Charles T. Trowbridge commanded of the sixty-two black recruits who embarked on the side-wheel steamer transport *Darlington*. The raid was under the overall command of Lieutenant Colonel Oliver T. Beard of the 48th New York Volunteers. The Union force landed at Butler's Island on the 6th and confiscated eighty bushels of rice while taking three prisoners at Darien. The next day, accompanied by the gunboat *Potomska*, a screw steamer under Lieutenant William Budd, the *Darlington* proceeded up Sapelo River. The five-gun *Potomska* carried too much draft to go all the way upriver, and thus anchored at Mallow (present-day Pine Har-

[218] *The War of the Rebellion: A Compilation of the Official Records of the Union and Confederate Armies* (Washington, D.C.: War Department, 1880-1901), Series I, 14: 189, hereafter cited *OR Armies*.

bor). Budd transferred to the *Darlington* and the raiding party proceeded to Fair Hope. En route, Beard's force was fired upon by Southerners from a bluff called "Spaldings" in the Union report. After landing at Fair Hope and Mallow plantations, the Yankee force returned to Belleville where they burned the buildings of the Hopkins plantation, then attacked the Brailsford plantation at Sutherland's Bluff before re-entering Sapelo Sound.[219]

Mallow plantation was owned by eighty-three-year old Reuben King. Also on the premises that day was his daughter, Sarah Amanda King Walker who recorded the events of the raid. Years later, Elizabeth Walker Quarterman compiled her grandmother's recollections, which serve as a revealing contemporary account of the incident from a personal perspective, that of a family caught amid the turmoil of war.[220] The log of the *Potomska* shows that Budd anchored his vessel off the King plantation at Mallow at 10:40 a.m. on November 7. In her recollections written soon after the events while they were fresh in her mind, Amanda King Walker noted:

"We were at the breakfast table, Joe, Isa, my father and myself, my poor mother being too feeble to join us, when the cry of 'Yankee vessels!' took us to the front piazza. There was a large vessel and gun boat just in front of the house, between Sutherland's Bluff and Creighton Island. The tide was high, the morning bright and lovely. The scene was altogether beautiful, and the vessels so novel a sight at Mallow that 1 was constrained in spite of myself to stop and admire the huge monsters, walking the water like things of life. When they got to Belleville they sent up a rowboat with a few negroes, who soon returned without firing a single gun. They then proceeded to Mallow at a rapid rate ...

"The men from the gun boat and vessel now landed [at Mallow]. I should say nearly one hundred men came up, most of them Negroes, all armed. Among them was a man differing from the rest in appearance, who had truly taken the 'livery of the court of Heaven to serve the devil ...' One whose

[219] OR *Armies*, Series I, 14: 191-92, Col. Beard's report, November 10, 1862
[220] Elizabeth Walker Quarterman, "At Home on the Bluff," typed ms., nd., GHS.

McIntosh County in the Civil War, from an 1864 map.

appearance was very much in favor came up to me and said, 'Good morning. Ma'am. I am captain of the blockading vessel that has been opposite your place for months. I have nothing to do with the slave question and would not have a negro on my vessel if I could help it. I feel very much for the South in this particular matter, and am sorry enough that things have come to this pass ... If they commence shelling your place, I would advise you to leave the house. Houses stand no chance. If they see a picket, they will certainly shell. Are you acquainted with Captain Brailsford? He has been the cause of this by going on St. Catherines Island and seizing and killing those Negroes. Since that time we have had orders to leave nothing undone on the coast.' I replied, 'The Negroes were found in arms against white men, and Captain Brailsford could not have done otherwise.' He said, 'You are mistaken; they were not found in arms against white men.' I said no more...

"My father and I stood on the piazza perfectly unconscious of the scene before us till we heard one of the men remark that Major Bacon, a very old man, had been taken prisoner in Darien. Some of the white men halted by the steps and spoke in a low voice. I heard the word prisoner — the men advanced and the captain ... stood in front of us. The idea for the first time

169

flashed into my mind that they were going to seize my father! I clung to him. I pleaded for him. I wept. I know not what I said and did! The Almighty saved him from the inhuman creatures who would not relieve me by saying they would not take him, but gradually dispersed and went off seeking what they might devour.

"They had by this time taken every Negro on the place down to the boat, with the exception of old Ma'am Rose whom they left at the Negroes' houses to die alone. They took off the large copper boilers, a quantity of leather, and everything they wished—helped themselves to oranges and sugar-cane which they carried away in bags ...The blockading vessel stayed at our landing while the gunboat [*Darlington*] went up to Fair Hope where they stole things from the house, broke up the salt-works and took Mr. [Daniel] MacDonald prisoner by a band of Negroes. On going up and returning they were fired on with much spirit by the McIntosh cavalry [between Mallow and Fair Hope]. They in return threw shot and shell thick and fast, but not a single man on our side was hurt. I expected they would stop at Mallow and shell us out, but both the vessel and the gunboat went on to Col. Hopkins' place at Belleville, which they utterly destroyed. They then went to Capt. Brailsford's, shelled there for about an hour, burned the outbuildings and set fine dwellings on fire, which was extinguished. All this we could see perfectly from Mallow. Night coming on ended their work of destruction for one day."

The unwarranted seizing of fifty-one-year old Daniel McDonald of Fair Hope plantation by the federals created considerable resentment among the area's citizenry. As to the incident at Brailsford's, there are attendant circumstances that require examination. Captain William Brailsford's cotton plantation at Sutherland's Bluff was the scene of Confederate military activity in the early part of the war. The site was a picket station and observation post by which the Confederates could monitor enemy naval movements in Sapelo Sound. In 1862 Sutherland's Bluff was also the headquarters for Brailsford's cavalry unit. Known for his flamboyance and temper, Brailsford had succeeded his friend, Savannah slave trader C.A.L. Lamar, as commander of the Savannah Mounted Rifles, a unit later known as Brailsford's Lamar Rangers, and still later, Company H, 5th Georgia Cavalry. It was at Sutherland's Bluff in the spring of 1862 that Brailsford recruited new members for his mounted troop.[221] McIntosh County citizens, including Alexander Baillie Kell, joined the Lamar Rangers; the unit later saw service around Savannah and the South Carolina lowcountry, and participated in the Confederate raids against retreating Union forces after the battle at Olustee, Florida. In the spring of 1864, the 5th Georgia Cavalry joined Wheeler's Cavalry, and Brailsford was captured by Union forces during operations in Tennessee.

Sutherland's Bluff was singled out as a target in the November 1862 Union raid for a reason additional to its being a picket station. Brailsford himself received attention for a retaliatory attack by the black troops accompanying the federal force. In the summer of 1862, Brailsford's force was engaged in a campaign to reclaim slaves owned by coastal planters that had been taken by Union occupation forces on the Georgia islands. In October 1862, Brailsford and thirty of his men landed at St. Catherines Island and killed or captured several black runaways.[222] The incident created animosity on the part of local blacks against Brailsford, thus making his Sapelo River plantation a particularly inviting target on the raid. After destroying Belleville on their return toward Sapelo Sound, the Union force stopped at Sutherland's Bluff where black troops landed and overcame a small contingent of defenders. The Union force then pushed inland up Bruro Neck for about half a mile, burning cabins, outbuildings and the Brailsford house. Some of Brailsford's former slaves, including Sam Miller who reportedly had been severely whipped by the "hot-tempered planter," were among those who landed at Sutherland's Bluff.

---

[221] Robert Manson Myers, ed., *The Children of Pride* (New Haven: Yale University Press, 1972), 1471, 1588.
[222] *Official Records of the Union and Confederate Navies in the War of the Rebellion* (Washington, D.C.: U.S. Navy Department, 1894-1927), Series I, 13: 196-97.

In a letter to the *Savannah Daily Morning News*, Brailsford noted:

"I see in the *News and Republican* a great deal said about very little with regard to the Yankees coming up the Sapelo river, and the two fights that is said to have taken place; and as the writer has put my name in his publication, and not wishing even our abolition enemies to suppose I am afflicted with the epidemic which is so prevalent both South and North, which is not being able to tell the truth, and being an eyewitness to the whole affair, I will give you the facts as they occurred. I rode down to one of my pickets stationed at Sutherland's Bluff, which is the first land upon the main. Two steamboats— one a propeller, the other the old *Darlington*, I think—came up the river about eight o'clock in the morning. The boats stopped about five minutes, and I expected them to shell, but they did not. The boats went up the river to Bellville, Colonel Hopkins' place, landed some men for a few minutes, then went on to Mr. King's place, stopped, landed a negro company, which they have had stationed at St. Simon's Island, and took all of Mr. King's negroes, with a few exceptions, and would have taken the old gentleman if his daughter had not clung to him as she did. The propeller stayed there, and the old *Darlington*, with her negro company and one gun, proceeded up the river to Mr. McDonald's place. As they passed White Bluff, Captain Hopkins' Company fired on the boat with their small arms; when the boat could bring her gun to bear she fired four or five guns at the bluff... [The Union force later returned to Sapelo Sound, but not before making the raid at the Brailsford plantation. Brailsford continues in his letter]: I had my men concealed about two hundred yards from the river [at Sutherland's Bluff] and took my position in the yard so as to see them when they landed. They shelled for one hour and a half, and the trees under cover of which my men were concealed, were riddled. All we did was to lay down and dodge shot and shell, and I think the only blood that was spilt on either side during the day, was a little bull calf of mine that was knocked down by a shell ..."[223]

The official Union account of Lieut. Col. Beard of the 48th New York, in command of the expedition:

"Friday, November 7, accompanied by the gunboat *Potomska*, Lieutenant Budd commanding, proceeded up Sapelo River. The gunboat could proceed no farther than King's. Lieutenant Budd came on board the *Darlington* and proceeded up the river with us to Fair Hope. At Spaulding's [west side of

[223] *Savannah Daily Morning News*, November 19, 1862.

Belleville between Mallow and Fair Hope] we were attacked by 80 or 90 of the enemy, who were well posted on a bluff behind trees. At this point the channel runs within 50 yards of the bluff. We killed 2 of the enemy ... At Fair Hope we destroyed the salt-works, some tan-vats, corn and other things that might be of use to the enemy. On return past Spaulding's we were again attacked by the enemy in greater force. We effected a landing and burned all the buildings on the place and captured some arms, &c. Five of the enemy were killed; we lost 3 wounded ... [Later] Under the guns of the *Potomska*, we landed at Colonel Brailsford's, drove [away] a company of pickets from his regiment, and destroyed all the property on the place, together with the most important buildings ... I started from Saint Simon's with 62 colored fighting men and returned to Beaufort with 156 fighting men (all colored). As soon as we took a slave from his claimant we placed a musket in his hand and he began to fight for the freedom of others."[224]

North McIntosh County Tax Returns for 1862[225]

James J. Garrison, 15 slaves, 600 acres; John Muller, 44 slaves, 1,475 acres (William J. King estate by marriage); C.J.W. Thorpe, 7 slaves, 1,000 acres; Margaret M. Harris, 73 slaves, 1,910 acres; Margery R. Forbes, 7 slaves, 350 acres; Charles C. Thorpe, 16 slaves, 494 acres; John A. Thomas estate, 45 slaves, 4,000 acres; William Hope estate, no slaves, 3,000 acres; Allen R. Johnston estate, 21 slaves, 6,711 acres; Daniel McDonald, 61 slaves, 1,600 acres; Edward W. Delegal, 33 slaves, 2,070 acres.

The Journal of Joseph S. Durant

Joseph Stiles Durant (1832-1897) was a plantation overseer who kept a record of events during part of the Civil War. The period covered in the journal excerpts that follow is 1862. Durant lived and worked at Bruro Neck, thus the

---

[224] OR Armies, Series I, 14: 191-92; see also Clarence Mohr, *On the Threshold of Freedom: Masters and Slaves in Civil War Georgia* (Athens: University of Georgia Press, 1986), 79.
[225] Extracted from McIntosh County Tax Digest, 1862, GDAH. The lands and plantation of Allen R. Johnson (1823-1859), cited in this listing, were at present-day Ludowici, a section then part of northwestern McIntosh County.

locales he most frequently mentions include Sutherland's Bluff and Shellman, owned respectively by William Brailsford and the late William Cooke. Also mentioned is Creighton Island, the upper end of which was only a short trip by skiff across Sapelo River from the Sutherland's Bluff landing. The upper half of Creighton, also owned by the late Cooke but, like Shellman, had been willed to his brother-in-law Charles H. Spalding, was under cultivation during the antebellum and early Civil War years. Durant, in his capacity as overseer for Spalding, spent much of his time supervising the Creighton operations. Durant may have been engaged by Cooke prior to his death in 1861, or perhaps later by Charles Spalding. Spalding would have required an overseer since the business of the war and his service with the coast defense forces occupied much of his time.

From his writings it appears Durant resided on and managed the Forbes plantation of fifty-nine-year old (in 1862) Margery Forbes near the White Chimney River west of Shellman. Durant's young wife, Susannah E. Durant, died in 1855 at the age of sixteen and was buried in the Forbes cemetery off the road to Shellman near White Chimney River. In 1990 the author found Forbes cemetery amid heavy undergrowth in a small grove of live oaks a few feet off the Shellman Bluff road. The plot contains only two marked graves; it overlooks the marshes of the White Chimney River and occupies land formerly comprising the Forbes plantation. The two headstones, both barely legible, are those of W.E. Cannon (1834-1861) and Susannah Durant (1839-1855). The latter headstone reads: "Sacred to the memory of Susannah E. Durant, wife of Joseph S. Durant. Died September 27th 1855 aged 16 years, 6 months."[226]

Another location mentioned by Durant is Travellers Rest plantation on

---

[226] Mattie R. Gladstone, et al., eds. *Cemeteries of McIntosh County, Georgia* (Darien, Ga.: Lower Altamaha Historical Society, 2000), 84.

Bruro Neck, situated north and west of Sutherland's Bluff, and west of Shellman. According to an 1867 survey, Travellers Rest comprised 1,831 acres. Travellers Rest was possibly another of the properties of William Cooke, then Charles Spalding. Joseph Durant spent time at Travellers Rest, apparently even residing there on occasion, based on comments in his journal. It is thus likely that Durant was the overseer of Travellers Rest. Selected journal excerpts and notes follow:

Tuesday the 4th of February A.D. 1862. Weather Cloudy & rainy this morning. PM no rain, clear at Sunset — I staid at home. One bale Cotton packed. Give the first Corn allowance today. Keeping Horses at Travellers Rest to-night.

Wednesday the 5th day. I went over to Creighton Island, gave Negroes allowance of Corn. Heard several heavy guns go off So. & So. East. I hear of hands sorting, moting, ginning & Packing Cotton at Shellman. All well thank God.

Thursday the 6th day. Weather — some clouds. No rain. Nothing more that I hear of. I staid at Home all day. D.J.E. Broughton stopped at Shellman a short while. [227]

Friday the 7th day. Some clouds, very warm, no rain. Unusually warm for this time of year, & has been for a long while. I went over to Creighton Island today, staid there a short time. Then returned to Travellers Rest via Southerlands Bluff & Shellman. Hands sorting, ginning Cotton at Shellman & cleaning up Corn lands on Island.

Sunday the 9th day. I staid at home all day. Soldiers from Southerlands Bluff went out to South Newport to be paid off. All well thank God.

Tuesday the 11th day. Weather clear & cold. Frost aplenty to be seen this morning ... first in several weeks. I went to Creighton Island, Shellman & Southerlands Bluff. Sent two Carts & four yoke Oxen to Mr. Allen Bass to help him in hauling Cotton to Rail Road.[228]

Wednesday the 12th day. I went to Shellman in A.M. I went to Mr.

---

[227] "Broughton," Daniel J.E. Broughton (1829-1868) of the 22nd G.M.D., McIntosh County, who lived in the household of James Deverger. He was a plantation overseer and son of Daniel S. Broughton of McIntosh County.

[228] "Mr. Bass," Allen G. Bass (1814-1884), overseer of the Spalding plantation at Sapelo Island, and brother-in-law of Charles Spalding's brother, Randolph. The railroad is the Savannah, Albany & Gulf running from Savannah to Thomasville.

Devergers. Col. Charles Spalding came to Shellman this morning.[229]

Friday the 14th day. Weather clear & warm. Sand flies bites very bad. I went over to Creighton Island, brought over one yoke oxen, & one Cow & calf. There is now all the cattle & horses taken from Island. I had a bad time getting Cow & calf into flat. Wm. Brailsford & Capt. Hughes went Drum fishing but caught nothing.

Tuesday the 18th day. Weather cloudy with light rain. Early in morning I went over to Creighton Island, gave Negroes allowance. Brought over Sugar. Governor Joseph E. Brown has issued a proclamation, ordering out or calling for twelve thousand soldiers to service for three years. If there is not enough volunteers then he will Draft for enough to make out said number. There will be very few men left in Georgia.

Saturday the 22nd. Cloudy but no rain. I went over to Island, then to Southerlands Bluff and Shellman. Then returned home and went to Post Office So. Newport.

Monday the 24th. I went to Shellman. Nothing new that I hear of. Hands sorting, moting, & ginning Cotton at Shellman. James P. Durant came home this morning.

Tuesday the 29th day of April. I went to Chappell to attend a meeting of the McIntosh Cavalry. There was a good many persons there. I returned home in P.M. Heard heavy firing this A.M. The Yankee gun boats went up Riceboro River on Sunday last & was driven out by Liberty Troops ... they fired a great many guns.

Monday, the 5th day of May, 1862. I went to Ridge & Thicket, returned in PM. Heard that Charles Trezevant has gone Crazey. [NOTE: Charles Trezevant, a McIntosh County farmer, born in 1812 at Contentment plantation. He was one of the men, with Joseph S. Durant, captured in the Union raid at Ebenezer Church in 1864]. Nothing new that I hear of. A few negroes belonging to Mrs. Day & Mr. A. Mitchel attempted to run away last Sunday

Tuesday the 6th day of May A.D. 1862. Weather Clear & cool. I went out to Reynolds Chapel early this morning to see Capt. Hopkins who was on his way to Savannah.

Saturday the 10th day. I went to Baisdens Bluff, returned home early in P.M. Hear that two Yankee gun boats went up to Darien yesterday, remained there a few hours, then went down to Doboy Island, they did no damage. Crops are looking very well generally. Most of persons plant nothing but corn & other kinds of provisions. The Lord sent us a good season that we may make a plenty of provisions. Corn is now selling at $2.25 per Bushel.

Thursday the 15th day. The McIntosh Cavalry was organized today by

---

[229] "Mr. Devergers," James L. Deverger (b. 1804), of the 22nd G.M.D.

Electing Capt. O.C. Hopkins as Capt., W.H. Atwood as first Lieut., Allen McDonald, second Lieut., C.H. Hopkins Jr. as third Lieut. Sergeants; 1st Charles Walker, 2nd E.D. Fennell, 3rd E.B. Poppell, 4th George McDonald, 5th John L. Deverger. Corporals to be Elected. I returned home after the Election via Fair Hope & Mallow. Nothing new that I hear of. All well thank God ..."

Durant refers several times to Reynolds Chapel. An integral part of the life of the planter families in the northern section of McIntosh County in the years just before, and during, the Civil War, was Reynolds Chapel, a Methodist mission church named for one of the early pastors of the Darien Methodist Church, Andrew J. Reynolds. The Chapel was located on what later became known as the Dean tract on present Highway 17 near the Pine Harbor turnoff, about twelve miles north of Darien. A survey of January 11, 1858 provides documentation relevant to Reynolds Methodist Chapel, indicating that the mission was constructed on a one-acre tract surveyed by county surveyor and large landowner, James J. Garrison. Garrison was a trustee of the Chapel, with William R. Townsend, Thomas J. Sheppard and E.F. Sandiford. The land on which the Chapel was built was given to the Trustees by James R. Calder and his wife, Sarah Elizabeth (Sandiford) Calder. Calder, brother of John Calder of Contentment plantation, had been granted the tract in 1817. The mission on the site was first known as McIntosh. When Rev. Reynolds died at the age of thirty-four, the name of the mission was changed to honor his memory. The chapel saw service until ca. 1920; the land and building were sold in 1922 to F.B. Dean who lived nearby. As noted by Joseph Durant in his journal, Reynolds Chapel was a meeting place for military and civic discussions during the Civil War, probably because of its convenient location in the center of the county.

The Seizure of McIntosh County Men at Ebenezer Church

After the destruction of Darien in June 1863, the courthouse and a loosely-organized civil government of McIntosh County was relocated to Ebenezer Church in the center of the county about nine miles north of Darien on the road to Sapelo Bridge. An incident there in August 1864 perpetrated by Union naval forces created almost as much furor among McIntosh Countians and their coastal neighbors as had the burning of Darien the year before. On the night of August 2-3, a Union contingent of 115 men landed at Sapelo Main (Baisden's Bluff, near present-day Crescent), marched overland several miles and made prisoners of twenty-six McIntosh County men who were meeting at Ebenezer. The church was established in 1857 as a mission branch of the Darien Presbyterian Church to minister to the black people, free and enslaved, in that section of McIntosh County (see map, page 188).

In the summer of 1864, Union naval officers kept abreast of local developments by reading the Savannah newspapers, through which source they learned of the meeting of the McIntosh men at Ebenezer. The local men, all of whom were too aged for front line Confederate military service, were meeting to discuss the defense of the coast in light of increasing pressure from the blockading federal forces. The men were taken by surprise at their meeting, rounded up with others captured at nearby Sapelo Bridge, and marched southeast to Blue and Hall's landing at the Ridge. There they were transferred to warships and transported to Union prisons in the North. Following is the action report of Commander George M. Colvocoresses of the U.S. sloop of war *Saratoga:*

"*Doboy Sound, Ga., August 6, 1864*—Sir: I have the honor to submit the following report of an expedition which left the *Saratoga* on the evening of the

2d instant: It was to surprise and capture the male inhabitants who had been ordered to meet at the court-house of McIntosh County, Ga., on the 3d day of August, for the purpose of forming themselves into a coast guard, which order I read in the Savannah Republican of the 27th of July, 1864. The expedition left the ship on Tuesday, August 2, 4:30 p.m. in seven boats, and reached the mainland shortly after 9 o'clock p.m. The night was very favorable to our design, there being no moon by which the enemy could discover our movements as we approached the landing. As soon as the expedition was landed [at Baisden's Bluff], I sent all the boats back to the ship, with an order to the executive officer to let them meet me the next day at the landing called the Ridge, some 7 miles distant from the first landing but nearer to the ship ... we began our march. We did not meet with any persons or see any house until 12 o'clock. When the signal for attacking was made we immediately charged at a double quick and completely surrounded the meeting, and all who composed it were captured except 3, who succeeded in making their escape. I gave the order for the expedition to again form into line and, placing the prisoners in the center, we started to return. The expedition arrived safely at the Ridge at sunset, but as my order in regard to the boats had been misunderstood we did not reach the ship until about noon next day. The following is a summary of what the expedition accomplished: We took 26 prisoners, 22 horses and buggies, destroyed 2 bridges, and burned a large encampment which the enemy greatly needed for the protection of his forces, and we did this in broad daylight and 15 miles from our boats without losing a single life or meeting with any unpleasant accident."[230]

Colvocoresses furnished Rear Admiral Dahlgren with a list of the captured McIntosh County men:

Joseph S. Durant, 33, planter and tax collector for McIntosh County.
William Summerline, 57, planter.
Converse Parkhurst, 51, merchant.
William Donnelly, 53, farmer and coroner of McIntosh County.
William Nelson, farmer.
Charles Trezevant, 50, farmer.
William R. Townsend, 58, farmer.
William J. Cannon, 60, farmer and salt maker.
William Thorpe, 46, farmer and justice of the peace for McIntosh County.
James R. Webber, 55, sawyer and farmer.
C. Bennett, 51, shoemaker.

---

[230] *OR Navies*, Series I, 15: 594-96.

George Young, 51, farmer and wheelwright.

Macgregor Blount, 52, farmer.

William Sallet, 58, planter.

William D. Rowe, 52, farmer.

James Slater, 53, engineer and machinist.

James D. McDonald, 50, farmer and salt-maker.

B. LeSeur, 32, salt-maker at South Newport.

Samuel R.J. Thorpe, 40, farmer.

John Hendrickson, George Johnston, 16; Daniel Lane, 16; Obed S. Davis, 20.

John Chapman, 55, planter.

Isham L. Johnston, 36, planter and justice of inferior court for McIntosh County.[231]

The response of the Confederate authorities, excerpted from the following letter to the *Savannah Republican*:

A Yankee raid in McIntosh.

"No. 3, Gulf Railroad, Liberty County, August 4, 1864. Editor: In obedience to orders previously issued by me, the citizens of McIntosh County assembled at Ebenezer Church, the present county site and court-house of the county, for enrollment and organization. About half past 10 o'clock the Yankees suddenly surrounded them with a force of from 50 to 100 men, sailors and negroes. The people broke to run, when they were fired on by the enemy. Some were captured; a number made their escape. About 10 o'clock they ambuscaded the Sapelo bridge, 4 miles this side, on the stage road, captured several there and took them to the church. Whereupon they took all the horses and buggies, rode in them, and made our men walk. As far as I can learn, none of our men was killed or wounded. The captain [of the Union force] stated that his orders were not to injure private property, but to capture the party assembled there, of which he had notice through the Savannah papers.

"After Darien, the county site, was burned, the last legislature authorized the inferior court of the county to select a new county site. They selected Ebenezer Church, 9 miles this side of Darien, on the stage road, with a good gunboat river at or near the Ridge, east 8 miles; Baisden's Bluff, 4 or 5 miles east, a good landing, with a fine river for gunboats; and Sapelo River, over which the bridge was burned, and navigable for gunboats to the bridge, thus

---

[231] Ibid., 596-98.

selecting a place flanked on three sides with rivers and landings suitable for gunboats. When I issued my order for the assembling of the people I was totally ignorant of the location of the church, but supposed it to be in the interior of the county. One of the justices, being present when I issued the order, requested me to assemble the people there as it was a safe place. I knew no better until Monday morning, when found on enquiry that it was located inconveniently near the enemy. I then stated to my friends that we would all be captured, but it was too late to countermand the order. On night before last (Tuesday night), at Jonesville, I met one of the justices, who informed me particularly of its location as above described. I remarked to him that we would all be captured on the morrow, and that the inferior court instead of being the guardians of the public should have guardians themselves or be put in the lunatic asylum. This justice went down with me yesterday, and when within two miles of the place we were informed that the bridge was burned and the church surrounded. Such unparalleled stupidity as the location of this court-house I have never met with before. Had 1 been ten minutes earlier I should have been in their hands. As the captain seems to be a reader of your paper, and I take this opportunity to make my compliments to him and to say that when he calls to see me again I shall be at home, and will try and give him a more respectful reception.
Respectfully yours,
Wm. B. Gaulden,
Colonel, A.D.C., Commanding Coast Guard.
"P.S. — I gather the above facts from Captain [Armand] Lefils, whom they captured and released on account of his great age, being 71."[232]

Two weeks after the capture of the men at Ebenezer Church and Sapelo Bridge, there was a skirmish between Union and Confederate forces at South Newport nine miles north of Sapelo Bridge. A Confederate company of South Carolina cavalry under Lt. W.L. Mole was on patrol duty in the South Newport area. On the night of August 16, 1864, the company was attacked while it was encamped by a federal force from the USS *Saratoga* (Commander Colvocoresses) that had come up the South Newport River under

---

[232] *Savannah Republican*, August 6, 1864, included in commander's report, OR Navies, Series I, 15: 611-12.

cover of darkness. About thirty Confederate soldiers were captured, along with several civilians, and the South Newport River bridge on the Stage Road to Savannah was burned. Following is Colvocoresses' report:

"Doboy Sound, Ga., Aug. 19, 1864–Sir: I have the honor to report that on the night of the 16th instant I landed with a small force at South Newport, McIntosh County, Ga., and did as follows: We captured a lieutenant and 28 privates of Company F, Third South Carolina Cavalry, dispersed the remainder of the company amounting to 40 more...burned their encampment and stables, destroyed two of the largest salt works on the coast, capturing at the same time the overseers of the works, numbering 6, and 71 slaves employed at the works. Also destroyed the large bridge near the main Savannah road, which connects the two counties, McIntosh and Liberty; also captured the mail and a Mr. L[achlan] McIntosh, who has always been looked upon as a violent secessionist..."[233]

Local citizens captured in this incident, and who petitioned for parole on August 28, 1864, were William A. Overton, Walter A. Overton, Charles Stebbins, Jr., William O. Brown, Wilson C. McMillain, Lachlan McIntosh, and Hugh F. Mitchell.

---

[233] *OR Navies*, Series I, 15: 631-34.

5

Reconstruction & Postbellum Harris Neck

Afterthe capture and occupation of Savannah by federal forces in December 1864 events of an unusual nature began to occur that would greatly affect the aftermath of the war in coastal Georgia. Major General William T. Sherman's Special Field Order No. 15 of January 16, 1865 set aside as reservations for former slaves the sea islands from Charleston to the St. Johns River, and the abandoned rice plantation lands from the coast to thirty miles inland. The Order stipulated that no white persons could live in these areas. In effect, the federal government was confiscating all the coastal lands owned by the pre-war planters for the use of the freedmen who would have exclusive management of their affairs on the islands subject only to U.S. military authorities.

Food was scarce in the coastal counties in the months following the end of the war in April 1865. The food-producing plantations were largely destroyed, and few farm animals had been left by the invading federal forces. The Bureau of Refugees, Freedmen and Abandoned Lands set up branch offices in the coastal counties as the process of Reconstruction began. These were initially expedited by U.S. Army officers who were later replaced by War Department civilian employees of the Freedmen's Bureau. The Bureau controlled civic affairs in coastal Georgia for five years until Georgia was readmitted to the

183

Union in 1870.

All six coastal counties had majority black populations before the Civil War, and consequently had large numbers of freedmen after the war, along with displaced white people; many of the freedmen remained on the plantations working with their former owners in a loosely-organized system of crop-sharing. In McIntosh County, the 1870 census showed that Darien's population comprised 111 whites and 435 blacks, figures substantially different from those of the 1860 census that had Darien with 315 whites and 255 blacks. Many of the white people in 1870 were living at outlying areas such as the Ridge after their homes in town had been burned in 1863. The county population in 1870 was 4,484, with blacks holding a majority of 3,288 to 1,196 whites. The 1860 census listed 4,063 slaves, 54 free blacks, and 1,429 whites in the county. Whites in coastal Georgia had little left but their land after the war ended. No matter their financial status before the war, many were now virtually destitute. There was little money for either blacks or whites. Norman Page Gignilliat reportedly said to his former slaves after the war that nothing had changed—he sent them back to the rice fields saying, "Roll up your sleeves, get back in the fields, make me one hundred bushels of rice, and I will give you one hundred acres of land." Thus, land served as currency for many planters, at least until economic conditions had stabilized and improved.

The freed slaves aspired to acquire their own land and assert their newly-gained independence. Many obtained property through the barter system or by wills and gifts from their former owners. Others bought land on credit and paid their mortgages from profits gained by working the land. the coastal freedmen thus became independent farmers sooner than many of their contemporaries on other parts of the South. Some left the plantations and "squatted" on land in the pine barrens where they built cabins for their

184

families and scratched out an acre or two for cultivation of crops.

The following document from the public records of McIntosh County contextualizes post-war Harris Neck and the events, often controversial, associated with the section over the ensuing 150 years:

Last Will and Testament of Margaret Ann Harris, 1865
"This is to certify that I, Margaret Ann Harris, of my own free will bequeath and convey to Robert Delegal, formerly my slave, now a freedman on St. Catherines Island, Liberty County, namely, Harris Neck, Dunham, Belvedere and Dillon Tracts on condition that the aforesaid Robert Delegal provide all that shall be necessary to make me and my son, namely Bright Harris, comfortable while we live. I have tried white men and they have cheated me, abused and driven off all my people. I now choose Robert who I have raised to take care of me and my son, and agree by this my last Will and Testament that all rights and titles vested in me to the aforesaid four tracts of land are on the above condition vested in the aforesaid Robert Delegal I hereby appoint as my Executors T.G. Campbell, general superintendent of St. Catherines & Ausabaw [sic] Islands, Georgia, & T.G. Campbell, Jun. I also convey all rights and title to buildings, tenements & houses to the aforesaid Robert Delegal. September 2, 1865."[234]

The Margaret Harris will was witnessed at St. Catherines Island by Freedman's Bureau agent Tunis G. Campbell, and Hamilton Delegal and Samuel Graham. Margaret died at Harris Neck in early 1866. Her historic document emerged from the origins of land acquisition by the emancipated black people of McIntosh and Liberty counties as the Civil War ended amidst the imposition of martial law on the Georgia coast by military authorities at Hilton Head. In March 1866 Sherman's directive was rescinded by the U.S. military authorities, on order of President Andrew Johnson, and the islands were restored

---

[234] Deed Book B (1865, re-recorded 1875), 76, RMCG. Bright B. Harris (1808-1875) was mentally infirm ("idiotic") according to the 1860 census. Margaret M. Harris was in her early to mid-90s when she died.

to their pre-war owners. By late 1866 Campbell was no longer associated with the Freedman's Bureau but remained on St. Catherines where his family taught school. He was later evicted from that island by the federal authorities for alleged "dishonest practices" in advising the freed people of the islands.

The above quoted document notwithstanding, McIntosh County probate records indicate that when she died in late 1865 or early 1866 Margaret Harris's estate devolved not to Robert Delegal, but to her son Bright Baker Harris. Nine years later, in 1875, Bright Harris died, the last of the long Harris line to live at Harris Neck. His estate was administered by William J. Wallace until September 1876.[235] Margaret Harris's properties were advertised at an administrator's sale in October 1875

"at the Court House door...the following property, to wit: Harris plantation on Harris Neck, containing 300 acres more or less, with one two story house and out houses, bounded on the north by lands of the estate of W.J. King and Thomas, east by salt marsh, south by land of the estate of W.J. King, and west Thomas. One tract of land on Eagle Neck [Dunham], containing 250 acres more or less, with dwelling house, bounded on the north by lands of the estate of Thomas [Baker tract], east by a creek, south by North Sapelo Creek [Julianton River] and west by the lands of the estate of W. J. King, and one other tract containing 1,200 acres, more or less, known as [Belvedere] on Eagle Neck, bounded north by South Newport River, east by lands of the estate of Thomas [Peru], south by lands of the estate of King and Thomas, west by lands originally estate of Thomas [Mosquito]. Terms of sale cash. Purchaser paying for titles. W. J. Wallace Adm'r on the estate of Bright Baker Harris."[236]

On October 5, 1875, the 250-acre Dunham tract was sold to Lachlan McIntosh for $350. The next day a deed was recorded for the sale of

---

[235] Probate Book 1 (1876), 135, 177, RMCG.
[236] *Darien Timber Gazette*, August 20, 1875.

the 350-acre Harris tract from the Bright B. Harris Estate to Margaret Bresnan of Chatham County for $350, the property described as "bounded on the east by Gould's River [Barbour Island River], South by lands of the estate of W.J. King, West by estate of Thomas, and North by Thomas and King."[237] On October 15, the Belvedere Island tract of 1,200 acres was sold to Charles O. Fulton for $410.[238]

Confusion prevailed as much on the northern McIntosh plantations during Reconstruction as it did around Darien. Edward J. Thomas recalled,

"I had not as yet, since the slaves were free, visited our old plantation home, Peru, in McIntosh County, but I had heard that a goodly number of our old slaves had returned and, without leave or license, simply considered it their privilege to come home, after they were scattered by Sherman's raid. They had taken up their abode in what cabins were left standing and had begun to cultivate the land."[239]

The chaos of the war's aftermath was largely that of economic upheaval. Damage to fields, and farm infrastructure in the absence of labor, was irreparable in Reconstruction conditions. Cotton crops could not be cultivated without labor. As Thomas noted, neither labor nor capital for repairs and wages could be easily obtained by the financially-strapped planters. The wartime changes are emphasized in McIntosh County population figures for 1870, reflecting a decline in total population of about one thousand persons since 1845. A description of the county's resources in 1870 refers to rice as the basic agricultural crop, and lumber mills as the only manufacturing

---

[237] Deed Book A (1875) 536-38, RMCG.

[238] Deed Book B (1875), 39, RMCG. See the article in the *Darien News*, August 9, 2012 for an analysis of the complexities involving the disposition of the Margaret Harris tracts in the aftermath of the war.

[239] Edward J. Thomas, *Memoirs of a Southerner* (Savannah, privately printed, 1923).

McIntosh County in 1870. Harris Neck is shown at upper right.

interests. In 1870 very few blacks owned land, a situation that would soon change. The census contains a telling phrase: opposite a list of enumerated houses appear the words "homes of the Thomas Place partly unoccupied." In 1878 only thirty per cent of the county's tillable land was cleared and ninety-five per cent of the farm laborers were black.[240]

While most of the county's farm laborers were African American in the Reconstruction period, an exception at Harris Neck was John Muller, a thirty-seven year old Swiss native who in 1870 was working the farm operation of his late father-in-law, William J. King, south of Gould's Landing. A community of black private land owners began to evolve at Harris Neck. From 1870 to 1880 the heirs of John A.

---

[240] U.S. 10th Census, 1880, McIntosh County, Agricultural Schedules.

Gravestone in the cemetery at Gould's Landing, Harris Neck.

Thomas owning portions of the former Peru plantation subdivided the land into small tracts which they sold to individuals, many of whom were their former bondsmen. An example of such a sale occurred in 1878 when Eliza H. and John W. Magill sold land comprising Lots 4 and 6 of the former Peru plantation to Frank Proctor. One of the earliest recorded transactions occurred in 1875 and involved Delegal land, not Thomas land, being William Delegal's transfer of property to Jack Sallins.[241] A burial ground for the freedmen and their descendants was established near Gould's Landing, the earliest marked graves being those of Mark Baisden and Kate Rice in 1882. In 1875, McIntosh County established a black school at Harris Neck, the location of which remains unclear.

---

[241] U.S. Civil Action File No. 56, Harris Neck Airfield Tract List, No. 137. Presumably, land sales at Harris Neck were concluded earlier than 1875. The loss of McIntosh County deed records in the 1873 courthouse fire included records of property transfers made between 1865 and 1873.

Dunham's store served the community, as did a later store operated by Edward W. Lowe (1855-1927), which may have been located on land later designated as Harris Neck Airfield Tract 150. Lowe is buried in the Gould Cemetery. In 1891, postal service was initiated at Harris Neck at Bahama near Gould's Landing. In 1896, the post office was renamed Lacey. Its location changed in 1908 and service was discontinued in 1914. In 1896, Philadelphia archaeologist Clarence B. Moore conducted field research on the upper end of Harris Neck. In his findings, published in 1897, Moore noted that the Bahama post office at Harris Neck had "lately been given the name Lacey."[242]

Establishment of the First African Baptist Church at Harris Neck occurred between 1875 and 1880. The surnames of white landowners frequently appear among the names of blacks acquiring Harris Neck land and in other areas of McIntosh County during the 1870s and 80s. The size of the rural community at Harris Neck varied over the years. By 1940, some 171 separate tracts of privately-owned land existed within the boundaries of the present-day Harris Neck Wildlife Refuge. Most of the tracts were small, with some amounting to less than one acre. Some individuals possessed enough property to permit fairly extensive farming activities. Limited quantities of corn, potatoes, oats, sugar cane and some livestock, primarily for home consumption or local marketing, represented the extent of the agricultural activity reported in the 1880 census. Cotton was grown in McIntosh County after the Civil War but in gradually decreasing amounts in the 1870s. However, unlike most of the rest of the South, private land ownership by blacks constituted the rule rather the exception in

---

[242] Civil Action File 56, Tract List, 150; Clarence B. Moore, *Certain Aboriginal Mounds on the Georgia Coast* (Philadelphia, 1897), 73.

coastal Georgia, particularly in Liberty and McIntosh counties. The numbers of black land owners in McIntosh steadily increased and by 1910, eighty-seven percent of the black farm operators in the county owned their land.[243] In 1900 the county population was 6,537, of which 5,081 were black.

There was one aberration amidst the development of African American settlement patterns at Harris Neck during the postbellum period. In the 1880s, a growing number of affluent Northerners had begun to discover the sea islands of South Carolina and Georgia, and their desirability as winter retreats. The islands offered privacy and seclusion amid a temperate climate, and the natural beauty of their ecosystems. Pierre Lorillard (1833-1901), a wealthy tobacco magnate from New York City, was a charter member of the Jekyll Island Club when it was formed in 1886. Lorillard complemented his tobacco fortune by being a Newport, R.I. yachtsman and a prominent racehorse breeder. Possibly in connection with his club membership, Lorillard, while on a yachting cruise along the southern coast, discovered a site that captivated him with its beauty and privacy, the upper end of Harris Neck on the South Newport River.

In 1889, Lorillard purchased river frontage at Harris Neck and developed a retreat: "Mr. Pierre Lorillard of New York has purchased a 30-acre oak grove on the Peru plantation, the old homestead of Major John Thomas...Twenty hands are at work beautifying the plat, where Mr. L. will at an early day erect cottages for himself and guests and stables for his racers."[244] Several weeks later, Editor Grubb of the local weekly again reported on the Lorillard initiative: "The great

---

[243] U.S. 13th Census, 1910, McIntosh County, Agricultural Schedules.
[244] *Darien Timber Gazette*, January 4, 1890.

Pierre Lorillard.

tobacco man is setting up a sequestered spot for himself near South
Newport river. He is building a club house with stables and all other
comforts for a hunter's lodge. Mr. L. will have all the hunting and
fishing he wants, or any of his friends."[245]

   Two women with whom Lorillard associated, Eleanor Van Brunt
Clapp (1862-1937) and Miss Lily Allien, also acquired Harris Neck

---

[245] Ibid., February 15, 1890.

land near the river during the period. According to deed records the first of the group to conclude a property transaction was the companion of Lorillard, Lily Allien, later Lily A. Livingston, of New York. A deed of December 28, 1889 recorded the conveyance from Malvina H. Thomas to Allien of twenty-eight acres on the South Newport River on the former Peru plantation. A second deed in February 1890 was concluded by which Malvina Thomas conveyed seven acres to Eleanor Van Brunt Clapp, also of New York.[246] In early March 1890, the *Darien Timber Gazette* noted that "Saturday's *Savannah Morning News* says the schooner *Charmer* arrived yesterday from New York, with a general cargo of merchandise. She had on deck a new steam launch, 60 feet long, named *Lillian*, for Pierre Lorillard, at Harris Neck. The launch is intended as a tender for Mr. Lorillard's steam yacht *Reva*. The launch is one of the newest and most improved vessels of its kind afloat and a complete description of it was recently published in the *Scientific American*. The launch was afloat in the river yesterday."[247]

Two weeks later, March 22, 1890, the *Timber Gazette* noted; "Mr. Pierre Lorillard of New York is erecting a $10,000 mansion at Harris Neck. The building will be completed in about a month. McIntosh County welcomes Mr. L. and all of his kind." The homes constructed on the north end of Harris Neck by Mrs. Clapp, and Lorillard with Miss Allien (Livingston) reflected the lifestyles of the wealthy northerners of the period. The Lorillard-Livingston house was particularly lavish, complete with outdoor fountains and pools. In large measure, these homes represented aberrations in the land-use

---

[246] Deed Book D (1889), 543; Book D (1890), 583, RMCG. The first transaction, although in the name of Lily Allien, was presumably on behalf of Pierre Lorillard.
[247] *Darien Timber Gazette*, March 8, 1890.

patterns associated with Harris Neck, for in no sense were they related to the agricultural life identified with the area. "During their existence the homes acquired considerable local significance, both as landmarks and as oddities. They clearly reflected the trend of the establishment of resort hideaways by wealthy Northerners which affected the sea islands of coastal Georgia during the 1880-1940 period."[248] The Clapp house was destroyed by fire not long after it was built,[249] then later rebuilt, and the Livingston house was dismantled upon the acquisition of the upper end of Harris Neck by the U.S. Fish and Wildlife Service in 1962. The houses overlooking the South Newport River near Thomas Landing on property now within the Wildlife Refuge have disappeared and few traces remain. There still exists, however, a pool and remains of some of the landscape structures associated with the Lorillard-Livingston house. As for Lorillard himself, his impact on Harris Neck was brief as he died a little over a decade after acquiring his land. Eleanor Clapp continued to live at Harris Neck until her death in 1937.

Supplementing the pursuit of subsistence agriculture, lumbering, turpentine distilling and related activities provided occupations for Harris Neck blacks. Federal interest in Sapelo Sound as a potential port and the development of the inland waterway increased after 1900. In 1910 the commercial use of Sapelo harbor consisted entirely of lumber shipments. In 1909-10, $750,000 value in lumber passed out of that harbor, representing a sizeable timbering operation. Landings maintained by three firms on the Front River,

---

[248] "Archaeology and History of Harris Neck National Wildlife Refuge, McIntosh County, Georgia," Cultural Resource Management, Inc., Interagency Archaeological Services, Atlanta, for U.S. Fish and Wildlife Service, 1979, 75-78. For the broader picture of the Georgia sea islands, see Buddy Sullivan, *The First Conservationists? Northern Money and Lowcountry Georgia, 1866-1930* (Charleston, SC: CreateSpace, 2016).
[249] *Darien Gazette*, November 10, 1894.

which fed into Sapelo Sound from the south served the area before 1910. Wharves no longer in use by that date had stood at Julianton and Belleville landings on the Sapelo River.[250]

Harris Neck people supported themselves with small farms and home gardens, yard or pasture livestock, lumbering, turpentining and commercial seafood activity. An oyster collecting shed occupied a lot (Tract 54) near the South Newport River in the 1930s and 40s. In 1906, the Shell Bluff Canning Company acquired Tract No. 34.[251] Other changes in the Harris Neck environment between 1880 and 1940 consisted of the construction of small homes and out-structures. Everything changed after 1940. In July 1942, the U.S. government filed condemnation proceedings for 1,200 acres of privately-owned African American land for the establishment of an air base at Harris Neck and the court issued its first taking declarations in January 1943.

In the fall of 1891 there was a smallpox outbreak in the Geechee community at Harris Neck. A report from McIntosh county commissioner James Walker noted that Dr. P. S. Clark had gone to Harris Neck where about 350 people lived. Most were vaccinated by Clark who reported fourteen infected houses. "There was difficulty of getting the negroes to submit to vaccinations," the *Savannah Morning News* of November 26, 1891 reported, "as one of their colored preachers having advised against it, saying it would kill more than the small-pox." The vaccinations did not claim any lives, but the smallpox outbreak did, as ten persons died.

---

[250] U.S. 61st Cong., 2d Sess., House Doc. No. 561, 1910.
[251] U.S. Civil Action File No. 56.

6

Twentieth Century Harris Neck

A s the twentieth century began, oyster harvesting was already an important economic pursuit and livelihood for a number of the Geechee community at Harris Neck. It was not a new industry to the southeast coast. Georgia oystermen harvested nearly 500,000 pounds of oysters in 1880, and for the next thirty years, Georgia harvests were among the highest in the world. In 1908, the Georgia harvest was a record eight million pounds, with fourteen canneries in operation. There was a dramatic decrease two years later with only three million pounds harvested in 1910, following which the industry went into a gradual decline for the next forty years, until an all-time low was reached in 1978 with only 38,000 pounds harvested.

Two of the leading Georgia canneries in the early twentieth century both had Harris Neck connections, these being those of Augustus Oemler (1857-1927) at Savannah, St. Catherines Island and Harris Neck, and the Maggioni family at Thunderbolt. Oemler was the leading commercial oyster producer in Georgia in the early 1900s. He established cannery operations at Wilmington and Wassaw islands in Chatham County, and on the south end of St. Catherines Island. Oemler's wife was Frieda Rauers Oemler (1879-1961), daughter of Jacob Rauers (1837-1904), owner of St. Catherines. In 1900, Oemler entered into a five-year agreement with Rauers by which Oemler, for

$600 per year, received rights to harvest oysters in the marshes surrounding the island. Oemler developed a cannery on Back Creek with three boilers and hired black workers to operate the cannery with housing provided in dwellings associated with the former South End plantation on St. Catherines. Oemler's Wilmington Island cannery produced 1.4 million cans of oysters in 1905. In 1928, after Oemler's death, the Rauers family leased oyster rights at St. Catherines to C. Philip Maggione and Joseph P. Maggione.

There are deeds and land plats among the McIntosh County records attesting to the oyster activities of both Oemler and the Maggiones in the Harris Neck area. In June 1926, George A. Morison of Milwaukee, Wisconsin, who owned Barbour Island, sold two acres of marshland on the east side of the Barbour River at Gould's Landing to Oemler, a tract that included "all that certain parcel of marsh land lying on Barbours Island River approximately opposite to Gould's Landing containing two acres more or less." The same agreement included a plat of this small tract opposite the northeast side of Harris Neck across from Gould's Landing. This "Map of a Proposed Factory Site for Capt. Augustus Oemler on Barbours Island in McIntosh County" delineates a two-acre rectangle in the Barbour Island marshes on which Oemler sited his oyster cannery.[252] Eighteen months later, another deed indicates further oystering activity at Harris Neck. In January 1928 Freda Rauers Oemler, widow of Augustus, sold for $5,000 to G. Phillip Maggione and Joseph O. Maggione the two-acre patch of high ground in the marsh opposite Gould's Landing that

"with the improvements of the above described lot of land consisting of buildings in which was conducted by Augustus Oemler an oyster canning

[252] Deed Book Y (1926), 109, RMCG. The oyster activities of Augustus Oemler at St. Catherines Island are documented in Liberty County Deed Records (1900, 1918), Superior Court, Hinesville, Ga.

factory known as the Oemler Oyster Cannery, together with all the machinery, tools and equipment located in said factory, including pipes, fittings, tanks, shucking houses, tongs, steam cars, steam chests, boilers, cans and oyster shells, located on said land; also all canning materials, boats, barges, batteaux, belonging to said cannery including one motor boat equipped with one 30-horse power engine, and all equipment, apparel and furniture used in connection with said boat; and four oyster bateaux located on St. Catherines Island."[253]

In 1933, The L.P. Maggione Company of Savannah purchased from Courtney Thorpe of Savannah an eight-acre tract at Gould's Landing for oyster processing. In 1949 the Bertram family purchased three-tenths of an acre on the Barbour River at Gould's Landing from E.M. Thorpe for use as an oyster house and public fish camp, an operation that continued until 1970.

In 1904, Edward S. Ripley of Chicago, Illinois sold to Robert S. Morison of Massachusetts Barbour, Oldnor and Wahoo islands, with their attendant marshlands. There were oyster beds along the streams associated with the islands — Barbour Island River from Sapelo Sound to Gould's Landing, Wahoo River, and Todd River, a tidal stream that penetrates the marsh between Barbour and Oldnor islands. The islands then went to George A. Morison of Milwaukee, either a son or brother of Robert S. Morison. George Morison, as we have seen, sold to Augustus Oemler land in the western marsh of Barbour Island on which to build a cannery. He also leased to the Maggione Company oyster rights around the highlands and marshes of Barbour, Oldnor and Wahoo islands. The Maggiones cultivated and harvested oysters for a number of years, processing them at the Harris Neck cannery they acquired from the Oemler Company in 1928. On July 1, 1936, Joseph O. Maggione sub-leased to Irvin Davis of McIntosh County

---

[253] Deed Book 1 (1928), 254-58, RMCG.

"the right and privilege of building houses and fences and keeping cattle and stock on said leased lands, as well as the right and privilege of planting or farming any cultivated lands covered by this lease. The lands to let being all those certain islands known as Barbours, Oldnors and Wahoo, being situated within a large body of marsh lands bounded North by Swains River and South Newport River; East by South Newport River; South by Sapelo Sound and Barbours Island River; and West by Barbours Island River. [The Maggiones] expressly reserve unto themselves the right to plant, cultivate, and harvest the oysters on said islands, as well as all oyster and fishing privileges connected therewith."[254]

In 1936, G.A. Morison sold Barbour, Oldnor and Wahoo islands to E.M. Thorpe and James M. DeFoor.[255] Barbour and Oldnor were later acquired by John C. Hull. The concrete bridge spanning Barbour Island River linking Gould's Landing to the two-acre tract in the marsh known as Pirates Point, which included only a small patch of vegetation, was not built during the oystering era of the Oemlers and Maggiones as some believe. The bridge was built later by the then-property owner, Dr. John C. Hull. Supervisor of the work was Francis L. Pipkin, with materials supplied by the Capital Concrete Company. In 1958, Hull, a Northerner, acquired 5,000 acres of upland and marsh comprising Barbour and Oldnor islands.[256] His intention was to develop the islands, plans that included the construction of the bridge across the Barbour Island River at Gould's Landing, and a causeway from that point through the marsh to Barbour Island. Hull began work in 1958 and the bridge was eventually completed. However, the causeway part of the project abruptly ended in 1962 when Hull was accidentally killed during construction work at the site. Ownership of the small Pirates Point

---

[254] Lease Book B (1936), 146, RMCG.
[255] Deed Book 7 (1936), 153, 261, RMCG.
[256] Deed Book 33 (1958), 20, RMCG.

tract devolved to Hull's widow, Mabel A. Hull, eventually being acquired as a protected site by The Nature Conservancy. The bridge over Barbour Island River to the hammock was dismantled in 1990; nothing remains of the oyster cannery once on the site.

At Harris Neck, traditional Geechee residents supported themselves in the first three decades of the twentieth century with small-scale farming and home gardens, yard or pasture livestock, lumbering, turpentining, and commercial seafood activity, chiefly oyster harvesting. An oyster collecting shed occupied a lot at Harris Neck Tract 154 on the South Newport River in the 1930s and 1940s. The Shell Bluff Canning Company acquired Tract No. 34 in 1906 for oyster processing that preceded the operations at Gould's Landing by Oemler in the 1920s and the Maggiones in the 1930s. There was a sizeable Geechee population on the upper end of Harris Neck between 1880 and 1942, with numerous small homes and outbuildings on the tract.[257] The Department of Agriculture's 1929 McIntosh County soil map delineated a well-defined pattern of sandy roads, and dwellings and outbuildings dispersed throughout upper Harris Neck.[258] Larger homes still remained, particularly those of Eleanor Clapp and Lily Livingston at Thomas Landing.

A chapter of *Drums and Shadows: Survival Studies among the Georgia Coastal Negroes* is devoted to Harris Neck and its African American residents, consisting of oral history interviews about traditional beliefs and customs, conducted in the late 1930s. Harris Neck was

[257] U.S. Civil Action File No. 56.
[258] Fuller, Hendrickson, et. al. *Soil Survey of McIntosh County*, Series 1929, op. cit.

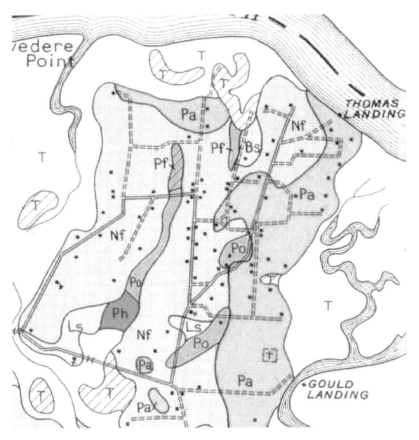

*Upper Harris Neck in 1929 with African American settlement
patterns, from the soil survey map of that year.*

much like many small settlements along the Georgia coast during

this era—remote, isolated, and mostly well-removed from the centers

of population and transportation:

"Turning off from the Coastal Highway, a tree-shaded dirt road leads
to Harris Neck, a remote little settlement connected to the mainland
by a causeway and located about forty-eight miles south of Savannah.
Narrow, rutted roads curve and turn unexpectedly through the
densely-wooded area. Set singly or in little clusters of two or three
and sometimes hidden by the trees and foliage are the houses of the

inhabitants. There is a peaceful atmosphere about the entire island; life flows along in a smoothly gliding stream; the people seem satisfied for the most part with a simple, uneventful scheme of existence."

Persons interviewed by the Georgia Writers' Project at Harris Neck were Ed Thorpe (1864-1940), Isaac Ba[i]sden (1877-1954), Liza Ba[i]sden (1867-1940), Josephine Stephens, Anna Johnson, and Rosa Sallins (1892-1956). Ed Thorpe noted, "Folks say duh road to Maringo [sic] is hanted. I use tuh lib at Maringo some time back, but I nebuh see no spirits. Once I tink I see one. Wen I git closuh, it tun out tuh be a big dog." On this same subject, Isaac Basden commented, "Yas'm I hab heah bout duh hanted road tuh Maringo on duh Young Man Road. Lots uh folks say deah is spirits roun deah. Wen yuh try to pass duh fawk in duh road, dub spirits stop yuh sometime an wohn let yuh by..." There were precautions that might be taken in such circumstances according to Liza Basden: "Mos of duh folks carry sumpm fuh pruhtection. These keep othuh folks frum wukin cunjuh on em. They's made of haiah, an nails, an graveyahd dut, sometimes from pieces of cloth an string..."[259] Upheaval for this community, though unforeseen at the time, began not long after the *Drums and Shadows* interviews were done.

In 1933, the L.P. Maggione Company acquired eight acres at Gould's Landing from Courtney Thorpe of Savannah for oyster processing. In 1936, Elisha M. Thorpe (brother of Courtney), who also held acreage on Harris Neck, moved his family to the King-

[259] Georgia Writers' Project, Savannah Unit, *Drums and Shadows: Survival Studies among the Georgia Coastal Negroes* (Athens: University of Georgia Press, 1940), 120-32.

The Livingston house at Thomas Landing.

Muller house that he had moved to his Spring Cove tract in the middle section of the Neck. Between them the Thorpe brothers at one time, held the majority of acreage at Harris Neck, including land within the present wildlife refuge, Spring Cove and the Julianton tract on the lower end of the Neck. In the mid-1930s, the Civil Aeronautics Authority (CAA) built Intermediate Airfield No. 8 on the upper end of Harris Neck under a renewable lease with E.M. Thorpe. Eleanor Clapp died in 1937, having lived at Harris Neck for nearly half a century. In 1939, the Coastal Electric Membership Corporation ran the first electric lines to Harris Neck, with power being installed at the Thorpe home at Spring Cove, the Maggione oyster house at Gould's Landing, and the CAA beacon.

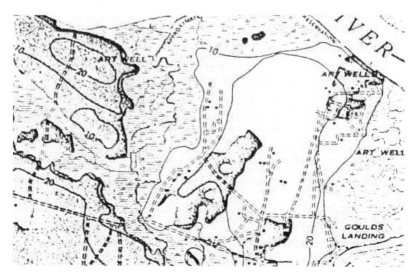

Upper Harris Neck in 1940, right, with location of artesian wells.

The Second World War and Afterward

The most intensive local military activity during the war was at the upper end of Harris Neck, facilities developed after the wholesale condemnation there of black-owned properties. In the mid-1930s, the Civil Aeronautics Authority, or its 1934-38 counterpart, the Bureau of Air Commerce, established a small, lighted intermediate landing field at Harris Neck to serve the Jacksonville-Richmond air route. Intended for emergency use, the airfield with runway dimensions of 2,600 feet (east-west) and 2,550 feet (north-south) provided no services and minimal support facilities.[260] The Harris Neck airfield appears on the 1938 state highway map of McIntosh County. The airfield was within the present wildlife refuge northwest of Gould's Landing. With clear approaches from every direction it was a logical site for an emergency field. After the Japanese attack on Pearl Harbor, government

---

[260] "Civil Aeronautics Bulletin," September 1, 1939, 16.

regulations concerning existing airfields began to appear.[261]

On January 15, 1942 the CAA airfield was closed to the public and the Civil Air Patrol initiated anti-submarine surveillance operations from Harris Neck. The advantages of the existing field made it ideal for air flight training, although it was considered somewhat vulnerable to attack. On July 6, 1942, the U.S. War Department filed condemnation proceedings for over 1,200 acres of mostly African American-owned land for the construction of two paved runways, and support facilities for a training facility. Additionally, the 3rd Army Air Force condemned fifty-six acres (Tract 143) of the Livingston property and thirteen acres owned by E.M. Thorpe (Tract 1408). The War Department later opted to lease the Thorpe tract for one dollar a year. The federal courts issued their first "taking" declarations in January 1943.[262] Nine Declarations of Taking for estimated fair compensation were filed in U.S. District Court, Southern District of Georgia from January 14 to July 19, 1943. The condemnation included 550 acres of land owned by E.M. Thorpe on the upper end of the Neck. Presumably the removal or demolition of structures began immediately, and "in a matter of months the community at Harris Neck which stretched almost two hundred years into the past, ceased to exist as a physical entity."[263]

The residents were awarded what was then deemed "fair market value" for their land but it was usually well below what the properties

---

[261] *Civil Aeronautics Journal*, March 15, 1942, Emergency Regulation 60-5951, 80.
[262] Civil Action File No. 56.
[263] "Archaeology and History of Harris Neck National Wildlife Refuge, McIntosh County, Georgia," Cultural Resource Management, Inc., Interagency Archaeological Services, Atlanta, for U.S. Fish and Wildlife Service, 1979.

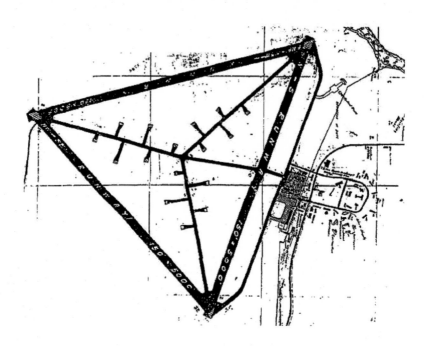

Harris Neck Army Airfield, from a 1943 military map.

were actually worth. Of greater consequence, and more traumatic, was the disruption of life as it had been known because of the dismantling of homes and the relocation of the people off the Neck to the adjacent mainland. Although the major part of base construction did not begin until August 1943, the Army Air Force had improved the CAA runway and added another runway by the end of 1942, with several support buildings. By the end of 1944, the War Department had constructed an assortment of permanent and pre-fabricated buildings. An additional runway and maintenance bays were built. The paved runways, now overgrown with weeds and underbrush, are still in place at the Harris Neck Wildlife Refuge. The buildings constructed were for barracks, warehouses, machine and repair shops, ammunition storage, latrine, and a non-commissioned officers club. The Livingston house at Thomas Landing served as the officer's club.[264]

The following selections from official correspondence attest to the flurry of military activity at Harris Neck during the war.[265]

Headquarters, 3rd Army Air Force, Tampa, Florida, to Division Engineer, Atlanta, Georgia, September 1, 1942: "It is requested that you take steps to acquire 55.8 acres of property at Harris Neck, Georgia belonging to Mrs. L.A. Livingston, and 13 acres of property at Harris Neck belonging to Mr. E.M. Thorpe for use for construction of Harris Neck Army Airport. Acquisition of this land and improvements thereon is a military necessity and it is urgently needed in connection with the construction of a third runway authorized by the Army Air Force which was not originally included in the Site Board Report. This land is required to provide clearance and safety zones, recreational areas, gasoline unloading facilities, and security of
military property. The estimated cost of the above property is $25,000 for the first parcel and $2,250 for the last."

U.S. Engineer, Savannah, Georgia, to Division Engineer, Atlanta, Georgia, October 22, 1942: "...Attention is invited to the fact that the 13-acre portion of Tract No. 140 lies adjacent to the gasoline landing pier. On these 13 acres is an existing commercial dock, the use of which by private commercial interests would interfere with the military use of the gasoline loading pier. The channel of Barbour Island River is too narrow to accommodate heavy commercial traffic concurrently with the delivery of water borne military supplies at the adjoining military dock. The distance of Harris Neck Air Base from existing highway and railway lines is such as to make necessary the delivery of much of its supplies by water."

U.S. Engineer, Savannah, Georgia, to Division Engineer, Atlanta, Georgia, November 19, 1942: "The Harris Neck Airfield occupies an exposed position...For reasons of military security the marsh land

---

[264] U.S. Air Force Archives, Maxwell Air Force Base, Montgomery, Alabama, Records of Harris Neck Army Airfield, Microfilm Reel B2269, Frames 1424, 1436.

[265] Extracted from documents pertaining to the administration and operations of Harris Neck Air Base, Georgia, 1942-44, in RG 18 (Records of the Army Air Force), NARA. Copies of these and other records relevant to Harris Neck Air Field are in Buddy Sullivan Papers, Collection 2433, GHS.

Brick ammunition building at Harris Neck.

should be acquired in order that military authorities might control all land and water approaches. Inasmuch as this Field is nearing completion, it is requested that the necessary action toward acquiring the marsh land be expedited."

Headquarters, Army Air Force, Washington, D.C., to Chief of Engineers, Washington, D.C., December 11, 1942: "You are authorized to proceed with the construction of the following facilities at Harris Neck, Georgia: Combination Theatre, Recreation Building and Chapel, size 37 x 99; Combination Service Club and Post Exchange, size 20 x 100; Storage Magazine, size 14 x 16; Post Engineer Office Building, size 20 x 60..."

Headquarters, 3rd Air Force, Tampa, Florida to Commanding General, Army Air Force, Washington, D.C., March 24, 1943: "It is requested that the construction of 19,000 square yards of additional parking apron be authorized for Harris Neck Air Field...predicated upon the occupancy of this station by one Dive Bomb Squadron (24 airplanes) and one over-strength Fighter RTU Squadron which will operate 36 single engine aircraft in the training of fighter pilots. The tactical complement of this station will consist of 75 officers and 350 enlisted men..."

Headquarters, 3rd Air Force, Tampa, Florida, to Commanding General, Air Force Eastern Defense Command, New York, New York, October 17, 1943: "...It is requested that a demolition

208

bombing target be installed at the Townsend Bombing and Gunnery Range for use by Third Air Force units stationed at Harris Neck Army Air Field..."

April 1, 1944: "Letter to Commanding General, Third Air Force, Tampa, Florida. Subject: Complaints by commercial fisheries as to bombing targets off St. Catherines and Sapelo Island, Georgia. Your comments are requested as to whether it would be practicable to schedule bombing practice during this period of the year so as to notify and allow commercial fisheries to trawl for shrimp in the bombing target areas when such targets were not being used by your command [aircraft stationed at Harris Neck]."

Following are extracts from an article which provide a picture of life at the airfield:

"Given the fallibility of human memory, the encroachments of time and decay, and the remoteness of the place, it is not surprising few people along the Georgia coast recall the Army airfield at Harris Neck. On December 7, 1941, a detachment of air guardsmen from Hunter Field [Savannah] took over the runway at Harris Neck built in the 1930s. For several years various Army squadrons used Harris Neck for maintenance and aerial gunnery training. There was a runway, a few support buildings, and an ill-ventilated post theater. In the fall of 1943, Harris Neck became a permanent auxiliary base of Dale Mabry Field, Tallahassee, Florida. In February 1944 the P-40 replaced the Aircobra for training purposes. Eleven pre-fabricated buildings and a hangar shed were started in March 1944, and the concrete ramp on the South Newport River was enlarged. An Officers Club was opened. In May 1944 there was a building boom. Pre-fab barracks for 125 men were erected. So too was an NCO Club, a supply building, a new latrine, maintenance and machine shops and pre-fab warehouses. The base historian observed that July [1944] was a very hot and routine month: 'A new floating raft with diving board has been anchored in the South Newport River about 30 yards from the floating dock where the two 42-foot crash boats are tied up. This has provided everyone with the opportunity to escape the torrid heat. At the present time there are many buildings on the field. The military personnel number 129 officers and 575 enlisted men.' In August 1944 Brigadier General Blackburn, commanding general of the III Fighter Command, spent a day inspecting the base. Local people attended an 'open house' and played softball games with teams from the base. Two USO Camp Shows and 'G.I. Movies' were shown along with three different motion pictures at the Post Theatre. Attendance was unusually large. Because of the isolated location of the field a shuttle bus operated on Route 131 to Highway 17. Harris Neck reached its zenith in September 1944 when 32 P-40s and five BT-13 planes were in use. September was an eminently routine month. Two exhaust fans were installed in the Post Theatre and, 'as a result the regular patrons were much more comfortable.' The [local] Women's Club continued their weekly meetings at the Officers Club [Livingston house]. The Club sponsored two events" a dance and a wiener roast. October was a month of cataclysmic change at Harris Neck...Personnel were near peak levels: 130 officers, 400 enlisted. But by the end of November, there were only 16 officers and 57 enlisted. The Orientation program was discontinued. But war summaries from UPI were put on bulletin boards and *Time*, *Life* and *Reader's Digest* were in the Day Room of the enlisted barracks. On October 18th the pilots evacuated all planes, and base personnel went over to Waycross by truck, bus and private car in advance of a hurricane that struck the coast two days later. Trees were blown down, roads blocked; the crash boat landing was damaged by the high tides and heavy winds. November marked the final decline of the base. Only a handful of officers and men were left. Harris Neck was deactivated in December 1944. All supplies, equipment, files and publications were shipped to Warner Robins and Dale Mabry Field. By December 31st, [almost] three years after the field was opened, the base was completely cleared and policed. Everyone was gone."[266]

On October 25, 1946, the U.S. War Assets Administration assumed accountability for 2,687 acres at Harris Neck, a routine post-war procedure for confiscated lands previously privately held. In an equally common action, the former air base land passed into the possession of McIntosh County. The structures and facilities at the air base were dismantled through official or unofficial salvage operations, or sold as surplus. An exception was the Livingston

---

[266] Charles Rippin, "Harris Neck Army Airfield," *Coastal Quarterly* (Savannah), Fall 1977.

house at Thomas Landing, which was not dismantled until re-acquisition of the tract by the federal government.

When the Second World War ended, the land on upper Harris Neck occupied by the former Army Air Field was turned over to McIntosh County with the understanding that the county utilize the tract as an airport. McIntosh County, however, would have little use for an airport in such a remote section and far removed from the county seat. In July 1949, the county commissioners became involved in a dispute with officials of the Union Bag and Paper Corporation of Savannah, which owned land west of Harris Neck. Union Bag constructed a barricade on the public dirt road linking Belvedere Island with the Harris Neck Road, a road providing access to the South Newport River where local blacks engaged in commercial oystering and crabbing. County commissioners W.H. Graham, G.C. Rogers, Jr., A.M. Durant, M.C. Middleton and J.A. Hardy responded by removing the barrier. Union Bag again padlocked the gate and notified the commissioners that if the obstruction was removed they would be taken to federal court. The commissioners refused to yield; their action was supported by the publisher of the *McIntosh County News*, Paul J. Varner, who wrote that "the people and the County have been good to this Corporation. The amount of taxes paid by this Corporation are negligible in comparison to the services received by the Corporation from the County. The County has practically bankrupted itself over a period of years by spending large sums of money in improving and maintaining roads for the use of this Corporation and its heavy equipment. We are astounded at the attitude and unwarranted actions and threats by this Corporation ..."[267]

After the legal and editorial contretemps, Union Bag "implied that they were considering the matter of the road favorably and the commissioners

---

[267] *McIntosh County News*, July 14, 1949.

believed the Corporation would re-open the road and place a cattle guard where the gate now is, without litigation."[268] At the time of the Belvedere incident another controversy was developing across the marsh at Harris Neck. Headlines in the July 14, 1949 McIntosh County News atop page one read: "Harris Neck Airfield Buildings are Robbed; Old Livingston Home Stripped of Valuable Equipment." The article noted the removal of fixtures and equipment from the Harris Neck properties amounting to $22,000 in value. The story continued:

"The Livingston property on the South Newport River, which is a part of the Harris Neck Airfield reservation, was found to have been stripped of windows and doors, and the electrical and pumping equipment from the Livingston powerhouse to have been removed. The hospital building [of the air base] has been wrecked from end to end. The boiler house was stripped of pipes and heating fixtures and steam radiators were removed from the main buildings. All of the pumping fixtures were removed from the theater building, and valuable motors, electrical switches and pumping equipment had been removed from the two water pumping stations on the base ..."[269]

In March 1948, Tom H. Poppell was elected sheriff of McIntosh County, succeeding his father, Adam S. Poppell (1875-1950) who had served from 1920 to 1948. Tom Poppell (1921-1979) was sheriff for thirty-one years, never losing an election. The July 14th News article noted that warrants had been issued for three persons in the Harris Neck incident and that Poppell had made one arrest with others anticipated. Three local businessmen were appointed by the county commission to manage the Harris Neck property; politics prevailed, however, and the commissioners were forced to assume direct management of the property. Varner opined that

"In view of all the circumstances in the history of this property and its manage-

[268] Ibid., July 28, 1949.
[269] Ibid., July 14, 1949.

ment, the News believes that the airfield should be closed and a guard placed at the gate until this affair is entirely settled. We also think the Commissioners should give a great deal of study to the question of developing this property along sound business lines and to utilizing it in such manner as will be of greatest benefit to the public at large."[270]

The following week, July 21st, Varner noted, "We invite the commissioners to furnish us with a prepared statement as to their position in this matter. We know the public would like to hear their side of the story as a large amount of County property is involved as the same is reported missing and unaccounted for."[271]

In 1951, Poppell told the county commission that he wanted to lease the Lorillard-Livingston mansion to run as an exclusive club. The lease was granted and the club was utilized until 1958. The Atlanta press picks up on this development in its reporting the death of Poppell in 1979:

"In the meantime, the Harris Neck property was being systematically stripped of anything of value. Furniture and equipment disappeared, as did houses and other buildings constructed by the military. Although several local people reported what was going on, the Federal government was in no rush to check into things. After several years of bureaucratic foot-dragging, the feds finally took action. [They] informed McIntosh County that its lease of the property to Poppell was illegal because the Federal government had never approved it. Three members of the County Commission, in the late 1950s, revoked Poppell's lease. The two other commissioners, both staunch Poppell supporters, were subsequently charged with fraudulently disposing of some of the Harris Neck valuables... The men were never tried because the charges against them were dropped by the sheriff's close political ally, Judge Mel Price. Because of McIntosh County's mismanagement of Harris Neck, the federal government reclaimed it and, in 1962, turned it over to the U.S. Fish and Wildlife Service to manage as a refuge."[272]

---

[270] Ibid.
[271] Ibid., July 21, 1949.
[272] *Atlanta Constitution*, August 16, 1979.

After years of alleged abuses and illegal activities by officials and private citizens, the Federal Aviation Administration reasserted its title to the airfield in 1961. In 1962, the federal government reclaimed the entire tract and designated it the Harris Neck National Wildlife Refuge, under the administration of the U.S. Department of the Interior, Fish and Wildlife Service. Pursuant to development of the wildlife refuge, the Livingston house on the South Newport River was sold for salvage in 1963 for $310 to Harry Wedincamp of Townsend, and the air hangar was sold as salvage to Irvin Davis for $50. Removal of virtually all structural evidence of the airbase, excepting the asphalt runways, was expedited.

In 1979, Edgar Timmons, Jr., Hercules Anderson, Chris McIntosh, Ted Clark and others at Harris Neck began an effort to assert Timmons' claim to restoration of family land within the refuge. Timmons, et al. subsequently filed an unsuccessful federal lawsuit in 1980 for reclamation of their lands. In 1982, the U.S. 11th Circuit Court of Appeals in Atlanta denied the Timmons appeal. Mike Wallace and the CBS program 60 Minutes visited the refuge and interviewed area residents in late 1982; the program aired in February 1983. After that, the issue lay dormant and unresolved for over twenty years until 2006 when the Harris Neck Land Trust LLC was formed to assist the descendants of the former Harris Neck land owners to reclaim their land. In 2012, a Briefing Document opposing "Congressional action sought by the Harris Neck Land Trust LLC to obtain lands within the Harris Neck National Wildlife Refuge" was submitted to Representative Jack Kingston by the Friends of the Savannah Coastal Wildlife Refuges, Blue Goose Alliance, Coastal Georgia Audubon Society, Georgia Ornithological

Society, Ogeechee Audubon Society, and the Coastal Group of Georgia Sierra Club. In 2013, a meeting was held with FWS staff, attorneys from the Regional Solicitor's Office, attorneys from Holland and Knight, and Representative Kingston to discuss the Land Trust's request to build permanent residences on the Refuge and to explore other options. In June 2014, Secretary of the Interior Sally Jewell visited Harris Neck National Wildlife Refuge to announce the change of the wood stork's status from endangered to threatened. Jewell and FWS staff met with HNLT representatives. Never during the process of re-designation in the 1960s was serious consideration given, either by federal, state or local entities, to return the lands to their pre-war African American owners, or provide fair compensation for the loss of the lands because of the World War II condemnation proceedings. Litigation and ongoing disputes over the controversy of the land ownership, concurrent with a passionate debate over land reclamation and fair compensation have ensued for forty years, at one point going all the way to the halls of the United States Congress. As of 2018, the federal government has shown no inclination to abandon the wildlife refuge, or return at least a portion of the land to the descendants of the traditional Geechee people of Harris Neck.

7

Early Twentieth Century Land Use

In 1911, a consortium of businessmen from Akron, Ohio formed the Fairhope Land Company and purchased 7,000 acres on the Sapelo River at the site of the former Mallow plantation, now Pine Harbor. Surveys were made, and lots, streets and public areas were laid out in a formal town plan. Deed records reflect the purchase in 1913 and 1914 of additional land by the Fairhope Company with the acreage being sub-divided into lots.[273] A second sub-division was added to Fairhope Township in 1914; a three-story hotel was constructed on the Sapelo River in 1915. The consortium hoped to turn the new town of Fairhope into a tourist mecca, with a transportation link provided by the Georgia Coast and Piedmont Railroad, which ran a spur track to Fairhope through the woods and marsh from Eulonia.

With the G.C. & P. running into Fairhope for a brief time, the community prospered for several years; there were two stores, a post office, a small steel and iron foundry, and a factory that manufactured ladders and novelties. There was a one-teacher school and the hotel with over one hundred rooms. G.C. & P. shuttles ran to Fairhope on the spur from Eulonia

---

[273] Deed Book J (1911), 577-81; Book L (1913), 220-25; Book L (1913), 364-68; Book L (1914), 411-12; "Township of Fairhope, McIntosh County, Georgia," (two plats), Plat Cabinet A (1913, 1914), slide 119, RMCG.

for only about a year and a half then, for lack of enough passengers and freight, the line suspended operations there. The ambitious Fairhope plan was based on speculation and high hopes, and never realized expectations. The hotel was unprofitable, and Fairhope struggled to survive. The father of McIntosh County historian Bessie Mary Lewis, Wilbert W. Lewis (1854-1933) from Hudson, Ohio was a charter investor in Fairhope. Bessie Lewis (1889-1983) moved with her family to McIntosh County in 1912 when she was twenty-three; in a *Darien News* column in June 1979 she recalled: "The families who still lived in the town were not without transportation by rail. Officials on the road left an old handcar at the depot and those of us who wanted or needed — to go somewhere rode that to the Stage Road or Eulonia. Of course, no one could take off on his own. There must be more than one person aboard the car, as two were required to operate it. In other words, if you wanted to ride the hand-car, you must be willing to work your way."

The Fairhope Land Company went bankrupt in early 1916. Over 3,000 acres around Fairhope itself and in the surrounding pine woods were purchased by the Georgia Land and Livestock Company, excepting lots that had been bought by individuals within the town site. In October 1916, the Fairhope tract, through a complicated transaction, devolved to E.M. Thorpe of the Newport Company then to J.R. Paschall of Richmond, Virginia, head of the Georgia Land and Livestock Company. The terms conveying Fairhope from the Newport Company to Georgia Land and Livestock provide a typical example of the real estate transactions that were prevalent in McIntosh County in the early twentieth century. Dated October 2, 1916, the indenture

"between Newport Company, a corporation with its principal place of business at Townsend, Georgia, of the first part and Georgia Land & Livestock Company, likewise a corporation with its principal place of business

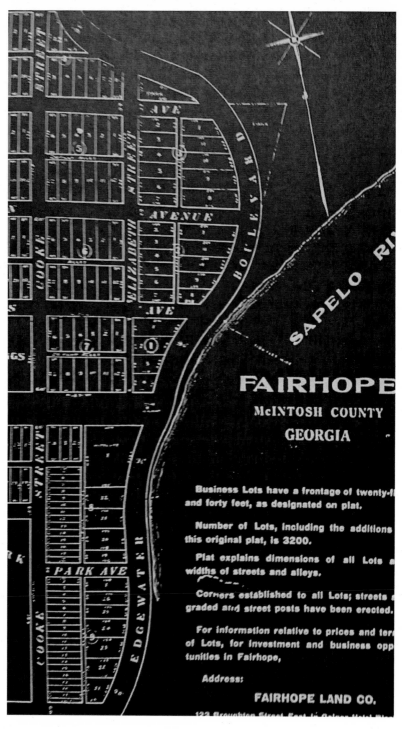

Plat of Fairhope Township, 1913.

218

at Townsend, Georgia, of the second part. Witnesseth that said party of the first part has granted, bargained, sold and conveyed unto the party of the second part all the following real estate, to wit: All that tract in McIntosh County formerly known as the Fairhope property of Joseph A. Walker made up of the original McDonald, or Fairhope tract, the said Joseph A. Walker's homeplace known as the Mallow tract, and various other tracts adjoining said two tracts above mentioned in the same immediate vicinity and being bounded as a whole on the north by the road leading from the Harris Neck Road to the White Chimney Bridge and by the White Chimney River; on the east and south by the Sapelo River; on the west by a public road known as the Savannah and Darien Stage Road and by the Harris Neck public road. The tracts of land hereinafter described being those tracts heretofore sold and conveyed by Joseph A. Walker to A.M. Holmes and M.S. Lang by deed dated January 7th, 1911. and thereafter conveyed by Holmes and Lang to Fairhope Land Company by deed dated November 9th, 1911 ... Together with all and singular buildings, fences and appurtenances thereunto belong excepting certain lots of land in what is known as the townsite of Fairhope, land off upon a portion of the land above described which excepted lots are known and duly noted on maps or plats as follows: That certain five acre tract fronting southerly for a distance of four hundred feet on the north line of Boulevard street, extending according to the plat to what is known as the 'First Addition to Fairhope' being the land and premises upon which is erected a factory and office building and a sawmill building ... having the following measurements; Beginning at a point on the northern line of Edgewater Boulevard [fronting Sapelo River] in Fairhope at the junction of the west line at what is called the Werntz factory site to the northern line of Boulevard, two hundred and fifty feet westerly from the northern line of the right of way of the spur track running to said property from the Georgia Coast & Piedmont Railroad, running thence northerly along the western line of said Werntz factory site, a distance of 510 feet. The president, vice president or secretary of Newport Company are hereby authorized and empowered to execute and deliver a deed in the name and behalf of the company conveying to the Georgia Land & Livestock Company all of the real estate owned by the Newport Company and constituting the former property of the Fairhope Land Company, excepting therefrom the town site containing approximately 323 acres as shown by a plat of the same made by Ravenel Gignilliat, dated July 1916. Signed sealed and delivered by Newport Company by E.M. Thorpe, its president and D.G. Thorpe, its secretary."[274]

---

[274] Deed Book N (1916), 464-71, RMCG.

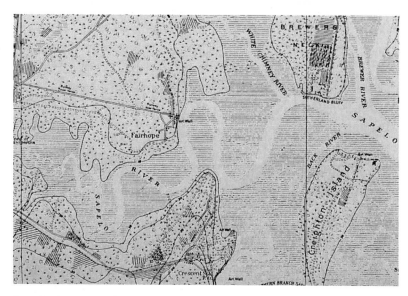

Sapelo River, Fairhope, Crescent, Bruro Neck, 1921 quad map.

Under new ownership, Fairhope acquired a new name, Pine Harbor, as suggested by Ravenel Gignilliat, a civil engineer who made the second survey of the tract. The name Pine Harbor appears on the 1929 soil survey map of McIntosh County. The G.C. & P.'s spur track from Eulonia was removed and sold; the pavilion in the park was dismantled, the railroad depot was moved to the waterfront and remodeled as a residence, and, in 1931, the hotel was torn down and its materials shipped to Savannah where they were sold for scrap lumber. The stores closed for lack of business. A photograph of the Pine Harbor waterfront ca. 1935 depicts a community practically devoid of residents. In the years ahead there would be homes and private docks constructed along that section of the Sapelo River as Pine Harbor settled into a quiet existence as a residential community. Bessie Lewis recalled an interesting aspect of her youth in the community:

"With the taking up of the rails and ties, the railroad was soon forgotten by almost everyone. Almost, but not quite, for one individual, four-footed, remembered it and observed the rules for traffic where railroads are

220

concerned as long as he lived. This individual was my horse, Rex. I bought him in Savannah where he had been bred and trained. All his life he had stopped, looked and listened when he came to a railroad track. And he had no intention of changing his habits when he came to live in the country. When I first drove him to Eulonia, he stopped and looked both ways when he came to the railroad crossing just north of the Dean home on the Stage Road. When the rails were removed it made no difference to Rex – he continued to look and listen when he came to the place where they had been. Whether under the saddle or in harness, to the end of his life, he continued to remember that this place was once a railroad crossing and to observe the traffic rules.."[275]

In 1918-19, a Compilation and Field Inspection by the Department Engineer of the U.S. Army Corps of Engineers resulted in the production in 1920-21 of a series of Grid Zone Tactical Maps of coastal areas. The "five-thousand yard grid system progressive maps" were compiled with overlays of U.S. Coast and Geodetic Survey charts and U.S. Geological Survey maps for the period. Four of the maps entailed areas of McIntosh County, and a number of features bear noting as they define the county's 1920s geography.

Two of the Corps maps are the Sapelo River and South Newport River quadrangles, published in 1920. They delineate areas then or formerly under cultivation on the upper end of Harris Neck, Barbour Island, several tracts on the road between Harris Neck and South Newport, Bruro Neck, the upper White Chimney River, part of Creighton Island, and land along the Cowhorn Road between Crescent and Eulonia. "Crescent Sta. P.O." is delineated at the curve of the G.C. & P. as it turns westward. Buildings are shown at Sutherland's Bluff, the upper end of Creighton, the south end of Harris Neck near the Julianton River, and on Front River at the former

---

[275] Bessie Lewis, "Low Country Diary," *Darien News*, June 28, 1979. For a biography of Miss Lewis and an edited collection of her writings, see Buddy Sullivan, ed., *A Low Country Diary: Bessie Mary Lewis and McIntosh County, Georgia* (Charleston, SC: CreateSpace, 2016).

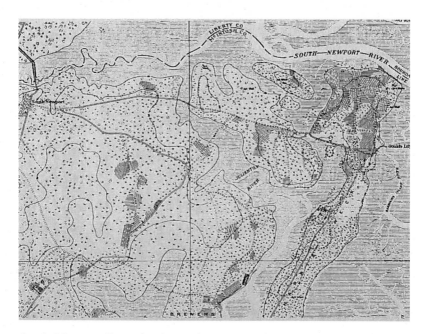

South Newport River (top), South Newport (l) to Harris Neck (r), from 1921 quadrangle map.

timber loading hammocks. "Sapelo" is delineated on the bend of the Front River east of Creighton. The town of Fairhope is shown, but not the railroad spur as the tracks were removed before the field inspection was made. Above Eulonia Station, the "Head of Navigation" of the Sapelo River is delineated. West of the "Dixie Highway" the G.C. & P. tracks go northwest from Eulonia to "Warsaw (Old Darien Jc.)" where buildings are shown around the intersection with the Seaboard Air Line tracks. Other buildings are shown at the former site of the Brickstone factory up the Seaboard track, and structures and two artesian wells appear at Jones Station. Between Warsaw and the Dixie Highway is Young's Island where several structures are shown. A tract of land abutting the west side of the Dixie Highway and fronting the marsh at South Newport is shown to be under cultivation. Deed records show this to be the "Baker tract", not to be confused with the Baker antebellum plantation some distance east near Harris Neck.

In 1925, the McIntosh County Board of Commissioners catalogued the county roads, all being dirt roads unless otherwise indicated. Those roads appertaining to the area of the county under discussion are as follows:[276]

County Line Road, west of Jones, being 1½ miles long and forming the northwest boundary between McIntosh and Long counties in the upper corner of McIntosh County; Jones-to-Townsend Road through Warsaw; Cox-to-Townsend Road; King Road, from the Long County line east to Townsend, then to Briar Dam Road, then to a junction with the Atlantic Coastal Highway; Darien and Macon, or River Road, from Long County line to Cox, then to Darien; Briar Dam Road, from River Road to King Road at Townsend; Eulonia-to-Townsend Road, from Atlantic Coastal Highway; Jones-to-South Newport Road; Harris Neck Road, west to Harris Neck from Atlantic Coastal Highway; Sutherland's Bluff Road from Harris Neck Road to Young Man's Road to Shellman Bluff to Sutherland's Bluff; Julianton Branch of Harris Neck Road, south to the Julianton River, down the Harris Neck tract; Young Man's Road, from intersection of Harris Neck Road and Sutherland's Bluff Road to junction with Atlantic Coastal Highway; Atlantic Coastal Highway, formerly known as the Stage Road, paved through county in 1926; Fairhope Avenue, from Atlantic Coastal Highway east to Pine Harbor; Belvedere Island Road, from Harris Neck Road to South Newport River; Sapelo Island roads.

[276] Public Road Register, Records of the McIntosh County Board of Commissioners, 1925.

The Georgia Land and Livestock Company

In the early 1900s, several land-investment companies controlled large amounts of acreage in the northern and western sections of the county. The first of these was the Sapelo Land and Lumber Company. In 1889, Sapelo Land and Lumber was formed as a subsidiary of the Hilton-Dodge Lumber Company, and was the first of the land combines that acquired acreage in western and northern McIntosh County; others followed, including the Newport Company, and the Georgia Land and Livestock Company. Sapelo Land and Lumber accumulated timberland in McIntosh and Liberty counties for timbering and turpentine production, lands later acquired by Georgia Land and Livestock, Warsaw Lumber Company, Union Bag Camp, and others. In the early 1900s, Sapelo Land and Lumber sold large tracts of its holdings as the fortunes of the parent company, Hilton-Dodge, waned.[277]

In January 1904 the Sapelo Land and Lumber Company, with its principal office in Darien, sold 12,675 acres of timberland in McIntosh and neighboring counties to C.H. Davis and Company of Townsend for $18,330. The tract was "penetrated by the Seaboard Air Line Railway, bounded on the North and North East by the Darien and Western Railroad, on the East by the lands of McIntosh, Robert Young, Sr., estate of J.E. Townsend, W.A. Wilcox and the King Road, and on the West and South West by the King Road

---

[277] For particulars on the Hilton-Dodge Lumber Company, and the Darien timber industry in general from 1865 to 1925, see Buddy Sullivan, *Early Days on the Georgia Tidewater*, all editions, op. cit.; Sullivan, *Environmental Influences on Life & Labor in McIntosh County, Georgia* (privately published, 2018); and Sullivan, ed., *High Water on the Bar, An Operational Perspective of a Tidewater Timber Port* (Darien, Ga., 2009).

[south of Townsend] and lands of E.R Miller." In a May 1905 transaction, Sapelo Land and Lumber sold 441 acres to F.H. McFarland for the nominal sum of $186.75, a tract known as "the Moses Jones Tract near the village of Jonesville and bounded by lands of B.B. Rozier, Henry Way and Savannah and Barrington dirt road," originally acquired by Sapelo Land and Lumber in 1894 in a mortgage foreclosure.[278]

With the breakup of Hilton-Dodge Lumber from 1912-16, many of the corporation's lands McIntosh and Liberty counties were acquired by two new companies started at the same time, often operating in tandem, and soon thereafter merged under a single corporate management. These were the Newport Company and the Georgia Land and Livestock Company. The Newport Company was a land investment and real estate entity incorporated in 1916 with its office of business at Townsend, and Elisha M. Thorpe as president and his brother David G. Thorpe as secretary. Also incorporated in 1916 was the Georgia Land and Livestock Company, a real estate firm initially comprised mostly of investors from Virginia. Georgia Land and Livestock was financially supported by the Virginia Trust Company of Richmond. The president of the G.L. & L.C. was J.M. Paschall of Richmond. There was considerable interaction between the Newport Company and Georgia Land and Livestock, and it was no coincidence that the primary offices of business for both firms was at Townsend in McIntosh County.

In 1916, the Newport Company acquired several large tracts, including 4,001 acres of the Sutherland's Bluff and Travellers Rest

---

[278] Deed Book H (1904), 320-21; Deed Book H (1905), 480-81, RMCG.

Lumber operations in the McIntosh County pine flatwoods, early 1900s.

tracts, and several thousand additional acres from the Fairhope Land Company on the Sapelo River at what later became Pine Harbor. Sutherland's Bluff, the former antebellum plantation tract, was owned by northern interests after the Civil War. Evidence of the interaction of the two real estate firms is seen in Georgia Land and Livestock's acquisition of the Sutherland's Bluff, Fairhope and other properties from the Newport Company almost as soon as the latter firm completed its own acquisitions of them. Deed records attest to a flurry of transactions in February and March 1921 involving both corporations. Much of the activity was associated with the merger of Newport Company's assets with those of Georgia Land and Livestock under the name of the latter. Most of the transactions by which the Newport Company was phased out and absorbed by G.L. & L.C.

were completed by the end of March 1921.

In February 1921 E.M. Thorpe sold to Georgia Land and Livestock 168 acres at Young's Island east of Warsaw, "said 168 acres being bounded north by lands of the estate of T.P. Pease, east by the lands of Margaret R. Rowe, south by lands of James A. Young and Samuel B. Rowe and west by unknown lands, but at the present time bounded on all sides by lands of the Georgia Land & Livestock Company; being the same lands conveyed by E.M. Thorpe by deed dated April 30, 1917."[279] The February-March 1921 deed activity saw Georgia Land and Livestock both sell land and mortgage land, some of it to Savannah Bank and Trust Company, in addition to leasing tracts of timberland for turpentine production.

Georgia Land and Livestock was starting what its Virginia stockholders envisioned would be a profitable cattle-raising venture on a scale to rival anything in Texas. Thousands of head of cattle were brought in to graze within fenced pasture lands scattered through the western McIntosh pine woods, particularly in areas west of Eulonia and in the Townsend, Jones and Cox areas. In February 1921 Georgia Land and Livestock gained title to a considerable herd of cattle from a corporation based in Atlanta. The herd comprised 4,235 head of cattle, in addition to 160 bulls, 538 calves and 4,963 sheep. In land, Georgia Land and Livestock acquired over 70,000 acres in McIntosh and Liberty counties in 1921 and 1922. Much of the acreage, gained by outright purchase or through lease, was to be used for cattle pasturage in the sparsely-populated sections of McIntosh County.

McIntosh deed and lease record books for 1921 are filled with

---

[279] Deed Book R (1921), 112, RMCG.

land plats and tract surveys documenting the acquisitions of Georgia Land and Livestock. The surveys were conducted in 1920 and included lands throughout the western sections of the county, and tracts along the South Newport River, in the White Chimney and Sapelo river areas, and in the Eulonia area. For example:

"Extract from Minutes of a meeting of the Board of Directors of the Georgia Land & Livestock Company held Feb. 24, 1921. Whereas the stockholders of the Georgia Land & Livestock Company have heretofore by resolution duly appointed a committee with full authority to make and complete the [transaction] of any property of the Company, and whereas the committee has sold the hereinafter described property to James Miller of Richmond, Virginia, now therefore be it resolved that sale to James Miller of approximately 35,540 acres of land out of the holdings of this company in McIntosh and Liberty counties at the price of $1,221,320."[280]

Also in February 1921, Georgia Land and Livestock acquired from the Newport Company title for the Sutherland's Bluff and adjoining Travellers Rest tracts, totaling 4,001 acres. This transaction was one of the instruments by which the merger of the Newport Company with Georgia Land and Livestock was effected:

"Extract from Minutes of meeting of the Board of Directors of the Newport Company held the 18th day of February, 1921. Resolved that the President or Vice President and the Secretary or Assistant Secretary of Newport Company are authorized, expressed and directed to execute a deed on behalf of the company to the Georgia Land & Livestock Company [for the tract] conveyed to the [Newport] company from Stuart H. Dodge et al. April 1st, 1920."[281]

After the merger of the two land companies, E.M. Thorpe served

---

[280] Deed Book R (1921), 126, RMCG.
[281] Deed Book R (1921), 119, RMCG.

Abandoned silo from cattle operations in western McIntosh County.

as vice-president of Georgia Land and Livestock, and the Company subsequently acquired thousands of additional acres in western McIntosh County. In 1917, G.L. & L.C. had constructed a series of concrete silos in the pine woods for the storage of silage for its cattle grazing. The silos still stand as silent monuments to the grand cattle-raising venture, scattered through the west and southwest sections of McIntosh County near Townsend, Eulonia, Jones and the Long

County line, some near existing roadways.[282]

The cattle-raising project by Georgia Land and Livestock was ultimately unsuccessful. Grand in concept, and seemingly well-organized, the idea failed possibly because it simply over-reached and was too ambitious. Cattle imported from Texas, Florida and Georgia were unable to adapt to the sandy, pinewoods environment of the coastal Georgia interior. The project lost momentum, and finally failed altogether. In 1925, the Georgia Land and Livestock Company sold or mortgaged 85,000 acres, and the company went bankrupt after having been active only nine years. The obituary of Georgia

Many of the lands held by Georgia Land and Livestock eventually came into possession of Union Bag Camp of Savannah in the 1930s and 1940s. In 1981, Robert A. Young, Jr., long-time county tax commissioner, offered useful insights on the Georgia Land and Livestock Company:

"We had a land company start here in about 1916, Georgia Land and Livestock Company. They got some big men from several Southern states, like Governor Stewart from Virginia, and they bought up thousands and thousands of acres of land, and back then, I remember my father sold a tract with big pine timber at three dollars an acre. Then they started shipping livestock in and fenced up pasture. They bought 93 miles of wire at one time to build pasture and then started pastures and built silos and started tobacco planting. Well, they made a failure in all their efforts. The cattle raising, they brought cattle in from ranges down in Florida and they just weren't doing well. They lost money. They had, I suppose, roughly 150,000 acres of land in this and some of the adjoining counties. They made a failure with that but they made money in the long run by the enhancement of the value of the land and the timber

---

[282] Author's interview with Jim Daniel of Eulonia, Ga., January 28, 1987. At the time, Daniel was a forest supervisor for Union Camp Corporation of Savannah.

on the land; they sold the timber so they made money in the long run. First Merchant's National Bank of Richmond, Virginia was the biggest land owners. The tracts of land which they had later, along in the 1920s and early 1930s, they went into the bag companies. They were consolidated. Now I suppose in this county we have the biggest consolidation of land by big owners than any county in the state. Union Bag had 70,000 acres of land in McIntosh County. International Paper had 40,000 acres. Rayonier had about 25,000 acres. But most of these tracts were assembled back when the Georgia Land and Livestock Company went out. That enabled the paper companies to come in and take these lands over and get the tracts assembled, which was very good. That was part of the growth of our county and we had from it the good timber and good turpentine. And now Union Camp in Savannah is one of the biggest mills of its kind in the world."[283]

The following extract from the 1929 soil survey contains contemporaneous information relating to agricultural and naval stores activities in northern and western McIntosh County in the 1920s and 1930s:

"Longleaf and slash pines are the principal trees worked for the crude gum, although a few loblolly pines have been worked but are usually very poor producers. The slash pine is preferred and is reported to produce more gum than the longleaf. Production is based on crops of trees, 10,000 trees constituting a crop. Production per crop and the quality of the product differ with the size of the trees and the length of time they have been worked, the height of production being about 40 barrels of turpentine per crop. The highest quality turpentine is obtained from freshly-cupped or virgin trees. The stand of trees ranges from 1 or 2 to 50 or more an acre, so that in the better areas 250 acres will constitute a crop and elsewhere from 400 to 500 acres are required for a crop. There is a noticeable difference in the manner in which trees are worked. The better and more conservative method, followed by many producers, consists of putting only 1 cup on smaller trees and working no trees less than 9 inches in diameter. However, it is common, more often on leased land, that trees 5 inches in diameter will have 2 cups and 18 or 20 inch trees 4 or 5 cups, the worked faces completely girdling the tree.

---

[283] *Ebbtide* I (10), June 1981, Frederica Academy, St. Simons Island, Ga.

It is reported that at least 75 per cent of McIntosh County's mainland area is in the control of turpentine and lumber companies, whose holdings range from a few thousand to more than 50,000 acres. Part of the area is conservatively worked and reforestation is being urged, but elsewhere the methods employed are destructive to the trees, and practically no second growth has developed on account of fires and livestock grazing.

"Most of the trees large enough for lumber have been cut, except on scattered small tracts. One sawmill, which is sawing about 60,000 feet of pine a day, is still operating at Warsaw [Warsaw Lumber].[284] The company owning this mill has cut both pines and swamp hardwoods but has shipped most of the hardwoods as logs. Another product of the county is deer-tongue, or vanilla leaf (*Trilisa odoratissima*), of which about 240,000 pounds a year are picked, the present price is about 7 ½ cents a pound, at which price the crop is worth about $18,000. The deer-tongue is shipped mainly to New York, Baltimore, Wilmington, and Richmond, from whence three-fourths to seven-eighths of the crop is exported to Germany and France. Deer-tongue grows principally on the Leon soils, but it is found in nearly all parts of the county.

"Elevation at Cox on the Seaboard Air Line Railway is 17 feet, and Townsend[285] and Jones are about 20 feet above sea level. In times of very high floods, water from the Altamaha River leaves the river swamp, breaks through the sand ridge in the southwestern corner of the county and submerges much of the western part of the county. At times Cox, Townsend, Warsaw and Jones are isolated, except by boat. The flood waters overflowing from the Altamaha River swamp move across the western half of the county to reach the ocean by way of Young's Island Swamp into Sapelo River, and by way of Big Mortar Swamp and Bull Town Swamp into South Newport River. Throughout the western part of the county, drainage canals and ditches would be necessary through the swamp areas to remove excess water...The population is densest along the coast, on Sapelo Island, and in small settlements along die railroad in the western part of the county...The Atlantic

---

[284] For the long-abandoned settlement of Warsaw, and its attendant railroad and lumber operations, 1915-1940, see Sullivan, *Early Days on the Georgia Tidewater*, all editions; Sullivan, *Environmental Influences on Life & Labor in McIntosh County, Georgia*, 682-87; and Buddy Sullivan, *Darien: A History of the Town & Its Environs* (privately published, 2020), 484-87.

[285] For the history of Townsend, see Sullivan, *Early Days on the Georgia Tidewater*, all editions; and Sullivan, *Environmental Influences on Life & Labor in McIntosh County, Georgia*, 677-82.

Coastal Highway, a paved road, passes through the county and is the principal transportation route for motorized vehicles. A State highway with a sand-clay surface extends west from Eulonia through Townsend...Formerly, considerable difficulty was experienced in securing satisfactory drinking water, but at present this is obtained from artesian wells in all parts of the county, including the islands. The largest industry in McIntosh County is the production of naval stores, of which approximately 7,000 barrels of turpentine of 50 gallons each and 35,000 barrels of rosin of 280 pounds each are sold annually at a value ranging from $400,000 to $450,000. These products are marketed through Brunswick and Savannah. The growing of sea-island cotton became commercially important early in the 19th century, but changing conditions have eliminated that type of cotton and none is now grown in the county...In 1919 there were 752 acres [of cotton] which reported 362 bales. In 1929, however, only four acres were reported...In 1930 there were 268 farms in the county comprising 11.7 per cent of the land area...Most of the land in the county is held in large tracts, ranging in size from 1,000 to more than 50,000 acres, by naval stores companies, lumber companies and individuals...The most outstanding feature connected with the soils and crops of McIntosh County is that only between 1 and 2 per cent of the county's 277,120 acres is under cultivation. 100 years ago, this county was one of the richest counties in Georgia...Practically all of the merchantable timber has been removed...Tidal marsh bordering the eastern side of the county extends into the mainland, merges with the swamps, and covers a large part of the county. Some of the marshland was cultivated before the Civil War and was later abandoned because of the change in economic conditions...The county is devoted primarily to the production of naval stores, lumber, coastal fisheries and allied products. The entire land area, including the accessible tidal marsh, is free range unless fenced, and it is used extensively for range cattle, hogs and goats."[286]

Eulonia

Eulonia, in the center of McIntosh County, had been known as Sapelo Bridge from the late eighteenth century, serving as the county seat from 1793 to 1818. In 1887, a post office designated as Sapelo,

[286] G.L. Fuller, B.H. Hendrickson and J.W. Moon, *Soil Survey of McIntosh County, Georgia*, Series 1929, No. 6, Bureau of Chemistry and Soils, U.S. Department of Agriculture, 1932, 412.

opened at Sapelo Bridge with Elisha McDonald as postmaster, followed by O.S. Davis.[287] Davis had moved to Sapelo Bridge in the late 1880s from Marion County, South Carolina in which was located a settlement named Eulonia, in an area that was home to a number of families named Davis.[288]

At Sapelo Bridge, Davis operated a store in a two-story frame building fronting the road to Savannah. The store was later owned by William Bacon and, still later, by D.E. McDonald. The *Darien Gazette* makes several of references to "Willie Bacon of Eulonia" in the late 1890s. In the spring of 1894, the *Gazette* noted that "Mr. O.S. Davis has been appointed postmaster at Sapelo, McIntosh county, by the post-office authorities at Washington. Mr. Davis is a good man and a staunch Democrat."[289] In 1895 Davis's application to change the post office designation from "Sapelo" to "Eulonia" was approved. As Sapelo Bridge's post office was in service when a post office opened at Sapelo Island in 1891, the island station was designated Inverness, Ga. In 1898, three years after Sapelo P.O. had become Eulonia P.O., a post office was opened to serve the shipping interests in Sapelo Sound, being designated as "Sapelo."[290]

Elisha M. Thorpe provides the story of how Eulonia got its name in a letter of May 2, 1946:

"When I was a boy Sapelo P.O. was in my Uncle Elisha McDonald's store right near Reynolds Chapel M.E. Church. In later

[287] Site Files and Register of Postmasters, Records of the U.S. Postal Service, RG 28, National Archives and Records Administration.

[288] Letter from Florence M. Bethea of Marion, S.C. to William G. Haynes of Darien, February 6, 1990, Haynes Papers, Ashantilly Center, Inc., Darien Ga.

[289] *Darien Gazette*, March 24, 1894.

[290] Site Files, RG 28, NARA.

years Mr. O.S. Davis had a big store about where the present Eulonia P.O. is located. Mr. Davis conceived the idea to change the name of Sapelo P.O. to Eulonia P.O. The reason was he had a brother in Marion County, South Carolina who was a merchant and his P.O. was Eulonia. So O.S. Davis got the Sapelo, Ga. P.O. changed to Eulonia, P.O. Later, Sapelo Island wanted a post office, and they secured a post office, Sapelo. The post office my uncle had was Sapelo. I notice now some spell it Sapeloe, but Sapelo was the old name. The mail prior to 1890 came from Fleming Station on the Savannah, Florida & Western Rail Road, now Atlantic Coast Line Rail Road. The mail carrier had on his route Riceboro, South Newport and Sapelo. I don't remember if there were any others at that time on the route. The mail came one day and returned the following day. The old South Newport post office was located at the old Lach McIntosh Place where Mr. Tom Proudfoot lives about 2 miles south of South Newport. As I remember, Miss Lucy McIntosh was Post Mistress.

"In the Nineties there was a post office at White Chimney in my brother Edwin's store. It was named McCants for my brother's wife's mother's maiden name — she was also step-mother to Mr. O.S. Davis. Townsend Station was first called Flotono. I do not remember if the post office there was ever called Flotono. I know the name was changed to Townsend and it was named for Mr. Joseph E. Townsend. I have been Post Master at Townsend, and before the present P.M. Miss Janie Ingram was Post Mistress for a long time. I have been told that the first post offices in McIntosh County were located at South Newport, Darien, Jonesville and Fort Barrington. This would have to be vouched for by the P.O. Department in Washington, D.C."[291]

Eulonia was a naval stores center in the 1940s and 1950s, particularly after similar activity at Townsend and Warsaw declined. Being on the Coastal Highway, it had convenient access to Savannah and Brunswick. The last of the large-scale naval stores operations in McIntosh County began at Eulonia in 1928. Charles Memory Williamson, Sr. (1883-1947) of Whiteville, North Carolina came to

---

[291] Copy of letter from her father's papers provided the author by the late Isabel Thorpe Mealing.

Eulonia that year as general manager of the turpentine operation for the Pine Harbor Naval Stores Company. Eulonia was in the midst of over 28,000 acres of rosin-producing slash and longleaf pine. Williamson constructed forty-two dwellings to accommodate over 100 forest employees, and rosin produced at the Eulonia distillery exceeded government specifications, being a product of a superior grade and quality. By 1946-47, the pine forest in the Eulonia region had been worked to its full limits, and the land was sold to International Paper Company. After yielding rosin and turpentine at great profit to the Pine Harbor Naval Stores Company, these tracts provided an ample supply of pulpwood timber for International Paper.[292]

The state highway department map of McIntosh County in 1936 delineates the dirt road from Ludowici to Townsend, it being shown as state road 99. The road bears north for several hundred yards at Townsend then turns again east to Eulonia (now known as Old Townsend Road) to its juncture with US 17 near the headwaters of the Sapelo River. At that time one necessarily had to travel nearly a mile south on US 17 to its juncture with the Cow Horn Road, then designated as state road 131. Later, the state eliminated the dogleg at Eulonia and constructed a straight road from the Cow Horn Road at US 17 west toward Townsend, re-designating the road state 99, including the Cow Horn Road. Parenthetically, the state road 131 designation was applied to the Harris Neck road from US 17 to a terminus at the upper end of Harris Neck. The 1936 state map shows numbers of dwellings on the upper end of Harris Neck, and "Harris Neck Airport," which preceded by several years the military airfield.

---

[292] Author's interview with Charles M. Williamson, Jr., June 20, 1989.

The Series 1959 USDA *Soil Survey of McIntosh County,* a revision of

the 1929 edition, had these observations relevant to the ecology,

economy and land use in central and western McIntosh County:

"Mixed forests of slash pine, longleaf pine, and loblolly pine and of cypress, oak, hickory and other hardwoods originally covered much of McIntosh County. The virgin stands of pine provided materials first for the naval stores industry, and later for the logging and lumbering industries. After most of the virgin stands were depleted, second growth stands provided materials for these industries. Large-scale cutting began about 1834 and continued until approximately 1935 when the last large sawmill was closed. In 1929, the naval stores industry produced 7,000 barrels of turpentine and 35,000 barrels of rosin. At the present time, only a few operations related to the naval stores industry are carried on in the county. Today's upland forests consist of open to thick stands of pine and hardwoods...Most of the forests are in large tracts. Commercial forests, of which approximately 130,000 acres are owned by pulp and paper companies, occupy about 171,600 acres in the county. Four mills where pulp and paper are processed [Savannah, Brunswick, St. Marys] are within short distances of most points in the county. Forest products taken from farm woodlands in the county accounted for 46.8 percent of the income derived from the sale of farm products in 1954. The products consisted mainly of pulpwood, saw and veneer logs, firewood and fence posts...

"The woodlands used for range in McIntosh County generally consist of slash, longleaf and loblolly pines. The woodlands are managed primarily to obtain wood products, but some grazing practices are beneficial, both for the production of forage and of wood. As timber canopies develop, there is a decrease in the volume of forage. Thinning, harvesting, and removing the undergrowth and weed trees promotes the growth of the useful trees and forage plants...Managed grazing of pine woodlands reduces the hazard of fire, contributes to the control of hardwoods, and helps the seeds of pines to come into contact with the soil. Controlled burning once in 2 to 4 years improves the quality of the native forage on woodland range. Saw palmettoes and gallberry bushes form the understory in large areas of woodlands in the county. These shrubs are not desirable for forage and crowd out desirable forage plants. Eradication by the use of chemicals has been limited, and machine clearing is the most effective means of control.

"Many of the soils of McIntosh County are not well suited to agriculture. Much of the county, or approximately 84 per cent of the acreage, is poorly drained. In 1959 there were 81 farms in the county. On most of these farms drainage was required...the farms averaged approximately 698 acres in size. Most of the farms are of the general type or are used mainly to grow products for home use. One dairy farm is located in an area of poorly drained soils. In 1959, a large part of the income from the sale of farm products in McIntosh County was derived from the sale of livestock and livestock products. There was a total of 1,812 head of cattle and 991 hogs on farms."[293]

---

[293] Hubert J. Byrd, D. Gray Aydelott, Daniel D. Bacon and Edward M. Stone, *Soil Survey of McIntosh County, Georgia*, Series 1959 (Washington, D.C.: U.S. Department of Agriculture, Soil Conservation Service, 1961), 34, 45, 59. This edition of the soil survey superseded the 1929 survey referenced earlier in this chapter. To date (2020), it remains the most recent soil survey for McIntosh County.

INDEX

ABOUT THE AUTHOR

Buddy Sullivan is a fourth-generation coastal Georgian. He has researched and written about the history, culture and ecology of coastal Georgia for 35 years. He is the author of 25 books and monographs and is in frequent demand as a lecturer on a variety of historical topics. He is a recipient of the Governor's Medal in the Humanities from the Georgia Humanities Council in recognition of his literary and cultural contributions to the state. Sullivan's books include *Georgia: A State History* (2003) for the Georgia Historical Society, and two comprehensive histories, *Early Days on the Georgia Tidewater* (revised and expanded 2018), for McIntosh County, and *From Beautiful Zion to Red Bird Creek* (2000), for Bryan County. The latter volume received the Georgia Historical Society's Hawes Award for Georgia's outstanding work of local history. In addition to the current monograph, his most recent books are *A Georgia Tidewater Companion: Essays, Papers and Some Personal Observations on 30 Years of Research in Coastal Georgia History* (2014), *Sapelo: People and Place on a Georgia Sea Island* (2017), *Environmental Influences on Life & Labor in McIntosh County, Georgia* (2018), *Thomas Spalding, Antebellum Planter of Sapelo* (2019), *Life & Labor on Butler's Island: Rice Cultivation in the Altamaha Delta* (2019), *Native American & Spanish Influences on McIntosh County, Georgia* (2019), *Darien, Georgia: A History of the Town & Its Environs* (2020), and forthcoming, *Postbellum Sapelo Island, The Reconstruction Journal of Archibald Carlisle McKinley* (2020), and *An Atlas of McIntosh County History* (2021). Sullivan has contributed 12 articles to the online *New Georgia Encyclopedia*, and wrote the coastal chapter for *The New Georgia Guide* (1996). He was director of the Sapelo Island National Estuarine Research Reserve from 1993 to 2013 and is now an independent writer and consultant living on his ancestral land overlooking the marshes and waters of Cedar Point, in McIntosh County.